Rens Muis & Pieter Vos

Arab Spring & Aaron Winter

The Work of 75B

nai010 publishers, Rotterdam 2013

Isn't This Something, 2000 – Ink on paper, 220 x 150 cm

I Was Thinking More Like This, 2000 – Ink on paper, 220 x 150 cm

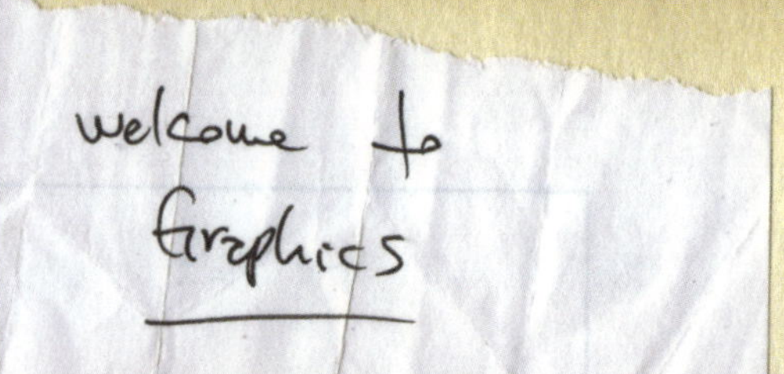

Photo, 1999

Now & Wow, interior logo, 2001

Ro Theater, poster *Wij zijn blij (We are happy)*, 2012

Ro Theater, facade banner, 2012

Ro Theater, sketch for *Wij zijn blij (We are happy)*, 2011

Metropolis M, cover of magazine #5, 2012

The Netherlands Foundation for Visual Arts, Design and Architecture, envelopes, 2002

Ro Theater, sketches for *Slaaf (Slave)*, 2012

theater, poster *Poeskafee*, 2010

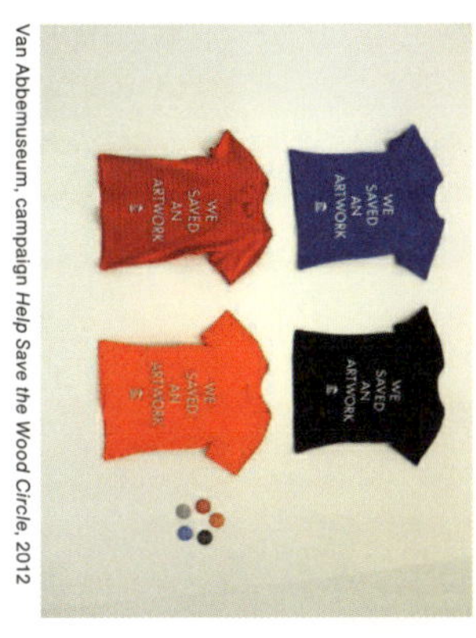

Van Abbemuseum, campaign *Help Save the Wood Circle*, 2012

Van Abbemuseum, campaign *Help Save the Wood Circle*, 2012

photo, 2009

Mint Film, poster *Kyteman Now What*, 2011

Mondriaan Fund, sketches for visual identity, 2011

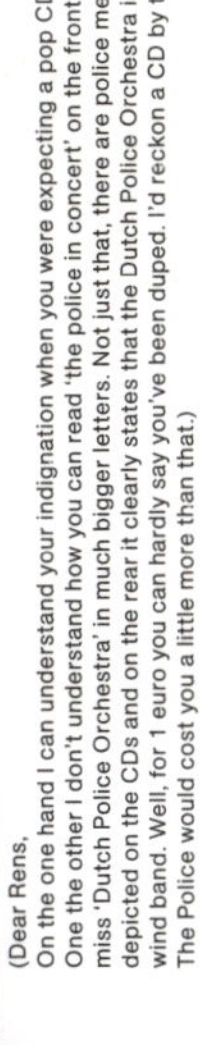

Beste Rens,
Aan de ene kant kan ik me jou verontwaardiging voorstellen als je je op een pop cd hebt ingesteld. Aan de andere kant begrijp ik niet dat je wel "the police in concert" leest op de voorzijde van de cd en niet nog groter afgebeeld "Nederlands Politie Orkest". Tevens staan er politie mensen afgebeeld op de cd's en op de achterzijde staat duidelijk vermeld dat het Nederlands Politie Orkest een symfonisch blaasorkest is. Ach en voor 1 euro ben je volgens mij niet bekocht. Een cd van de popgroep The Police is volgens mij iet wat duurder.

Vriendelijke groeten,

Erik Schipper.

(Dear Rens,
On the one hand I can understand your indignation when you were expecting a pop CD. On the other I don't understand how you can read 'the police in concert' on the front of the CD and miss 'Dutch Police Orchestra' in much bigger letters. Not just that, there are police men and women depicted on the CDs and on the rear it clearly states that the Dutch Police Orchestra is a symphonic wind band. Well, for 1 euro you can hardly say you've been duped. I'd reckon a CD by the pop group The Police would cost you a little more than that.)

NAi Publishers, publication *Charlotte Schleiffert. Feel No Shame*, 2006

Totem pole, 1998

5

Verloren woorden (Lost Words), logos, 2011/2012

Lighthouse, 2012 – iPhone drawing on inkjet print, 220 x 150 cm

Windmill, 2012 – iPhone drawing on inkjet print, 220 x 150 cm

Photo, 2006

Netherlands Architecture Institute, mascot *Maak ons land* (Shape Our Country), 2008

Institut Néerlandais, sketch for map, 2011

Lowlands Festival, video-performance, 1999

Photo, 2006

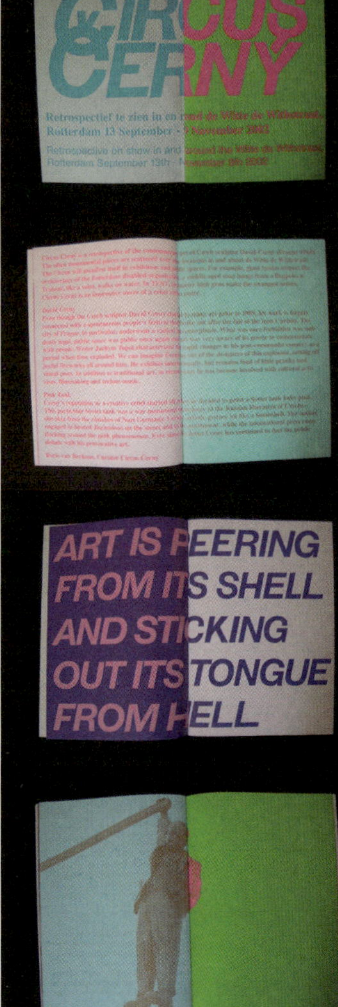

Showroom MAMA, publication *Circus Černý* 2001

The Netherlands Foundation for Visual Arts, Design and Architecture,
business cards, 2004

Club RoXY, rental brochure, 1998

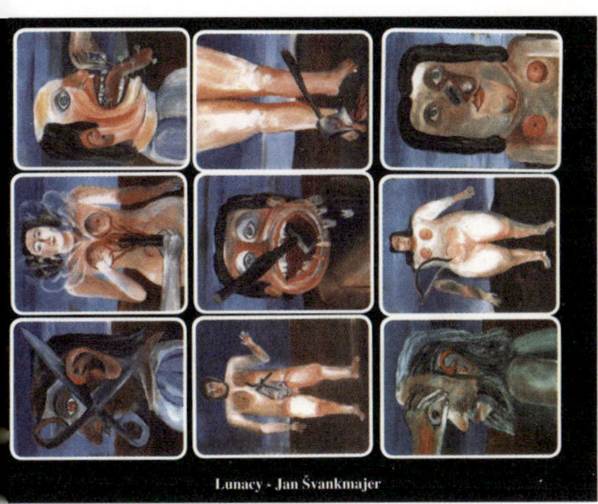

ctbureau Euro 2000, *Crazy Goals!*, 2000

Projectbureau Euro 2000, *Crazy Goals!*, 2000

Sketches for *Crazy Goals!*, 2000

Erik van Lieshout, logo, 2002

Have a Gay Day!, sticker, 2011

(75B psychiatrists
The small venue wasn't full
There aren't enough young people in the museum)

Photo, 2006

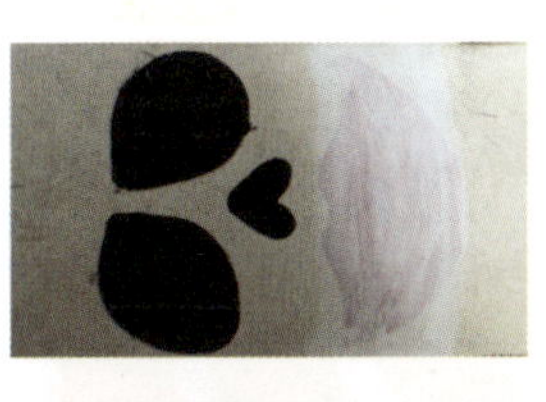

Tronies, 2011

Tronie #03, 2011 – Paint on refrigerator door, 60 x 60 cm

Tronie #02, 2011 – Paint on hardboard, 120 x 120 cm

010 Publishers, *Exactitudes – Ari Versluis & Ellie Uyttenbroek*,
publication first and second editions, 2002

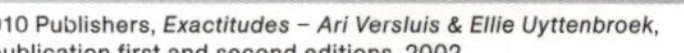

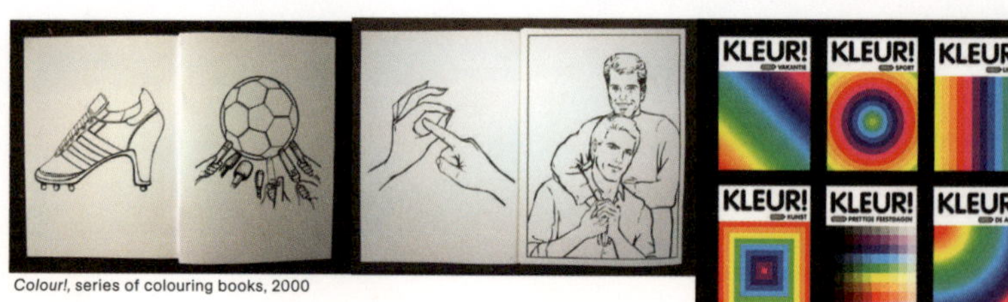

Colour!, series of colouring books, 2000

Colour!, submissions, 2000

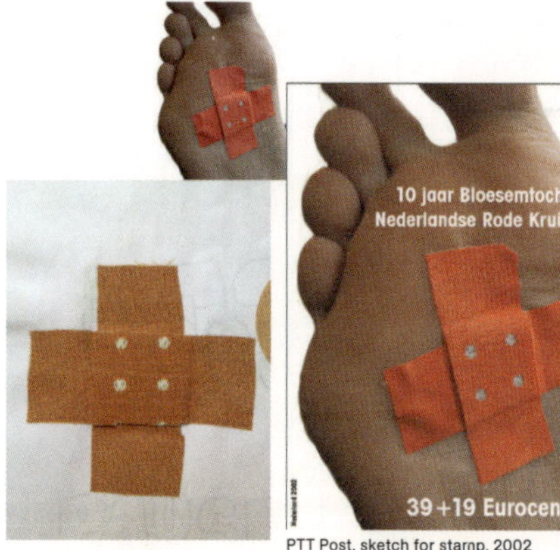

PTT Post, sketch for starnp, 2002

Ro Theater, poster *Slaaf (Slave)*, 2012

WMDC (World Music & Dance Centre), logo, 2006

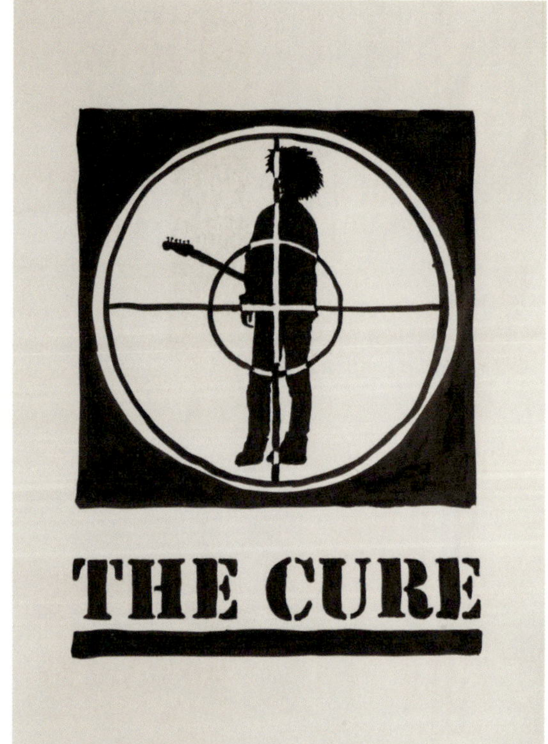

It takes a nation of millions to make us not cry, 2006

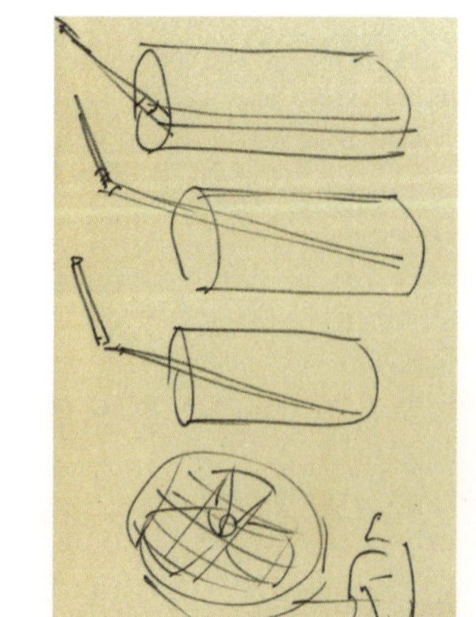

Trekvogels (Migratory Birds), sketch, 2011

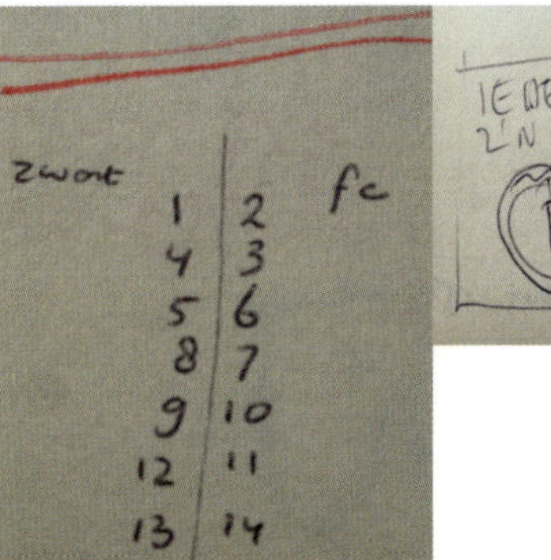

Boomerang Freecards, *Happy Holidays*, 1997

The Netherlands Foundation for Visual Arts, Design and Architecture, application forms, 2005

Art Center College of Design, Pasadena, poster for lecture, 2006

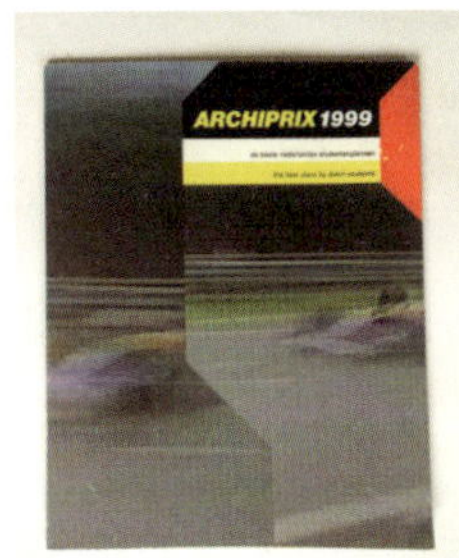

010 Publishers, publication *Archiprix*, 1999

Tronie #06, 2011

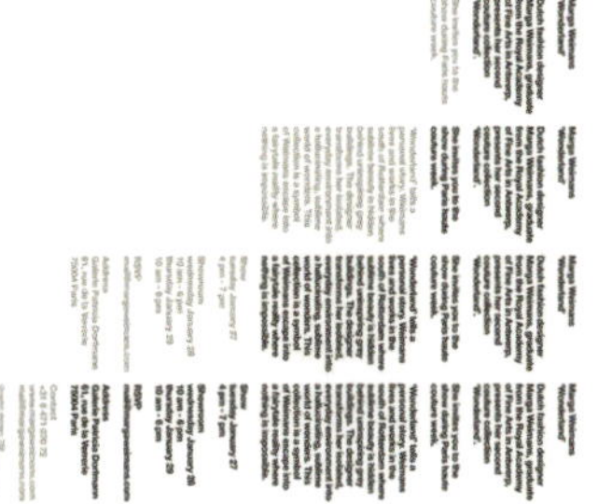

Marga Weimans, invitation *Wonderland*, 2009

Aesthetic Terrorism (Museum Boijmans Van Beuningen, Rotterdam), 2000 – Silkscreen and coloured varnish on paper, 300 x 300 cm

Artoteek Schiedam, *Colour! on the road*, Benin / Burkina Faso / Casa Blanca, 2000

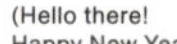

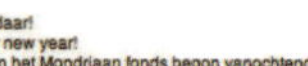

(Hello there!
Happy New Year!
Our year started this morning with the entrance of the stationary. Nice!
And great that it's just all done! I made a mini expo in the hall for my
colleagues. The oeuvre prize cards entered later, also beautiful.
Greetings, Mirjam)

Hallo daar!
Happy new year!
Dat van het Mondriaan fonds begon vanochtend met het binnenkomen van de huisstijl. Mooi! En geweldig dat het ge
allemaal! Ik heb voor de collega's een mini expo ingericht in de hal. Later kwamen ook oeuvreorijskaarten binnen, o
Groet, mirjam

Photo, 2010

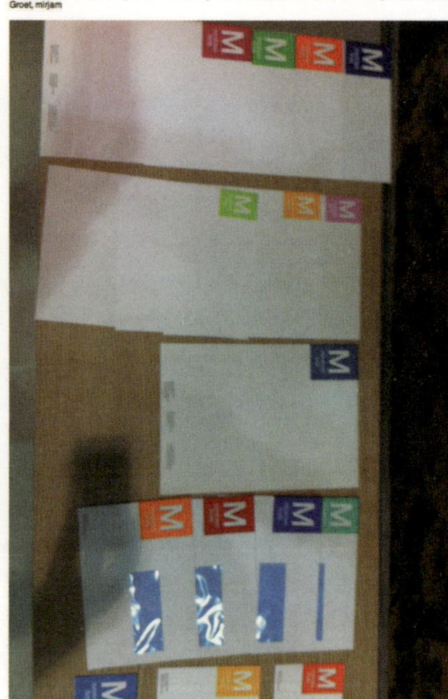
Mondriaan Fund, visual identity, 2012

Sonor, *(On)zichtbaar vakwerk ((In)visible community work)*, 2010

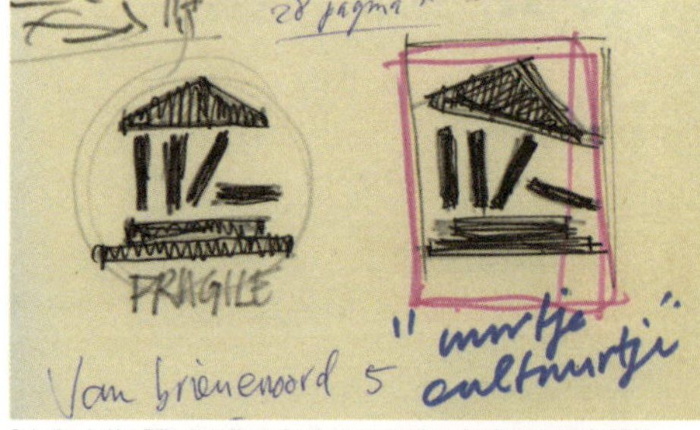
Schuilen In Het Rijks (manifesto for the preservation of culture), sketch, 2011

CBK Rotterdam, exhibition design *Cor Kraat, Made in Rotterdam*, 2012

Mondriaan Fund, sketches for visual identity, 2012

Colour! The Exhibition, visitors, Artoteek Schiedam, 2000

Sculpture International Rotterdam, performance *Anita Gets a Good Going-over*, 2011

Sketch, sketches of logo, 2009

Colour! The Exhibition, Artoteek Schiedam, 2000

Anishinaabemowin, 2011 – Ink and acrylic on paper, 70 x 50 cm

Untitled, 1998 – Silkscreen on paper, 1189 x 841 mm

PTT Post, stamp, 2002

Van Abbemuseum, entrance *Heartland*, 2008

Incoming, 2006

Incoming, 2007

Sculpture International Rotterdam, poster *Cascade*, 2010

Now & Wow, flyer, 2004

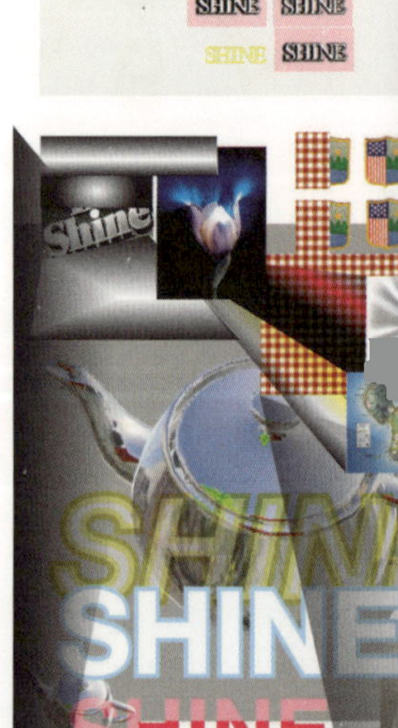

NAi Publishers, sketches for publication *Shine*, 2010

20

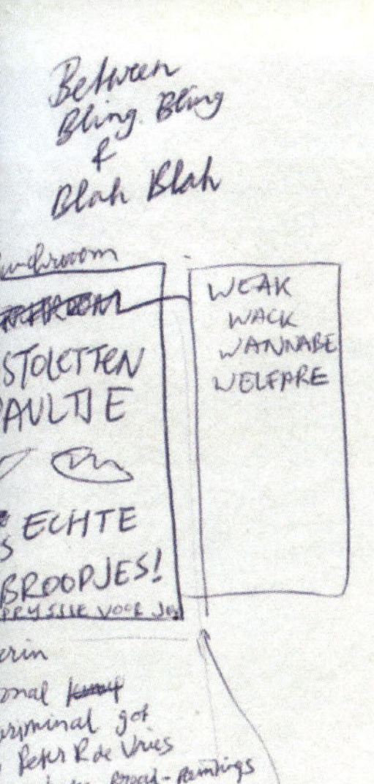

FASHION
VICTIM

ON THE
DOWNLOW
LOW PROFILE

BUSINESS CLASS
WANNAHAVES

IDOLS

CASE
MACARONIVLEES

NAi Publishers, publication *Shine*, 2004

International Film Festival Rotterdam, campaign items 41st edition, 2012

ck-face, sketch, 2010

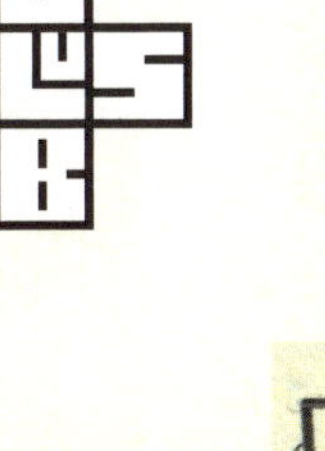

Holland International, exhibition *Mooi maar goed (Beautiful but good)*, Stedelijk Museum Amsterdam, 1999

Holland International, exhibition *Mooi maar goed (Beautiful but good)*, Stedelijk Museum Amsterdam, 1999

99 Miles from L.A., 2007 – Plastic foil and paint on paper, 150 x 220 cm

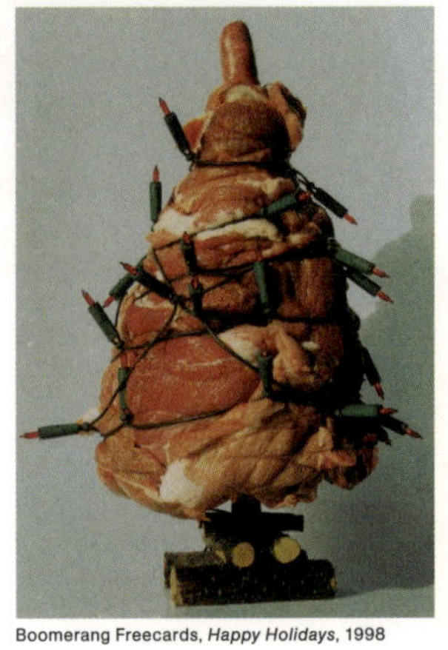

Boomerang Freecards, *Happy Holidays*, 1998

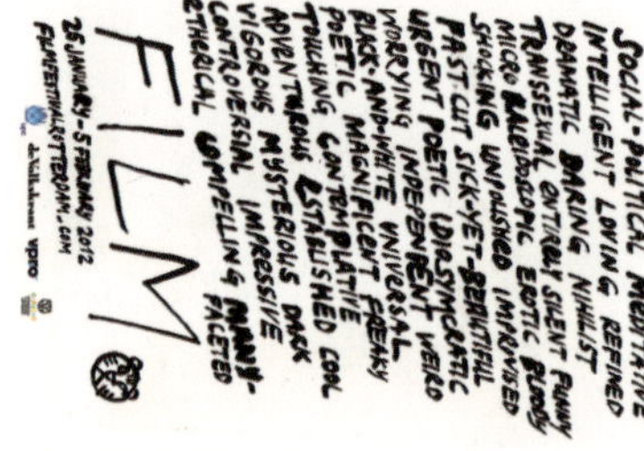

International Film Festival Rotterdam, sketches for 41st edition, 2011

Ro Theater, sketch for *Wij zijn blij (We are happy)*, 2011

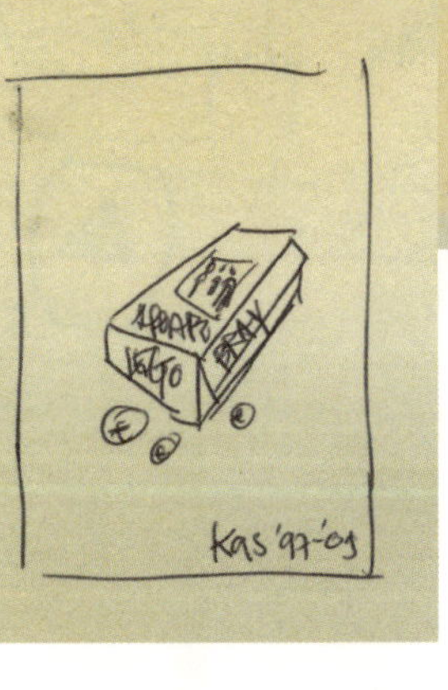

Kas '97-09

75B 12.5 years, ticket, 2009

Van Abbemuseum, posters *René Daniëls*, 2012

International Film Festival Rotterdam, poster 39th edition, 2010

Van Abbemuseum, poster *Vanuit hier / Out of here*, 2011

Van Abbemuseum, wall text for *Time Machines – Reloaded*, 2010

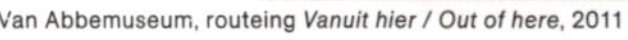

Van Abbemuseum, routeing *Vanuit hier / Out of here*, 2011

...ed, 1998

Six Lanes of Fame, 2006

...kunst, facade design, 2003

Van Abbemuseum, poster
Vanuit hier / Out of here, 2011

War Stars (Los Angeles), 2006 – Intervention on Hollywood Boulevard

The Ghost of Christmas Yet to Come (Rotterdam), 2010 – Intervention on transformer kiosk

International Film Festival Rotterdam, sketches of logo, 2008

CBK Rotterdam, sketch for campaign Cor Kraat, Made in Rotterdam, 2012

Camouflage Commercial, 2006

Photo, 1999

Van Abbemuseum, sketches for poster Lissitzky+, Victory over the Sun, 2009

Hootchie Cootchie, unrequested stationery, 2008

Now & Wow, magazines, 2005/2006

Now & Wow, grid, 2001

Photos, 2012

Framing Nature, production, 2012

Photo, 2001

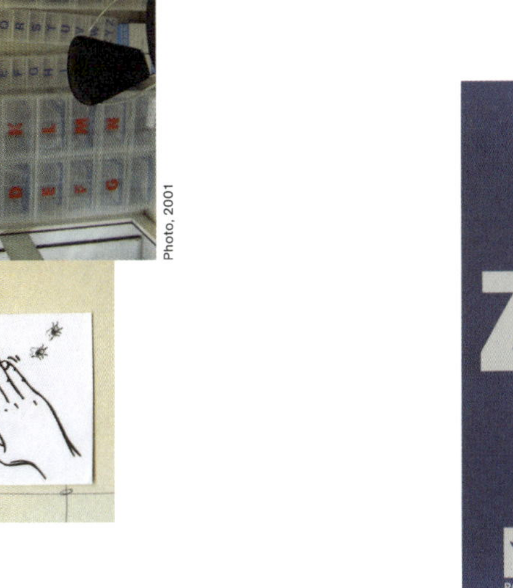

Ro Theater, poster Wij zijn blij (We are happy), 2012

Metropolis M, covers and spreads, 2011/2012/2013

Van Abbemuseum, sketch for routeing, 2012

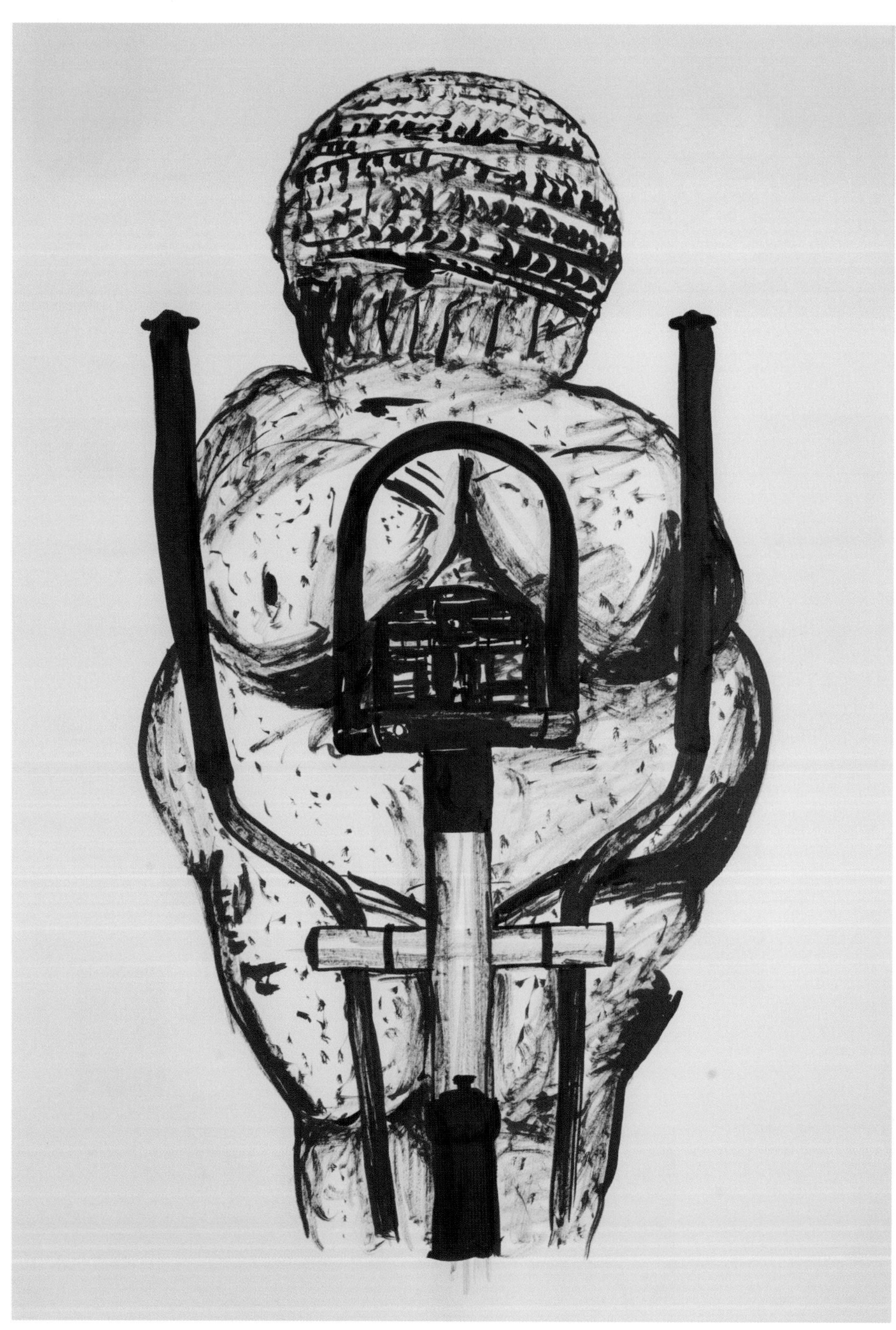

Willendorf's Gym, 2006 – Ink on paper, 100 x 70 cm

Ingres' Tramp Stamp, 2006 – Ink on paper, 100 x 70 cm

------ Forwarded Message
From: Noel Arendain <noelarendain@artcenter.edu>
Date: Wed, 12 Jul 2006 14:52:37 -0700
To: Steve Kim <stevekim@artcenter.edu>
Cc: Computing Labs Staff <ComputingLabStaff@Artcenter.edu>
Conversation: Fake Signs
Subject: Fake Signs

Steve,

Apparently, there is a Graphic Design 1 class that has been hanging fake signs around the lab area over the last couple of weeks. Vivian Wu and the other lab assistants have been taking them down. I've personally seen two signs so far falsely identifying staff as points of contact for fake events. For example, there was a sign stating that Dick Cheney was coming to Art Center to show off his watercolor art and that the contact person was Megan Webster. We have another sign in our office saying that Internet Pornography can be viewed on one of our lab machines and that they can get assistance from the Computing Lab Staff.

Do you know who the instructor for the class is and what can be done to stop this? We don't want false information to be passed on to the students as the signs look legitimate.

Sincerely,

Noel Arendain
Jr. Systems Administrator – Computer Labs
ArtCenter College of Design
1700 Lida Street; Pasadena, CA 91103
Phone: (626) 396-127796

------ End of Forwarded Message

Art Center Pasadena, fake signs between the real ones, 2006

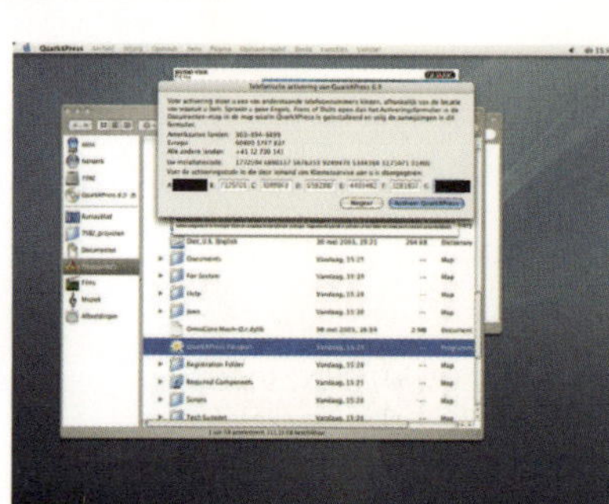

Centraal Museum Utrecht, poster *Pipilotti Rist -54-*, 2001

Untitled, 2010

Van Abbemuseum, welcome sign, 2008

Ro Theater, poster *Hondsdagen (Dog Days)*, 2010

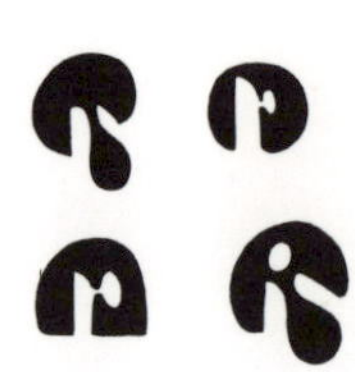
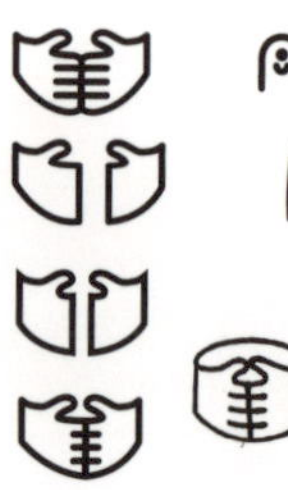
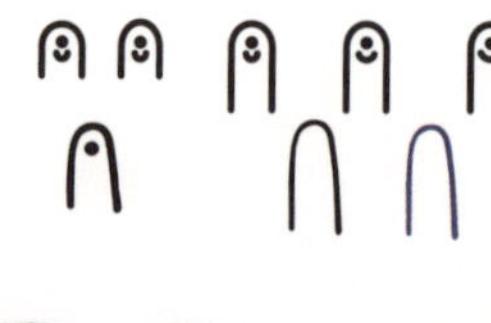
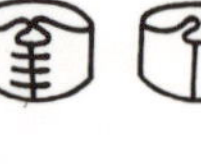

Johnson & Johnson, sketches for *OneTouch*, 2010

(Giants) in atelier and Rotterdamse Schouwburg, 2011

Posters i.c.w. ZUS, 2012 (Permanent Transience, Who will buy the City, Do Mongering, We appreciate depreciation)

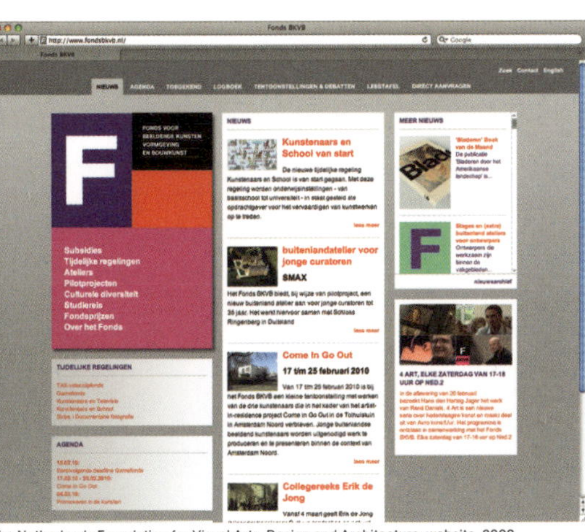

The Netherlands Foundation for Visual Arts, Design and Architecture, website, 2009

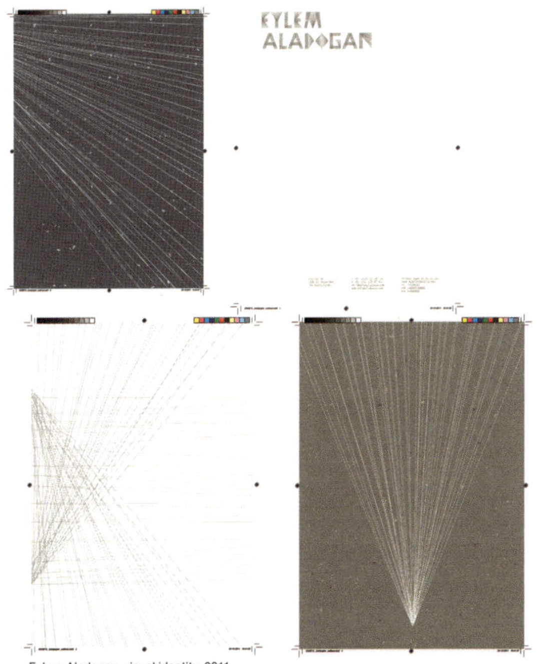

Eylem Aladogan, visual identity, 2011

33

Skatepark Westblaak (Rotterdam), 2000 – Acrylate resin on asphalt

Now & Wow, posters *Flirt*, 2001-2006

Studio, 2002

BCG-Matrix		relatief marktaandeel	
		hoog	laag
groeipotentieel	hoog	star	question mark
	laag	cash cow	dog

(Phillips nail)

Mint Film, poster *Kyteman, Now What*, 2011

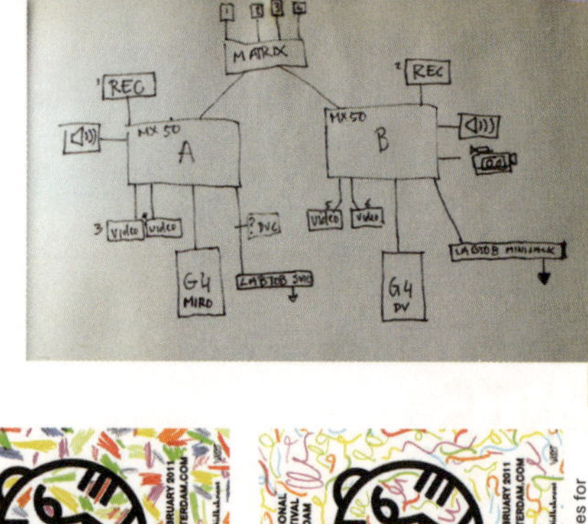

International Film Festival Rotterdam, sketches for campaign 40th edition, 2010

International Film Festival Rotterdam, sketches for campaign 39th edition, 2009

Publication *75B LAX*, 2008

White Light / White Heat, 2006

LantarenVenster, ad, 2012

Institut Néerlandais, poster, 2012

Institut Néerlandais, poster, 2011

War Stars, 2006

(Made possible by me and you)

Historisch Museum Rotterdam, posters JONG! (Young!), 2000

XXX, 2010 – Ink on paper, 40 x 55 cm

Rexona (Hotel Centraal, Rotterdam), 2010 – Installation

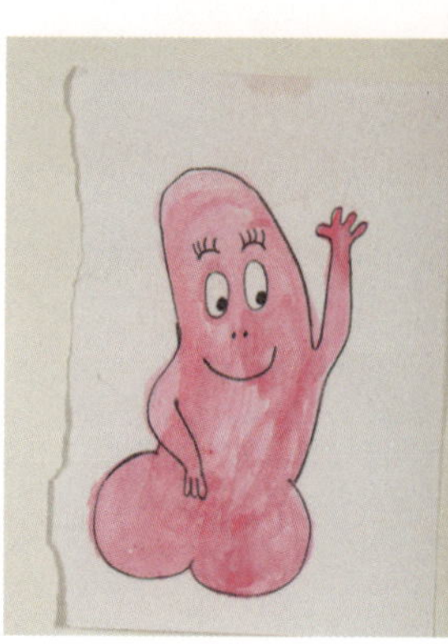

Ro Theater, sketches for posters, 2009

Mondriaan Fund, annual report, 2012

Ro Theater, facade design Rotterdamse Schouwburg *Ro Festival*, 2009

Schuilen In Het Rijks (manifesto for the preservation of culture), sticker, 2011

International Film Festival Rotterdam, sketches for visual identity, 2008

Art Center College of Design, Pasadena, lecture poster, 2007

International Film Festival Rotterdam, campaign 41st edition, 2012

(Remember this, guys?
From the last century, wasn't it?
Anyway, we'd love to see whether we really
can make something of this design!
Expect a call from me
greetz, Julius Vermeulen)

Post, proposal, 1999

Passage Publishers, cover *Vaandrager – Sleutels, een straat-collage*, 2012

Now & Wow, poster, 2006

International Film Festival Rotterdam, merchandise, 2009

Centraal Museum Utrecht, sketches for *Pipilotti Rist -54-*, 2001

0/1, 1998 – Offset print on paper (series of 16 posters), 100 x 70 cm

Trinity, 2006

Muze, 1993

Marga Weimans Wonderland, wall text, 2010

Codarts, poster Open day, 2010

Passionate Magazine, literary magazine, covers, 1997/1998

44

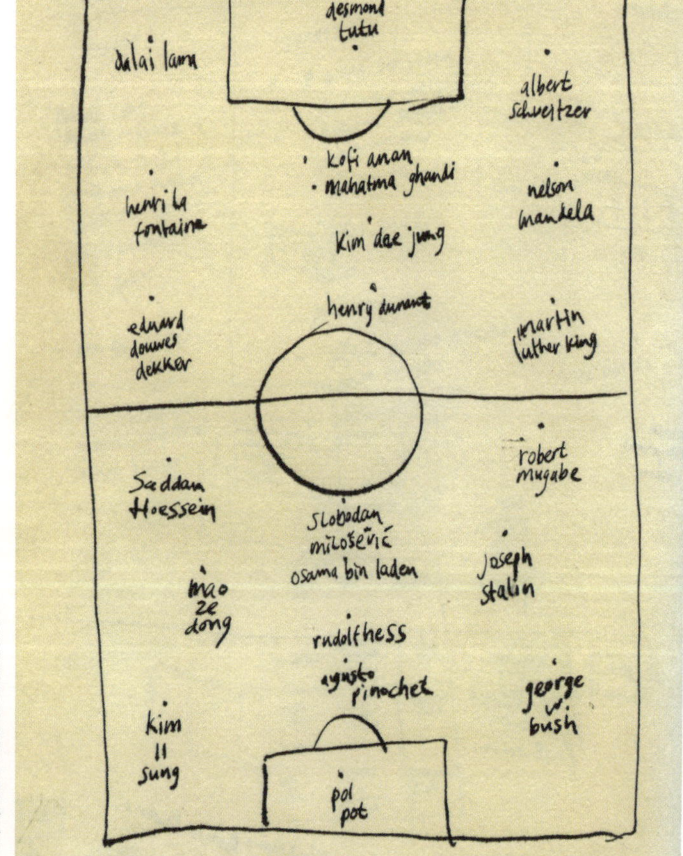

The good versus the bad, 2006

De Unie, projection De staat van de staat, 2012

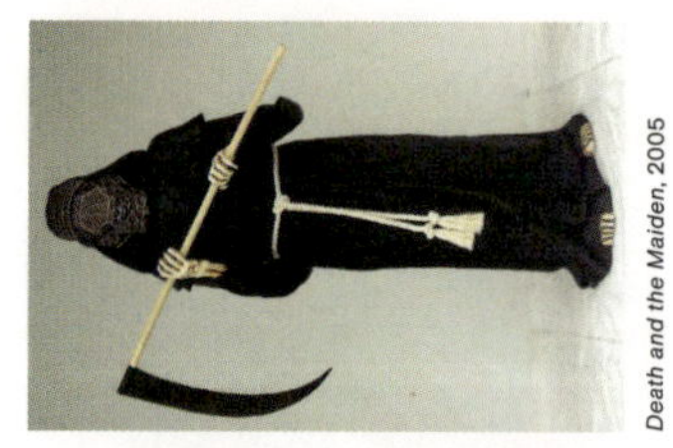

Death and the Maiden, 2005

The Netherlands Foundation for Visual Arts, Design and Architecture, envelopes, 2001

Ro Theater, poster *King Lear*, 2010

Netherlands Architecture Institute, poster *Maak ons land (Shape Our Country)*, 2008/2009

Now & Wow, sketch for T-shirt, 2004

Danger, 1996

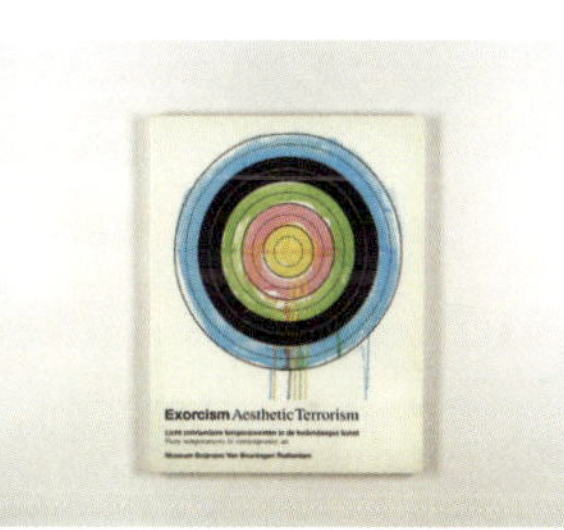

NAi Publishers, publication *Exorcism / Aesthetic Terrorism*, 2000

...eum Boijmans Van Beuningen, production *Aesthetic Terrorism*, 2000

De Unie, website, 2010

Sculpture International Rotterdam,
sketch for T-shirt, 2011

Ro Theater, T-shirts, 2009

I Always Had a Ph.D., 2010 – Acrylic, ink and plastic foil on paper, 220 x 150 cm

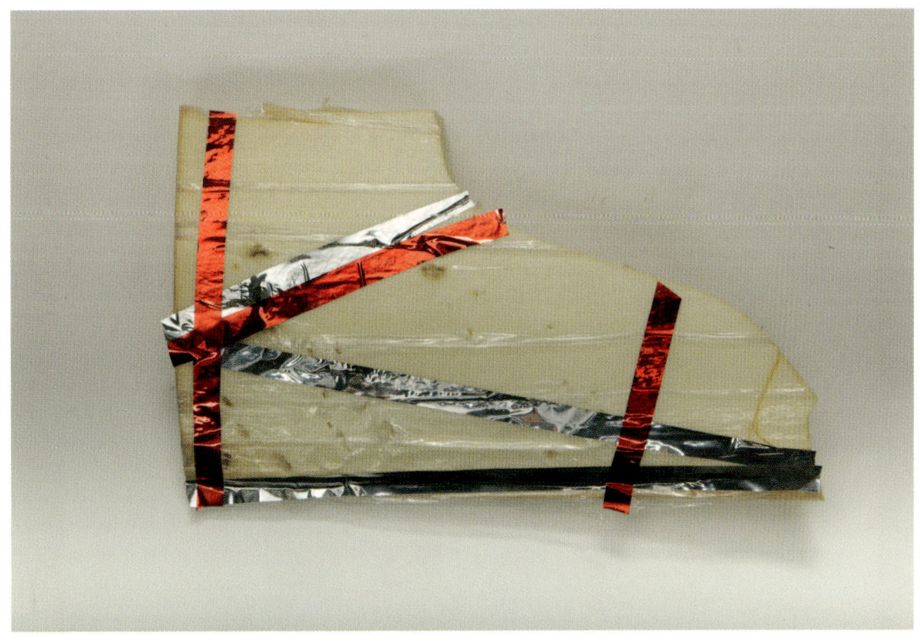

Sneakers, 2010 – Foam and plastic foil, 20 x 30 cm

Ro Theater, poster Amazones, 2010

Vitruvian Dancer, installation on roof of Art Center College of Design, Pasadena, 2006

De Unie, poster, 2010

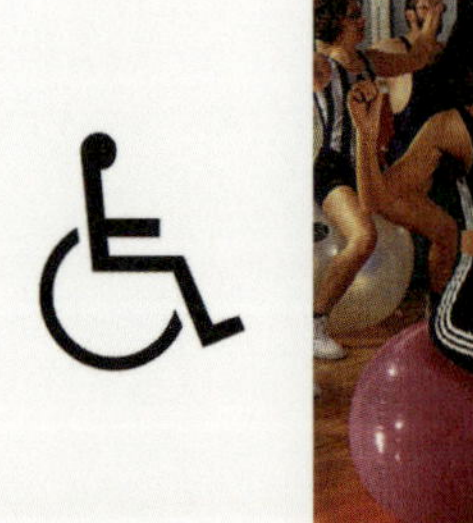

Spreads *75B Pictobook*, 1997

The Netherlands Foundation for Visual Arts, Design and Architecture, invitations, 2001–2011

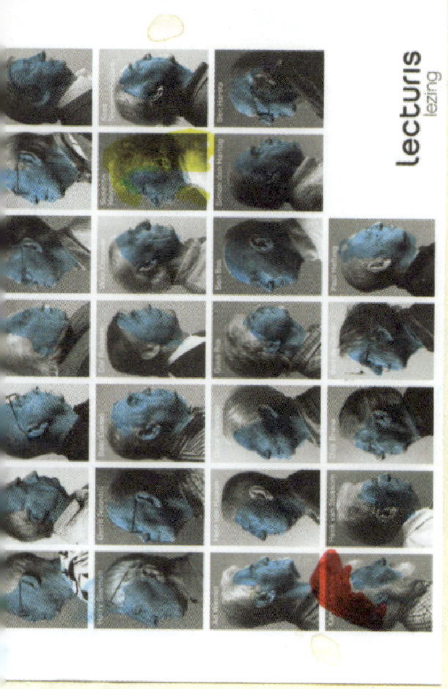
Designers, 2012

ZUS, campaign presentation Luchtsingel, 2011

International Film Festival Rotterdam, facade design Oude Luxor Theater, 2010

CBK Rotterdam, sketches for campaign Cor Kraat, Made in Rotterdam, 2012

Historisch Museum Rotterdam, sketches for JONG! (Young!), 2000

TENT, publication Paramaribo Perspectives, 2011

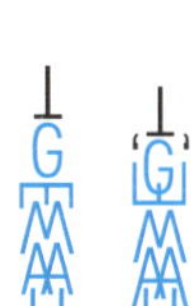

Het Gemaal, sketches for visual identity, 2009

Grid, 2012 – Photo print, 60 x 45 cm

Everything Will Be Fine, 2012 – Silkscreen on paper, 1189 x 841 mm

Photo, 2013

The Association of Associations,
logo, 2006

International Film Festival Rotterdam, poster campaign 39th edition, 2010

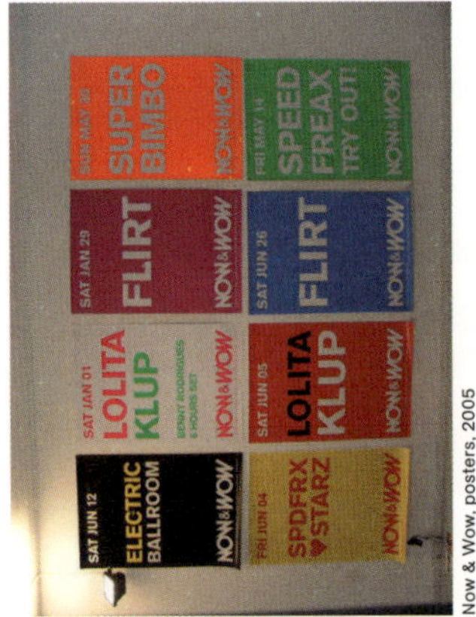
Now & Wow, posters, 2005

Art Center College of Design, Pasadena, poster for lecture, 2006

Ambidexter, 2011

Now & Wow, flyer, 2004

Entertainment, 2006

52

Ro Theater, poster *Dieven (Thieves)*, 2011

Schuilen In Het Rijks (manifesto for the preservation of culture), posters *Boijmans Bezet*, 2011

LANTAREN VENSTER

LantarenVenster, logo, 2010

Historisch Museum Rotterdam, crest, 2010

nai010 Publishers, publication *Cycle Space*, 2012

Blackest Black, 2010 – Offset print full colour on paper (#1/3, edition of 100), 70 x 50 cm

Blackest Black, 2010 – Offset print full colour on paper (#3/3, edition of 100), 70 x 50 cm

Codarts, posters *Open day*, 2009

Historisch Museum Rotterdam, sketches for *ANNO*, 2007

Van Abbemuseum, projection *Heartland*, 2009

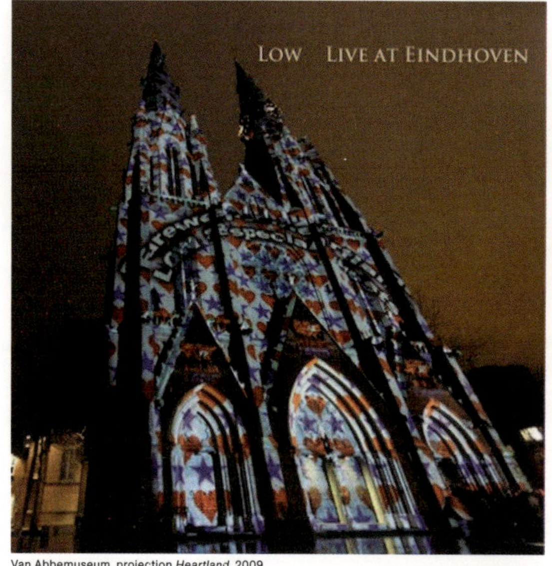

The Dummy Speaks, covers, 1999

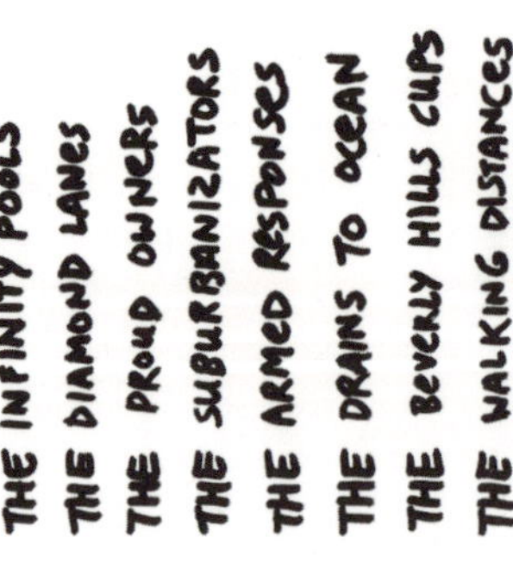

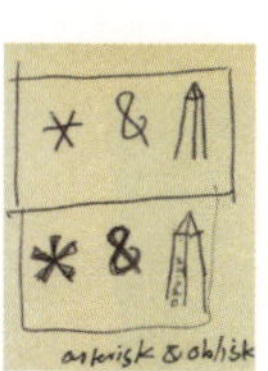

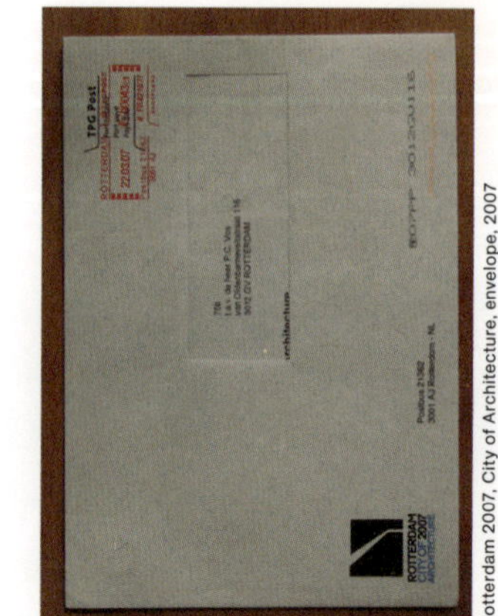

Rotterdam 2007, City of Architecture, envelope, 2007

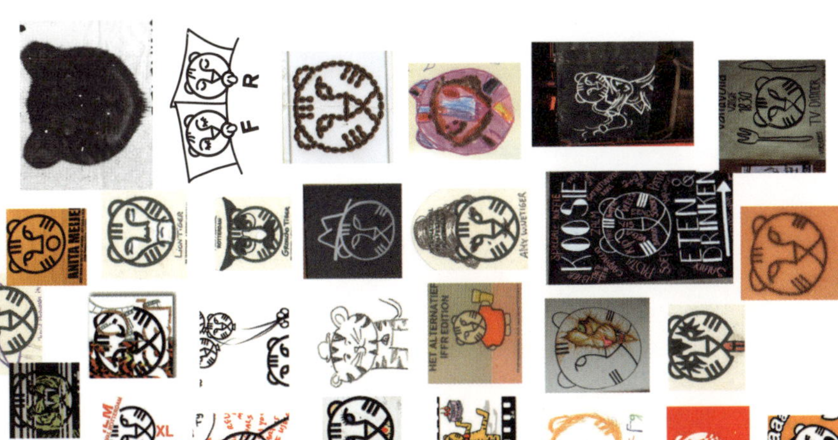

Tiger interpretations International Film Festival Rotterdam, 2008–2013

Ro Theater, posters *Oedipus*, 2013

Van Abbemuseum, posters *René Daniëls*, 2012

Photo, 1999

Ro Theater, posters *Ro Festival*, 2011

Giants, 2011 – Silkscreen, ink and paint on paper (series of 600), 70 x 50 cm

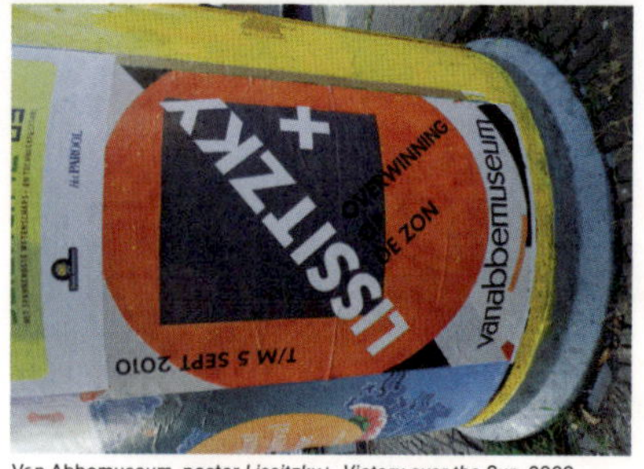
Van Abbemuseum, poster *Lissitzky+, Victory over the Sun*, 2009

Metal Detector Award, 2010

60

Art Center College of Design, Pasadena, poster for lecture, 2006

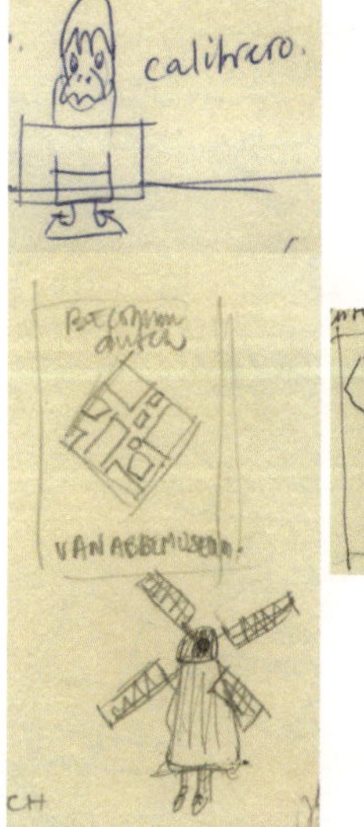

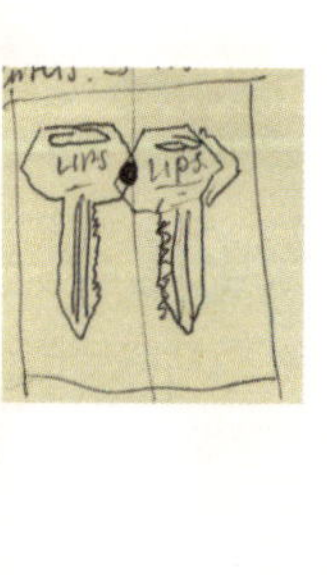

Ro Theater, sketches of logo, 2009

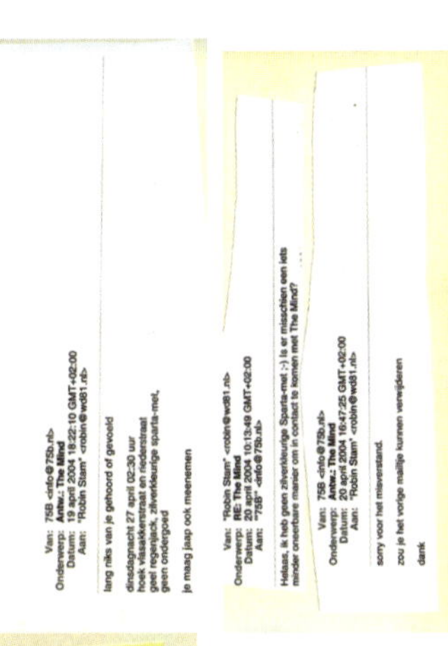

Boomerang Freecards, *Happy Easter*, 1999

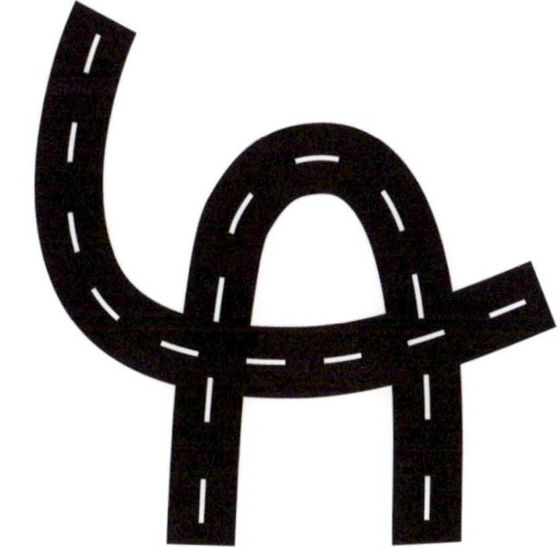

L.A., logo, 2006

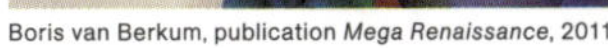

Boris van Berkum, publication *Mega Renaissance*, 2011

Van Abbemuseum, covers *Radically Yours!*, 2012/2013

Kijk hier es naar (Take a Look at This), Fons Welters Gallery, 2001

NAi Publishers, publication *Exorcism / Aesthetic Terrorism*, 2000

Rotterdam 2007, City of Architecture, posters, 2007

Is Everybody Happy?, 2005 – Spray can paint on polyester, 80 x 120 cm

Last Day, 2011 – Objet trouvé, 70 x 50 cm

International Architecture Biennale Rotterdam, campaign *The Flood*, 2005

Hardcore, publication *Stoep*, 1996

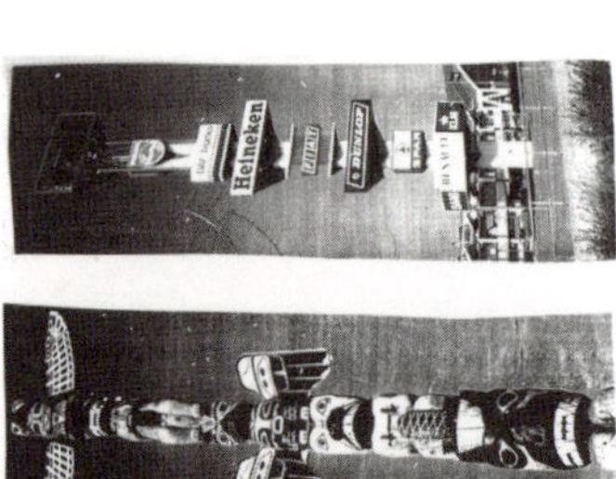

Rotterdam 2007, City of Architecture, flags, 2007

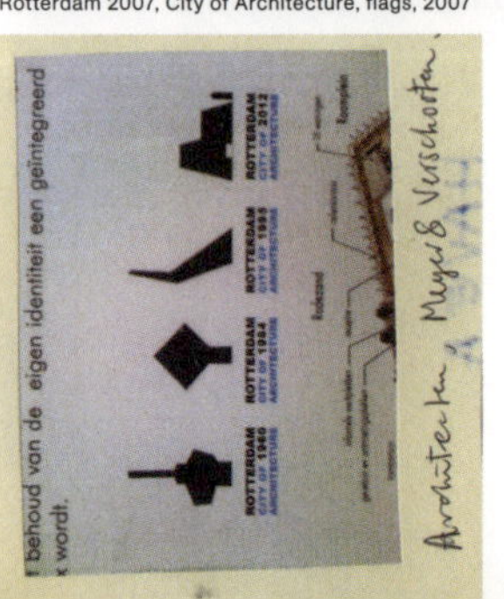

Meekers, T-shirts, 2012

Codarts, sketches for visual identity, 2005

Der Ernstfall des Laupvogels

Rens Muis

I

'How do you do, Ernst. I understand that you are responsible for designing the museum's communications.' Barbara van Schutterstaert was the new head of PR & Communications at the Tax and Customs Museum. 'I hope I will soon know all there is to be known about the marketing communications here,' she continued. 'It's a tremendous challenge setting up our new marketing plan.' The museum's Director, who had introduced them moments before, slipped away.

'People really like the present look, but I wonder if it's clear enough that we're a museum?', Barbara asked. 'I should think so,' Ernst replied, 'the word museum is there in the logo, isn't it?' He pointed to a paper napkin on the bar table, running his finger over the letters of the logo. 'Tax and Customs Museum,' he read aloud emphasizing the last word.

Ernst had supplied design work to the Tax and Customs Museum for years on end, and no one had ever criticized his typesetting. Indeed, he had developed a strong bond with the lady from PR & Communications who had been his contact hitherto. They had needed few words with each other. Sometimes he would help her out with a small job, say converting a computer file, without even charging for it. Today was her farewell reception and Ernst had just presented her with a framed poster on behalf of his company Laupvogel. It bore her name in the house style of the museum.

'In my last job at the HEMA, we worked a lot with studio Prima Zo. Do you know them?', Barbara van Schutterstaert asked Ernst. 'The name rings a faint bell but I can't say I know them well,' Ernst lied in reply. What a stupid name, he thought. What kind of idiot calls a studio Prima Zo, 'Just Fine'? Ernst cared little for the rising tide of communications agencies sporting frivolous names like Plik-Plok, Yo-Lite, Studio Okie Dokie, Deedus and Fresh! For Ernst the so-called unorthodox efforts of these creative entrepreneurs yielded a crop of utterly interchangeable and insipid designs.

The director of the Tax and Customs Museum had chosen Laupvogel years ago because he had been taken with their designs for a literary magazine, of which he happened to be one of the 28 subscribers. He asked Laupvogel to apply the same kind of design approach to the museum whose director he had just become. Once the main style features were established, the director took a background role emerging only to take an active interest in big projects. Day-to-day implementation of the house style became the duty of the head of PR & Communications. It was all very professional, in Ernst's opinion. The situation could have continued for years were it not for the head of PR&C reaching pension age.

Ernst Laupman ran the graphic design firm Laupvogel together with Arjan van der Vogel. They formed a general partnership and were registered in the creative services category. Their office was on the first floor of an old premises in the city centre. They shared the stairs with an administrative branch of the Eye Hospital, a beauty salon, the Skin Bar, and a black tennis instructor called Andy Ample. To the right of the premises, the ground floor was occupied by the Appola Gay and Lesbian Youth Association, and the upper floors by Back On Track, a charity dedicated to counselling young people with behavioural problems. In the slightly smaller premises to the left lived an elderly couple, Mr and Mrs Futselaar, with whom the staff at Laupvogel got on with very well.

Ernst and Arjan had deliberately sought a workplace among ordinary people and had spurned the space allocation scheme touted by the city's Planning Department. Inspired by an American urban scientist who argued that the creative professions were a catalyst for civic prosperity, the official plan earmarked several zones for creative industry development; and designers were on the list of professions considered to be creative. Officials from the municipal services regularly approached Laupvogel with invitations to view the smartened-up premises in the 'creative' zones, in the hope of persuading them to relocate. Most of these premises were former industrial buildings such as warehouses or power plants which had been tastefully converted into multi-company facilities, leaving some of the original elements on view. The visible victory of design over industrial brutalism was presumed to appeal to the creative soul. But, quite apart from the high rents, Ernst and Arjan did not feel at home in the tribal reservations set aside for them and their kin. On one of the promotional tours intended to fill the many empty units, their guide from the real estate department told Ernst and Arjan: 'There's a quite a lot of artists already renting space in this building.' Artists? Nonsense, Ernst thought. 'There are no artists here', he replied, 'they are somewhere else.'

'What do you mean? We've got the Full Service Web Agency and Boing!, the design marketeers. And then there's Rottenall & Dropperdog, the creative communications people. All of them are creative artists like yourselves.' Ernst cringed.

Laupvogel's working premises had an ample floor area and a particularly high ceiling. From the shared entrance hall of the building, an interior door led into a wide corridor, off which there was a kitchen and a toilet. Parallel to the corridor was a large office space containing eight hefty workbenches that did duty as desks. Adjustable office chairs were scattered between the benches, on whose massive tops large screens with built-in computers stood. It all had a basic, no-nonsense look to it. At the end of this office there was a conference area which could be closed off by a glass door. One wall of this space was occupied by a room-wide storage rack of several metres in height, which contained plastic crates full of office supplies and Laupvogel's archived work. Set into the storage rack was a inconspicuous little door, which led into a spacious concrete room with four tiny windows equipped with grilles to prevent break-ins. This room was what Ernst and Arjan designated their atelier. A visitor to the office with the workbenches would scarcely suspect that another large room lay behind the storage rack. Ernst imagined parallels between their surreptitious atelier entrance and the famous Secret Annex at the rear of Anne Frank's house.

Following a meagre night's sleep, Ernst slumped onto the gigantic claret-coloured leather corner sofa in the atelier. Arjan and Ernst had found this piece of furniture abandoned in the street, and dubbed it the Kalou sofa after seeing a newspaper photo of the Ivorian forward Bonaventure Kalou lounging on a similar monstrosity, seemingly the sole furnishing in the apartment his club had provided him. Arjan wasn't there that day. They usually worked on alternate days so as to avoid getting in each other's way. But Ernst could still see traces of Arjan's activities from the day before. There were large green plastic tarpaulins lying on the floor with bits cut out of them somewhat in the shape of frogs' legs. Thin wooden sticks were stuck into the openings and joined together with red thread. Sheets of white A4 paper with pictures of deer on them were folded double and hung over the threads. Arjan had stopped halfway, evidently dissatisfied with the result. Ernst had several projects under way simultaneously. Presently he was engaged in developing chocolate miniatures of the monolithic heads of Easter Island. In search of a suitable producer for his idea, he punched a number he had found listed under 'Patissiers and Chocolatiers' into his phone.

'Good morning, Confectioners and Chocolaterie Speckle, how can I help you?' The businesslike but astringent voice was, he gauged, that of a woman of about 55 years old from one of the new suburbs. Clearly, this was not just any confectioner but one of the high-class establishments.

'Good morning madam, my name is Ernst Laupman, from Laupvogel. Is this a convenient moment to ask you something?'

'Yes of course, ask away.'

'Good, thank you, I'm ringing about a business proposition to jointly introduce a new concept in your branch. You see, I have been thinking about the stone statues of Easter Island – you know, those huge carved heads.'

'What about them?', said the woman.

'Well, I was thinking about those huge heads on Easter Island. They have always have been something of a mystery. And I thought about having them moulded in chocolate.'

'Umm, I don't think I can help you there, sir.'

'I'm not trying to place an order. I'm asking whether your business would like to consider collaborating with mine to get those heads reproduced in chocolate or some other sweet-tasting stuff. Perhaps in different sizes.'

'No, thank you, I don't believe we're interested.'

'But surely they would go down marvellously at Easter time, with slogans like...'

'Er ... no. No thank you.'

Well what about your head in chocolate, Ernst muttered to himself, concluding that the effort was hopeless. But instead he said 'Thank you so much for your time,' and hung up.

He remained there for a while sunk in the Kalou sofa and staring into space. The confectionery branch had no ambition and probably no capacity to reflect on itself. No critical discourse; regrettable, most regrettable. It then struck him that he had forgotten to mention that the heads could be filled with marzipan or some other confection which they could decide on together. What a missed opportunity!

Since the days when they started collaborating at the art academy, Ernst and Arjan had worked in two distinct veins: commissioned work and autonomous work. In both areas they were purists. They were never confused about which context applied to their activities at any given moment, now if only because the two alternatives were spatially separated: applied art in the office with the workbenches, and autonomous art in the atelier. The claims made by others to blur the boundaries between the two disciplines amounted in their view to mere opportunism. Their hackles arose as soon as designers started bandying terms like the interface, the twilight zone or the frontier territory between autonomous art and applied art. Was it fish or fowl? More to the point, was it good fish or good fowl? The more one complained about the compartmentalization of creativity, in their experience, the less convincing the resulting output became. No, it was important to keep a clear idea of your intentions in that regard whenever you were at work.

The commissions for applied work had quickly risen out of hand. To reduce the load on themselves, Ernst and Arjan brought in assistant designers and, ultimately, a business manager. This allowed the two partners to shut themselves off in their atelier in the Secret Annex for much of the week without distractions from the daily running of the practice. They could now devote a great deal of time to freely creative work and to developing ideas and products without an immediate utility or goal. Looking for a name to give this messing about, which was important to them, they came up with the idea of labelling it Research & Development. In no small part this was to appease the business manager, Monique van Crumbstein, who saw little connection between their backroom activities and the 'real' business.

For the others working at Laupvogel, it was quite a relief that the two owners regularly devoted themselves to their projects in the R & D cubby-hole. At last they could do their designing in peace without having to listen all day long to Arjan and Ernst's comments. Besides, Statler and Waldorf, as the staff liked to call the partners, were inclined to plague them with sardonic quips and vent their views on current affairs, sports, the media and so on. After several years in the firm, they were able to design independently, as intended, and if anything with greater efficiency and organization than Arjan and Ernst themselves. The young designers could cope perfectly well without those two Muppet oldies, Ernst reasoned. The partners each kept two clients for themselves, however. Arjan continued his work for Rowit & Sludgemüller, a firm of architects, and for Circus Arts, an advanced vocational training school for big-top artistes. Ernst still took responsibility for Spatt!, a dance theatre company, and for the Tax and Customs Museum. Monique the business manager was of the opinion that the four clients served by the owners did not really make much of a difference financially. But Ernst and Arjan felt the design challenges were too valuable in creative terms to let these clients go. Monique had also advised them to precede the name Laupvogel with the word 'Studio'. It would look more professional and suggest a larger company than just Laupman and Van der Vogel, she argued. Ernst and Arjan both rejected this idea. For them Laupvogel was enough. However, they did comply with Monique's request to add an extra line to their business card describing what Laupvogel did. The extra line read 'Full-time Amateurs & All-round Specialists'.

II

How wonderfully ugly it all is here, Ernst thought as he looked out through the atelier's barred window. Everything in the vicinity was earmarked for demolition in five years' time to make way for high-rise development. The slick artistic impressions of how the area was supposed to look when finished was complete gave Ernst sombre premonitions of a sanitized social environment.

The area in its present state at least made an impression of a location largely untouched by official planning, of a neighbourhood evolved over time. The new master plan had no doubt been tossed off in a couple of days just to meet some deadline. Architects invariably spoke of the 'task' to which they were committed. To Ernst this sounded as though they were talking about school homework; or perhaps they saw their brief as a divine injunction to which they were about to dedicate their life's endeavours. 'No dogs and no architects please', Ernst had printed on the invitations to a celebration of Laupvogel's first ten years. The upshot was that far more architects turned up than ever. They either ignored his admonishment, or took it merely as a joke. At least dogs know when they are wanted, Ernst concluded.

All morning he had been heaving pieces of scrap plywood he had found in the street, with the idea of using it as the support for a new work. Sweating from the exertion, he pulled on the old overalls they kept in the studio.

'Would you like some coffee?' an unfamiliar female voice enquired.

'No thanks. Actually, I never drink coffee, so in future please don't ask,' Ernst replied to the brand-new student trainee standing in the doorway. She scanned the room with an expression that suggested she had just caught Ernst in the process of hiding an illegal abbatoir. 'Oh? Why not?', she asked. Ernst had no wish to waste effort thinking of a plausible explanation for the umpteenth time, while no such explanation existed. 'I've never really liked it,' he answered. He had read somewhere of a famous performer who, as a child, had vowed never to drink coffee 'because the coffee ritual was a shackle of adulthood'. Ernst could scarcely imagine himself sticking to such a principle. But he did try to shed more and more facets of his daily life that wasted time and did not give him the least satisfaction. The tedious chitchat during coffee breaks was certainly one thing he could do without. Another was the TV set which he had thrown out of his home some years earlier. That felt good. Not that he no longer watched televised programmes, but he chose whatever programmes or podcasts interested him on the internet, so that he and not the TV was in control. The very thought of killing time was anathema to him. Anyone who got in his way, or anything technical that worked against him, put him in a bad mood. When that happened Arjan preached patience, which calmed him down somewhat.

Ernst was on the point of painting a discarded fridge door with black outdoor varnish when he heard the voice of Freddy Hoonstam coming from the office. Freddy was the artistic director of the dance theatre company Spatt!, for which Ernst still did design work. He often arrived at the studio without warning, fresh from the fitness centre or some trendy lunch counter. His deep, throaty voice came ever closer, while he was no doubt taking his time to ogle and flatter the girls on the studio staff.

Ernst and Arjan had agreed that only Ernst would have to speak to him because Arjan could not stand the man. They had persuaded Freddy that Arjan suffered from eighty percent hearing loss in both ears and therefore found it too exhausting to be involved in business discussions. On every contact, Ernst was astonished by the sheer volume of ludicrous and contradictory statements that this man managed to utter within a few minutes. But his intentions were good, Ernst assumed.

The voice came ever closer until the familiar face, framed by a blond coiffure, black moustache and little beard, peered around the door. 'Knock, knock. Not disturbing you I hope?' Freddy grinned.

'You always do,' Ernst replied. 'Never mind, come and sit down.'

Freddy always wore the same seventies tracksuit top over a denim jacket. Complementing this outfit was a neckband of thick, black thread with tiny round stones, and – despite the miserable weather – a pair of sunglasses tilted back on his head. A new communications assistant from the theatre company, the third to appear this year, entered in his wake. No doubt Freddy had recruited her in a bar somewhere. She thrust out a hand to Ernst and introduced herself: 'Eveline van Diggelen'. Eveline looked fresh and wide awake, as though she had come straight from the shower to her work. Her hair was gathered back in a pony tail, and her ears sported silver trumpet-shaped earrings, like minute Christmas-tree ornaments. She was clad in a blazer, jeans and high-heeled boots. Ernst speculated whether she had a tattoo somewhere – a ladybird or a little elephant, he guessed, which she now regretted and made every effort to cover up.

Ernst was unsure how to operate the office espresso machine so he always asked visitors if they would like tea. Nine times out of ten they politely acquiesced but occasionally some bright spark would insist on coffee. Then he had to arrange a cup of coffee, usually with help from someone from the office. After all, he would break out in a sweat at the very sight of the espresso machine, which had a small LCD screen and two openings to put stuff in. Something would go wrong as soon as he touched it. Thankfully, this time both his visitors wanted tea.

'Ernst, we are planning to work very differently for the new show,' Freddy began. 'Something with special colours so it's obvious to everyone it comes from Spatt! You know, like Ikea with its blue and yellow. And Coca-Cola red, you know.'

'I do know, Freddy,' said Ernst, 'but their budgets are of a different order. In your case, who would recognize your colours? After all, the furthest you get is three black-and-white ads per year. In a manner of speaking.'

'I see your point,' Freddy replied. 'You know what, I'll pinch a bit from the props and costumes budgets. Enough to pay for colour posters. And we'll stick them up all round the city. What do you think of that? It's going to be big this time, a real smash.'

'What about your props and costumes then?'

'I have all the props we need in my shed, and the players can perform in the nude,' Freddy said. 'We can scrap the wigs and makeup too!'

'What's the piece called then?' Ernst asked.

'It's called *Here Are the Facts You Requested* – provisionally, at least,' Freddy replied. 'I'll give you the lowdown on how it's going, and fill you in on the staging and the performers,' he added.

Tell me all you like, thought Ernst, but it won't make a damn of difference to the design. 'Go ahead,' he said.

Freddy launched into his story. Ernst pretended at first to take notes now and then, thinking meanwhile about theatre posters. There was a special prize you could win for those. In fact, the design business had a prize for practically everything that could be printed. The awards were generally organized by a variety of professional and stakeholder organizations, including international ones. The designers' clients fortunately had not even the faintest idea of the actual status of a particular prize, but they were pleased with the recognition regardless who gave it. It meant they had chosen to work with an award-winning firm!

Ernst and Arjan had been honoured in the past with awards for the best designed annual report, the ultimate compliments card, the best flyer of 1998, the best-produced book, the best-folded brochure and several others.

The artistic tradition in the theatre poster genre was dominated by quasi 'in the raw' photography, generally involving a combination of nudity with some or other prop that was intended as a metaphor for something. For example, Ernst thought of the poster with the naked black man holding a yellow Dutch clog before his private parts, and the one with a mature actress posing in a white slip and glaring with visible irritation at the camera; the text of the poster was painted on her bare skin. Designs like these were in his view often ludicrous and dated in their effort to come across as artistic and shocking. Still, it surprised him that there were still so many special-interest groups, especially those from the religious margins, who raised a fuss about poster images like that. It was a ridiculously outdated attitude. And something that was completely incomprehensible to him was that certain organizations took the protests seriously and were afraid to burn their fingers on bad publicity. Quite apart from the fact that a controversy could deliver more publicity than the client could ever gain by other means, he thought it was cowardly. Maybe it was time for a second sexual revolution, even if many of the 1960s generation had fared poorly from the liberating experience.

'So you think you can make something that gets to the core of our new production, do you?' Freddy asked. 'And will make a big splash when people see it?' Eveline added.

'Probably,' replied Ernst, 'At least I'd like to have a stab at it.'

'Make sure people know that we are a musical theatre company, and they know where the performance is. We don't want people to go to the wrong place,' Eveline said.

'How on Earth could it be anywhere else,' Ernst asked, 'you haven't moved have you?'

'No, of course not, it's in our own theatre,' Freddy answered.

'Then it should be no problem,' Ernst reassured Eveline.

'It needs to be legible, and my name must be in big letters,' Freddy said. 'And it must have photos of all the actors – otherwise I'll get the usual load of guff.'

'Wouldn't it be enough to show the actors' names in the text?' Ernst asked.

'Also possible,' Freddy replied, 'but not lettering only, like last time, if you don't mind. People thought it was boring, more like a poster for a flea market. We don't need to pay an expensive design agency to make us something like that.'

'On the contrary,' Ernst said. 'Otherwise it wouldn't have looked as good and we would never have won an award at the Hungarian Poster Biennale.'

'The Hungarian prize was nice, but it doesn't fill any seats in our theatre,' Eveline said. 'We'll also be doing the social media, of course. Do you have all the icons for on the poster? We'll need at least FaceBook, Twitter and YouTube. And what about Flutter, Rupper en Skoepi?'

'It would be a good idea to put a QR code on the poster too,' Freddy added, to demonstrate his familiarity with technical matters.

'A QR code? That's so 2011,' Eveline smirked. 'No one uses QR codes any more.'

'Nobody has ever used QR codes,' said Ernst.

'Thanks, Ernst,' Freddy said getting up. 'Eveline, check out the schedule with Monique, would you? I'm going for a quick workout and a sandwich. Cute little trainee you have there, by the way,' he winked at Ernst.

Meals were often an irritation to Ernst when he was occupied with work. His thoughts and activities were interrupted three times a day. Liquid nutrition was quicker. So he always breakfasted on a plate of Brinta, a Dutch wheat porridge a bit like a quick-setting cement of fibre and milk. That kept him going until about 2 p.m. Then he would take lunch in the studio, which had a well-stocked larder of supplies from which the trainee made him sandwiches. To cut the time wasted on cooking an evening meal, he bought several dozen pots of baby and toddler food every few weeks. He had developed some favourites over the years. Nutricia spinach with beef (for age 3+) was pretty tasty. Olvarit pasta with cheese and tomato sauce (8 months and above) wasn't bad either. He would boost the flavour by stirring in some extra salt before microwaving the delicacy. Some of the products were labelled organic, which made Ernst feel a little better. He generally followed the main course by a portion of fruit yoghurt, vla or another dairy product of similar consistency. On occasions such as business receptions or exhibition openings, he would consume enough of the snacks on offer to satisfy his own nutritional needs.

When Ernst entered the Secret Annex about 10.30, he encountered Arjan operating a vacuum pump to seal some substance in plastic packaging. It looked like pieces of mummified excrement such as he had seen in the Natural History Museum. 'There's an artist who's already done that,' Ernst said. 'Wim Delvoye if I remember correctly.'
'No, that's an author,' Arjan said.
'Wrong. You are thinking of Tom Lanoye.'
'It doesn't matter. This isn't art, it's a product design,' Arjan replied. For years he had been trying to develop a product that would provide them both with a comfortable income; something totally useless, perhaps, but which would sell like hot cakes. When Arjan held forth on his vague ideas, Ernst found himself beguiled by the prospects of an easy fortune. The problem was that all the products hitherto were hilariously incomprehensible and inappropriate. No shop had ever laid in a stock of anything of the kind. The only place to offer the articles for sale was their own web-store. Yet Arjan was invariably convinced of the business potential of his latest product. He would work out the putative profits for the benefit of Ernst: 'If we print a hundred *So sorry, you're gay* stickers and we sell them for five euros each, that gives us five hundred euros. But if we print five hundred, it won't cost much more but we'll earn five times as much. Let's see, that 2,500 euros!' Who would buy the product and where it would be sold was irrelevant to him. What is more, he would express irritation every time a pallet of products was delivered to their studio. 'What am I supposed to do with these?' he would cry. 'Put them in the archives, and don't show or give away too many of them because we need to conserve our stock.'

Monique was keen to unleash her underutilized marketing skills on the products, so as to free up storage space and bring in some real money. But Arjan was implacable. 'People must come to the studio themselves if they want any,' he would say. Ernst saw a close resemblance to the fate of his own artistic work, so he had no hesitation about describing Arjan's unwanted and useless products as Art. With a pinch of good will, after all, you could see an implicit social critique in them. Arjan did not care what Ernst called the products: 'The name isn't important, as long as there's a gap in the market.'

The plastic crates in the racks were full of such products. There were three boxes containing 490 *So sorry, you're gay* stickers (Arjan had given ten away and kept a record of the recipients names), as well as boxes of transparent wallpaper, dummy coins, geometrical soft toys, handleless shopping bags, child-friendly cigarette lighters, little bags of coloured sand and countless stickers with baffling slogans like *If you're not doing it now you never will succeed in doing so* and *If you have a bungalow with a balcony, just jump!*

Ernst tried for his part to persuade Arjan that they both had qualities as fine artists. Few people were capable of seeing beyond the superficial. But he was. It was not in the technical sense of 'I can see something you can't,' but of associative seeing: being able to analyse and interpret things. Every day Ernst practised by unconsciously drawing conclusions about what he saw, and by considering how original or authentic a particular image was. Arjan steadfastly refused to call himself an artist. But when it came down to it, Ernst could find no other term to describe their activities in the Secret Annex.

When Ernst himself set to work in the atelier, he made a lot of things in parallel and at breakneck speed, without trying to make something more beautiful than he could make it, and without entertaining the idea that anything could fail. He felt like a genius in every action he undertook. Sometimes he made things that were so strange that he felt unwell as soon as the heady excitement of work was over. He tried to delve deeper for his thoughts or to shake off any rational inclinations during whatever it was he was doing. He had no need of bronze, marble, tubes of oil paint or pre-stretched canvases for his work, but of something which he could bring to life, which could develop and survive of its own accord. He could do this with any material he had available – a pen, a sketchbook, anything. The state of agitation in which he worked felt similar to an irresistible urge to defecate. Afterwards he would leave everything standing, and not look at it again until several days later, when he would scrutinize it with fresh eyes. Then he would select those pieces which he felt merited exposing outside the Secret Annex.

A week later, Barbara van Schutterstaert came to pick Ernst from the reception desk of the museum. He had entered the building by a back door. The museum had been closed for nearly two years because of major renovations to the reception area, cloakroom and toilets.

'I'd like to brief you on our campaign focus for communicating our reopening to our target public,' Barbara said. 'I engaged a consultancy to help us through a process to identify our core values. We dedicated some long meetings to figuring out who we actually are now and who we want to be.'

'OK, so who are you?' Ernst asked.

'The results have proved very valuable,' Barbara said. 'The communications consultants have boiled them down into a brand profile and a mission statement of our values.'

Ernst could see a rectangle of black foamboard on the table with a A3 sheet stuck on it. The paper was printed with a column of seemingly detached words, and the foamboard was held upright by a folded cardboard stand. Ernst had seen similar displays on sale in an arts and crafts shop which promoted itself as a 'Center for Creative Supplies'. It struck him that the sheet was printed in an ugly typography with little feeling for layout.

'Is that it?' Ernst asked, nodding towards the foamboard display.

'Yes, that is one of the mood boards which were the final result of our session,' Barbara replied. 'Dynamic, catering to all ages, challenging, out-of-the-box, accessible, positive, energetic, multi-coloured and fresh,' she read out aloud.

It was not the first time Ernst had seen a list of this kind. He had read at least twenty of them. Mentally he composed his own mood board for a different type of organization: inward-looking, monochrome, cynical, static, lazy, limited, inaccessible. What kind of design was appropriate to that? Probably the same as we are going to do now, he concluded.

'We are also planning a smartphone campaign,' she said. 'Look, there's already an app called Diper which lets you take a photo of a magazine article and get more information on your smartphone. Although you do need the latest OS because otherwise you can't download it.'

Ernst suspected gadget-freaks who liked playing around with that kind of thing of were masking their lack of confidence by doing something with the phone – in the same way as smokers try to strike a pose with a cigarette in hand. 'Anyway', Barbara continued, 'it was normal practice in my last job to launch a pitch contest for a campaign.' Ernst had not heard of a pitch contest but he felt certain Barbara was about to tell him. 'A pitch contest is a competition where various designer firms each hold a pitch for their creative ideas with a price tag attached,' she continued. 'Then the client commissions one of the designers. It gives the client a chance to find out which of the designers fits in best with the organization's profile. But the director doesn't consider it necessary in your case because he has confidence in your studio's work.' Indeed, it struck Ernst as an unnecessary waste of time. Besides, it took only a minute to see what kind of design results a firm produces. The real question was whether the client was sufficiently design-aware to decide whether those results fitted their needs.

'Could you email me your ideas tomorrow, Ernst?' she asked. She seemed to be in a hurry, although Ernst could not imagine why.

The design firm of Arjan and Ernst had grown steadily over the last decade. They used the same typeface, Standard Bold, for all their designs. Ernst had once tried a different font but the proposal was rejected. So he changed the face back to Standard Bold and everything went ahead. Apart from that, they had no written design philosophy. As long as Ernst or Arjan approved the work then it was in order. A crucial test was to show the proposed design to Monique. If she couldn't understand it, then it was generally OK, and vice versa.

Sometimes their designs looked so simple that others thought it would be easy to do something similar themselves. It was just a matter of the typeface and the colours, it seemed, so why go to the expense of a design studio? Our in-house paste-up specialist could do just as well, the client reasoned. But the results were always inferior. They showed no feeling for composition or for a hierarchy of information. It was immediately obvious to anyone: this was the work of an amateur, a mere parody of a Laupvogel design. It was at times like this when Ernst noted with surprise that their work was a professional discipline, indeed a gift. Their designs had so often been imitated by other designers or even by their own clients, yet the results were embarrassing, devoid of sensitivity, talent or whatever it might be. Laupvogel collected the most obvious imitations or straight copies of their designs in a box file.

They had never had to canvass for clients. What is more, they often put people off. However, that proved to work to their disadvantage; they would always be phoned back by someone who insisted on a Laupvogel design.

When selecting new designers to reinforce the staff, Ernst paid attention first and foremost to the candidate's taste in music. After all, music played all day long in the studio. The partners also chose new employees on the basis of the work they showed and their comments about it, of the correctness and politeness of their speech and of their capacity to stay silent when there was no reason to speak.

The young men who entered their employment would often be desperate to prove themselves. The young women, on the other hand, tended to start off in a reticent way but gradually revealed their talent as designers. In the long run all Laupvogel's staff designers were female.

Ernst was not an entrepreneur by nature. Maximizing profit was a secondary consideration, and he found doing business rather mundane. It was an aspect of their studio which had more or less descended on them unasked. The staff worked normal daily hours but the studio was closed on Fridays. Arjan and Ernst were happy to be surrounded by people who shielded them from all the trivial problems of their clients. They had taught their employees all the tricks of the trade, in particular their arsenal of techniques to defend a good design. They decided that in the long run it was in the client's own best interests, even if the latter did not realize it. One such technique was to present the design at the last possible minute, just before it was due to go to the printers, thereby leaving no time to make major changes. Another was to present a rejected design again unchanged; the client would usually find it much improved over the first attempt and approve it unreservedly. And another was to make the lettering smaller than normal on the first presentation, because you know that people always ask for the lettering to be larger; the result was that the text ended up at the desirable size. It was a little sneaky, but the motives were good. One day they would be thankful to Laupvogel.

III

'Coffee?' asked the artist Jonas Kreupelstorm. Ernst peered at the small coffeemaker teetering on the edge of an old sink unit. There appeared to be little choice. 'Okay, why not for once,' Ernst replied.

The artist had two old armchairs upholstered in corduroy fabric and a battered stool that served as a table. The studio occupied a classroom in a dilapidated former school. It had a high ceiling that left room for an entresol. An oil stove provided heating. One wall was kept empty and painted in pure white, an ideal backdrop for presenting work to visitors and for photographing it in a museum-like setting. Jonas had just returned from an artist-in-residence period at a large American ceramics factory.

'What caused the explosion then?' Ernst asked.

'Well, they have an enormous kiln measuring one hundred and fifty metres long. The toilets and washbasins all go in at one end and come out at the other. My work was fired along with their own products.'

'So what was wrong with your objects?' Ernst asked.

'The recycling bin is full of unfired clay products. Greenware, as they call it,' Jonas answered. 'They look weird, all those misshapen toilet pots. So I rescued some of them from the bin and moulded them together a bit, although I didn't change them much. I assumed that they had all been dried out enough in the drying cabinet, but the clay was too thick so it was still relatively wet. The result is like throwing water on a pan of hot frying oil.'

'And that explodes in the kiln, of course,' Ernst said.

'Yes, and it blasts all the surrounding pottery products. Even the tiniest fragment hitting one of those beautifully glazed pots makes it unsalable, so they weren't very pleased. Experts from the insurance company were all over the place. Actually I had made holes in my object to be on the safe side but it wasn't enough. Moisture and heat, you know: that's always bad news. I was lucky that nothing hit the conveyor rails, because otherwise they would have to send someone in to chip off the bits of dried clay; and that would mean waiting for the kiln to cool down. The kiln is meant to run continuously, 24 hours a day, so it would have been a real disaster.'

'Was anything left over of your own work?' Ernst asked.

'Yes, three of the twenty pieces came off unscathed, and they are fabulous. I'll show you in a minute', Jonas said.

Ernst drank his coffee, tempered with ample milk and sugar, from an old mug with a broken handle. There were a few artists living in the city whose work Ernst frankly admired. He could not say the same about graphic design studios, which always irritated him with their predictable, facile output. It was for this reason that he avoided going to social events and professional meetings organized for the design fraternity. Now and then he visited some of the artists he appreciated in their studios. Most of these were spaces in decrepit former school buildings provided by a foundation for providing accommodation to artists. They were studios for artists whose existence was totally unknown to the municipal property agent, who was incapable of distinguishing artists from creative entrepreneurs. On studio visits, Ernst listened to the answers to his questions and looked attentively at the works shown to him.

'How are you managing to survive,' Ernst asked.

'I'm living at my girl-friend's place, and she has a job. I had a part-time job myself at Museum Borselaar Bizaksium, working in the exhibition construction team. It didn't last though. We were building up a blockbuster show of one of the Flemish Masters when we played a little joke on the curator. We hid a couple of the canvases and told him they had been stolen. They didn't take kindly to that and didn't renew our contracts. Now I deliver post and work part time in a pharmaceutical warehouse putting pills in bottles all day. And I'm working on a new subsidy application,' Jonas replied.

'What about your gallery?' Ernst asked. 'It has a good reputation doesn't it?'

'They don't do a damn thing. They never put me in the art fair shows. It'll be another two years before I'm in line for a two-man show. If they sell any works of mine, I have to phone them a hundred times before I get my share of the money – and they keep fifty percent of it. I'm not allowed to sell anything without them as middlemen. They even kick up a fuss about exchanging work with other artists. It's bad for your career, they say, but their real concern is that they don't earn anything from the transaction. So even that I have to do secretly.'

Ernst would have liked to buy a piece of work on some of these studio visits, as much to show his appreciation for the work as to enjoy the thrill of possessing it. That was beyond his means however. He had heard about artists acquiring works of art through exchanges with others. But he felt embarrassed to suggest this himself. Could it ever be a fair exchange? After all, his work was the work of a split personality. He was half designer – not a bad designer, admittedly, but still a somewhat self-willed layer-out of other people's messages. It was his main source of income, and, as Arjan always said, you are what you earn. Would an artist really care to exchange a work of his own for something from Laupvogel's atelier?

'Ernst, I wonder whether you actually read our briefing? This design doesn't seem have the look and feel we wanted. We all had a look at it, and our education manager thought it had something fascistic about it, with all those sharp-cornered letters and the black and red colour scheme. Then

we all saw it the same way. It's a bit Nazi-like.'

You can't say those guys didn't have a knack for marketing and communications, Ernst thought to himself. And the logo wasn't at all bad. 'So it does make an impact, doesn't it?' Ernst asked, hoping to rescue something positive from the situation.

'Yes, sure, but it isn't the kind of impact we want to be associated with. It certainly doesn't harmonize with our USP,' Barbara said, audibly frowning at the telephone mouthpiece. 'We are looking for a real bit of proactive marcom which shows some out-of-the-box thinking.'

'If this is your definitive proposal,' she continued, 'I think we had better hold a pitch contest after all. When I used to work at the HEMA, Studio Prima Zo used to pay attention to how we wanted things to be done.'

 'It's just an initial idea, but I'll put some more work into it,' Ernst said. 'You know what. I'll come along myself to present you and the director with my next proposal on my laptop and digital projector.' Ernst hoped that she would be impressed by this mention of expensive hardware, compared to that scrap of paper mounted on foamboard which the consultancy had produced. But it seemed to be of no avail. 'Can we fix a date?'

'Of course, I'll put you through to Monique,' Ernst replied, and transferred the call as quickly as possible. Just in time, he thought. He felt his ire rising and pictured himself pelting her with HEMA smoked sausages.

'Yes, another graduate of the University of Know-nothing,' Ernst replied. 'It doesn't harmonize with their USP.'

'Hm, USP. Isn't that the parcel delivery firm with black vans?' Arjan asked.

'No that's UPS. USP stands for "unique selling point",' Ernst read out aloud, having just spotted it in the Google results on his laptop screen.

'The unique selling point of the Taxation & Customs Museum?' Arjan paused for a moment and thought of the characteristic blue envelopes in which Dutch tax communications arrive. 'How about putting the invitations in blue envelopes?' he said. 'Wouldn't that be something?'

'That occurred to me too,' Ernst replied, 'tax-demand lookalikes as teasers.

I suggested it to them but they thought the associations were too negative.'

'I hear the frog is talking to the Chinaman again,' Arjan said.

Ernst and Arjan had made a sport of inventing colourful new expressions to ridicule the complete lack of logic they encountered. These were generally variants on the bucolic idioms with which colloquial Dutch is so generously endowed, such as the saying about pincers and pigs. The game was to find a pair of unrelated concepts that suggested the paradox in the most graphic and poetic way possible. Their verbal inventions served them as shared imagery which they both recognized as metaphors for the dualities between marketing and graphic design, between graphic design and art, between high and low culture, and sometimes between their own characters. The alternating experiential worlds into which they both ventured related to one another as a Venetian blind to a squirrel. Or as Nelson Mandela to an exhaust pipe. Or the Arab Spring to Aron Winter.

Their first exhibition had been on the invitation of a gallery owner who had noticed the final examination project of Ernst and Arjan. He had obtained a subsidy from one of the many national art funds which redistributed money on behalf of the government. This collectivist principle had been on the decline since the consequences of the banking crisis became clear. And although artists were not directly culpable for this situation, there was no strong argument against making cuts here as in other areas. Peer to peer reviewing in the national subsidy system proved to be a snake that consumed its own tail. Peer pressure had the effect of creating a reservation of insiders of the same mentality who understood only one another. The outside world, with little patience for this incomprehensibility, wondered why money had to be spent on them. And no one could explain why. Let them seek sponsors and private individuals for support, was the conclusion. Sports clubs functioned that way, didn't they?

Ernst had heard countless far-fetched arguments to defend the arts in these times of austerity. Among them were that it would be good for the economy, that it would foster integration and social interaction, that it would enhance the functioning of democracy and that it would improve school exam results. They were all attractive-sounding excuses which tried to justify art as a tool, as serving some external goal. Why couldn't art just be art, without serving any other purpose?

If the government refused to continue financing art, Ernst thought, I can think of no argument that would justify a subsidizing policy. It had no social function or utility, in his view, or at least none that was applicable in all cases. That, when it came down to it, was perhaps the only valid argument in favour of funding art: that there needed to be space where no kind of imposed value, utility, logic, social aspiration or financial motivation prevailed. It would be terrible if artists were obliged to adapt to, and satisfy, the expectations of others. Plenty of sponsors were keen to cut a dash with large, successful organizations, but not to take the risk of supporting an 'R&D department' of the arts.

Arjan and Ernst were loading a rented van with four pieces of work from the Secret Annex. They were destined for a group exhibition in the south of the city. Laupvogel was the only artist duo. Apart from them, six individual artists (one of whom was as yet unknown to Ernst) were taking part in the show. Ernst had chosen two works from a series of nearly eighty faces he had painted on all kinds of waste materials. They were like smileys, the most innocent and positive graphic symbol that Ernst knew. The neurotic grins of Ernst's versions gave them an insane look. In some cases, they had a facial expression which reminded him of Tommy Cooper. In sombre moments he needed only think for a few minutes of the hilarious conjuring of his hero to roll on the floor laughing until the tears ran. Arjan had a new product in the pipeline but was as yet unwilling to reveal the final result of his work, fearing that someone might steal his unpatented idea. He had therefore chosen to show a work that depicted the basic principle of action of this gap in the market. It was something with carpet tiles on which old table fans were arranged, and were supposed to have a certain effect when they reached a certain angle. The idea was incomprehensible to Ernst, but never mind, it did not look out of place among the other work appearing in the exhibition.

Ernst pondered over what might be the shared themes of their work. At first it was mainly reactivity: they make pastiches and parodies of everything around them. Nowadays that had changed; Ernst's inspiration came more from himself but without being autobiographical. In reflecting on his own work, nowadays, he thought of it above all as stylish, distinctive but always mischievous play. He recalled how he used to play with his boyhood mates by launching folded paper arrows into people's open windows using a length of plastic tubing from the DIY store. Rolled up inside the darts were small obscene drawings, often accompanied by absurd legends such as 'This arrow is a public service from Mayor E. Laupman.'

Before the firm of Laupvogel occupied its present premises, their office was in a small attic storey a few streets away. An ascent of eight flights of stairs brought the visitor into a space beneath a pitched roof where the structural wooden beams were fully exposed to view. An old door led to a gutter between two adjacent roof slopes and sported an illuminated green panel identifying it as the emergency exit. Ernst's and Arjan's artistic activities necessarily took place in the open central area between the computer desks. Their found materials and the pungent fumes of the paints they used ran contrary to the businesslike image of the design practice. This was a thorn in the side of Monique the business manager. The final straw came when the head of postage stamp development at the National Postal Company, lured at long last into their office by every inducement, received a nasty bruise in the backside from a pallet that fell from a precarious art installation then under construction.

In the period that followed, Laupvogel took abode in a succession of so-called anti-squats. Office blocks that had remained vacant for longer than a certain minimum time would be filled with temporary tenants, making squatting effectively illegal since the building was now 'occupied'. The estate agents and property owners who offered this service feared the potentially lengthy legal battles to evict squatters, who were moreover prone to trash the interior when finally forced to leave. The anti-squatting scheme attracted all kinds of characters whose largest common denominator was seeking an ample floor area for a low rent. The tenants included many artists – although of patchy quality, Ernst thought. The hopeless daubing of the lesser among them, in his eyes, was proof that the creative urge could never be completely repressed. He had read somewhere that an artist in Auschwitz had painted Snow White and the Seven Dwarves on the side of one of the barracks. Even in hell, apparently, there were people who just had to make art. Maybe that was the Unique Selling Point of humanity with respect to the animal kingdom: making art, whether anyone else wanted it or not.

People will always make art and the demand for it will arise of its own accord. Or it won't. Or too late. Meanwhile, you had to keep body and soul together, with or without subsidies. But hey, who's to blame? The anti-squatting situation was far from ideal. Ernst and Arjan were forever cycling back and forth between the design studio and their 'atelier', loaded with bags and boxes. Often they were needed only for a moment in the studio, and some items like cameras were needed at both locations. The anti-squatting atelier proved to be a time-waster of major proportions. Furthermore, most of the premises were unheated, so in winter Ernst and Arjan would be padded like Michelin men. There was always a carry-on with the different keys to the huge number of doors, as well as with the code-controlled security systems which were supposed to be enabled once everyone had left the building. Ernst had been locked in one night in a huge, empty office building after a co-tenant had actuated all the electronic door locks. The toilets were generally inoperative, so one would have to leave the building to relieve oneself. The biggest drawback was the unpredictability of the tenancy. The notice period was only two weeks. Emptying the atelier and moving all the collected leftover materials to a new anti-squat in cost at least two days: hiring a van, lugging boxes up and down stairs and so on. The contract required the tenant to pay a deposit to cover potential damage, but Laupvogel never obtained a refund because some or other trace of their activities was invariably visible.

IV

'Lovely, those tree-thingies or whatever they are,' said Freddy, the artistic director of Spatt!, plunging onto the Kalou sofa. Eveline remained standing, having squinted distastefully at the leather monstrosity. In one corner of the atelier, Arjan had filled a number of pillow-slips with expanded insulating foam and mounted them on bamboo poles. They were covered with stuck-on pieces of green plastic tarpaulin. There was indeed something of trees about them, Ernst agreed. 'Maybe I can use them as scenery,' Freddy continued.

'I'd have to ask Arjan,' Ernst said, pouring three cups of tea.

'I came to talk about the stuff you sent us.' Ernst looked inquisitively at Freddy. 'I mean your proposal for the poster for our new production.'

'Of course, the poster for *Here Are the Facts You Requested*,' Ernst recollected.

'Exactly, although the title has now changed to *Strange Infatuation*, by the way. Anyway, it's cheerful and fresh with those nursery colours, but we don't want people to go thinking it's a children's production do we?' Freddy said. 'Josje agrees with me on that.'

The last piece of information was one which Ernst would have preferred not to hear. Josje was Freddy's wife, who also worked for Spatt! If everyone were to base arguments on the consent of his or her spouse, Ernst thought, we would never get very far. This remark and the fact that his wife worked in the same organization and that their dog was also often to be seen there was, in Ernst's view, the very picture of amateurism. It was fortunate that Freddy never brought his dog along to the studio because otherwise Freddy would be bound to ask the dog's opinion too, Ernst feared.

'It's too much like something for *Miffy, the Musical*,' Eveline said, standing with arms folded.

To Ernst this analogy was a compliment because he was a great admirer of Dick Bruna. But he feared that his esteem for Uncle Dick, as he always called Bruna, would fail to convince this pair.

'Besides the fact that I don't cater for children,' Freddy said, 'you have to realize that the protagonist of this piece has the tendons in his feet severed, he tears out his own eyes, he murders his father and he screws his own mother. Not suitable for under-eighteens, you could say. Never mind, Ernst, would you mind taking another look and designing something different for us, something that fits the content of the piece better? Eveline suggested holding a pitch competition for various designers. You know what that is, don't you Ernst?'

'Of course I do,' Ernst replied, 'although it seems superfluous in the present situation.'

'I also think we should go for a viral marketing campaign,' Eveline said.

'Tell me more,' said Ernst.

Freddy looked at his protégée with pride. 'A viral campaign,' Eveline explained, 'is when your message reproduces itself of its own accord, like a virus. People see it in the social media and post it to friends through their network. It's more personal kind of marketing and communication.' More sneaky, you mean, Ernst thought.

Arjan entered, but he had not allowed for the presence of Freddy and Eveline. Ernst saw a slight panic in Arjan's eyes. Ernst gestured at him with his hands, saying 'Fred ... the trees ... wants them ... for the theatre ... OK?'

Arjan nodded vigorously. 'Was that a yes?' Freddy asked.

'It was,' replied Ernst. 'Indeed, he's enthusiastic.'

'How lovely that you two have learned to communicate so well over the years,' Freddy said. 'I'd like to base a theatre piece on that some time.'

To Ernst, 'marketing' meant a pseudo-academic way of talking about selling things to people. He understood of course that art organizations need an exalted kind of sales promotion in their struggle to attract visitors. But applying for-profit marketing strategies to actual works of art was misguided, in Ernst's view.

The intention of marketing consumer goods was to place the product with people. In art, things worked quite differently: the intention was to attract people to the 'product'. And this product, the work of art, never accommodated itself to the wishes of the consumer. If it were to do so, it would no longer be a matter of art but of entertainment. The 'product' is thus inviolable and constant, and a public must be sought for it. In commercial marketing, on the other hand, the product is seamlessly adapted to the wishes of the consumer. Is it too big for the target group? Then make it smaller. Does the target group prefer blue? Then the product is blue. The consumer does not like surprises or risks: he chooses blue. But in the case of art, you never know what you will get or what value it will be to you. If it does have a value for you, then it is an abstract value such as insight, revelation or experience. It satisfies multiple needs or none at all – immediately, or not until you get it home, or ten years later while you are on the train. The experience is wholly individual; everyone experiences something different. And individualism is anti-marketing. When Laupvogel announced an art event, there were two groups to be reached: their professional peers, who sat on committees that dealt out the subsidies and wrote reviews in the papers, and a public with a longing for something unknown. The public's decision on whether to go or not began with the first glimpse of the flyer.

In their third year at the art academy, the senior lecturer assigned Arjan and Ernst to the LBD studio as a form of punishment. It was a place where students could work on real projects that were commissioned from the academy. The LBD studio was a small classroom in an otherwise empty temporary building, several streets away from the main academy. LBD stood for 'learning by doing'. None of the students were keen to work there.

There was invariably someone in some low-budget organization or company who would come up the idea of turning to the academy for help. It would probably be inexpensive and students could allegedly learn something from the experience. In the main building, student assignments generally related to fictional projects, which were idealistic and had no deadlines. For example, Ernst once spent six months working on a record cover for his favourite band, The Pixies. Arjan was banished to the LBD studio because he had returned several library books two-and-a-half years too late, and had failed to pay the fine. Ernst, for his part, had been summoned to the director's office because he had placed a fake announcement on the noticeboard promising study credits to interior design students if they would be so kind as to paint the walls of their classrooms black instead of the customary white. Ernst and Arjan were assigned two design projects: a house style for a psychiatric care home, and another for the Netherlands Institute of Aircraft and Space Vehicle Development.

One day the director of the academy appeared unexpectedly in the LBD Studio. An obituary notice was needed quickly for the national newspapers: a famous American artist who had once half-followed a course of evening classes at the academy (and after whom the academy was later to be named) had just died. Could Ernst help him out? It was an honour Ernst could not refuse. Knowing that the artist was a noted abstract-impressionist, he roughed out a bold design in a corresponding style. When the director came by again an hour later he was aghast. Couldn't Ernst make something more conventional? Ernst reluctantly agreed, secretly wishing he hadn't taken it on in the first place. Meanwhile Arjan had followed most of the conversation through the thin partition that divided them, and came to Ernst's rescue as soon as the director was out of earshot. Neither the director nor Ernst had been aware that Arjan previously studied at a graphic crafts school, and that he had ample experience of practical typography and computer layout. Arjan and Ernst lost no time in arriving at a result behind which they both stood. The director was full of praise for the result.

The unplanned collaboration in the temporary building, where they had both commenced reluctantly, led eventually to Arjan becoming involved in the flyers that Ernst was covertly making for a Gothic music venue on the academy's computers. Ernst similarly offered his critique of the surfers' magazine on which Arjan was working. Prior to the postmodern period it would have been inconceivable for a happy-go-lucky, surfing-obsessed teetotaller to collaborate successfully with a melancholic, fatalistic shoegazer. Arjan possessed many qualities that were lacking in Ernst, and vice versa. On their way to a goal, Arjan would take a left turn and Ernst a right turn, but they would arrive together at the same result. To Ernst, music was everything; to Arjan it meant nothing. Arjan was tidy and well-organized in his work; Ernst was sloppy and chaotic. Arjan was direct and black-and-white; Ernst was circumspect and nuanced. Arjan loved detail; Ernst the broad gesture. Ernst was morose but Arjan effervescent. Paradoxically, their collaboration resulted in an effective modus operandi which rose above their capacities as individuals. They were both capable of making good work as individuals, but perceiving and frankly accepting each other's better qualities proved more productive. The academy lecturer who had forced them together had turned out to be a chemist with psychological insights: he had set off a violent but high-yield reaction between two highly concentrated reagents. It reminded Ernst of the Jagger-Richards relationship – or, more precisely the Jagger-Richards transaction – even though Arjan probably had no idea who those names referred to.

Following the incident with the falling pallet, the postage stamp manager, who had suffered a bruised rib, phoned Laupvogel to thank them for the basket of fruit they sent. At the same time he mentioned that he was opting for another studio; a consultation had taken place with the working committee, in which six persons had declared their interests. What a lot of people to be involved in such a little piece of paper, Ernst thought. In the sixties and seventies, when a many public services and corporations were still publicly owned, there had been ample time and room for a well-founded, public-elevating design philosophy. The postal service was an excellent example of this era. A tradition of modern design had developed in the Netherlands, giving the large nationalized institutions a highly progressive image. The banknotes, among other things, stood out for their clever, iconic designs. Since then, the country had shed most of the public corporations. Privatization was more or less complete by the time Ernst graduated. Public commissions for designs like those displayed at the academy and published in the glossy design magazines no longer existed. Disappointment was widespread when the new Euro banknotes replaced the much-admired modern designs of their Dutch predecessors. Nothing was happening in the design world, yet everything seemed to run its course unperturbed. Dutch designers proved to have been living in an illusory soap bubble. To Ernst, the images of subcultures from abroad were more exotic than the 'normal' Dutch design, which was exemplified by the cover of the official school atlas. Ernst remembered how bored he was by the Bosatlas on his school desk, and how his thoughts wandered to the record cover of an American indie band which he had at home. The design style of Laupman had unconscious roots in the solid national collective design tradition, but conscious ones in foreign subcultures: Total Design meets Raymond Pettibon.

Ernst was reading the papers. The tremendous clutter that filled the atelier tended to trigger his dust allergy, setting off a salvo of sneezing. Instead of politely holding his hand before his mouth, he took pleasure in sneezing wholeheartedly into the open newspaper. The effect resembled a photo of the universe with its countless galaxies and planetary systems. Thousands of moist droplets glittered like stars. Could the origin of the universe be traced to God having an allergic attack? Ernst had an album by Red House Painters playing when Arjan entered clad in a red woollen padded jacket of a kind supposedly made for polar expeditions but now sold as outdoor fashion. 'Jeez, who's funeral is it?' he said. 'No one,' Ernst replied, 'and believe it or not this is one of their more cheerful numbers.' Arjan began tidying up. Ernst had long lost interest in that. The activities of the last few weeks, involving dragging the found materials around and painting over them, had left a huge mess. The only consolation was that no one could see the ravages from the studio as long as the little door was closed. It was a bit like the kitchen in a typical nineteen-seventies' family home, before the vogue for open kitchens and cooking islands left the mess for all to see.

Monique stormed into their domain and cried, 'Time to get moving! You have an appointment with the accountants.'

Ten minutes later, they both sat perspiring from the hasty bicycle ride face to face with the worthy accountant. He must have explained the financial and fiscal niceties to Ernst and Arjan some two hundred times, but invariably, the instant they stepped out into the street, they could no longer remember exactly what he had told them. 'No, the profit is no longer taxed, it's only your income.' 'Yes, but why doesn't he deduct the costs then?' After failing to resolve their incomprehension together, they would leave matters for what they were and proceed to the order of the day. Ernst pictured how, once they left his office, the accountant and his colleagues would roll on the floor laughing at the inane questions of the Laupvogel partners. Once, when Laupvogel had to register with the Chamber of Commerce, the man at the desk had asked them to state the proposed purpose of their company. Arjan and Ernst came up with all kinds of ideas to describe their goals but could not arrive at a conclusion as to which was the most apt. The official, shaking his head wearily, at last cut them short: 'To make a PROFIT of course!'

Back at work again, Ernst pondered. He had stacks of dummy books, their blank pages filled with rough sketches of his ideas. He found it reassuring that his thoughts had been set down safely on paper, and accepted that life would be too short to work them all out in further detail much less to realize them. Once he had selected one of them to implement, he would fume with impatience and wished he could complete the whole business instantly. There were other times, however, when he was too lethargic to think of anything that had to do with work. It made him sick to think of it. He imagined himself starting a new career in some fresh, respectable field – something medical, perhaps. He would be an independent specialist in a white coat, working in aseptic conditions. He would mean something to people at large, and would naturally earn way above an average income. Of course, he would first have to study for six years. He had already encountered mankind in all its perishability on the visits he had made to a hospital. The interior was always clean, white and uncluttered, like an art gallery, but it was populated by ugly, nicotine-stained, poorly dressed, malodorous characters who all had something wrong with them. The idea of asking them to undress or looking into their mouths – well, no, that didn't appeal to him. And as for that charming, stylishly clad, educated woman in her early forties, with whom he would first chat about the fine arts and about the lovely resorts along the West Corsican coast, and whose pain he would then relieve by massaging her suntanned skin with fragrant oils – well, no, she sought treatment elsewhere. All you got were wheezing, flabby warehouse labourers with no vocabulary, a horrible dialect and a gold chain around the neck. You had to feed a rubber tube into their mouth, pull it out again at the other end, and wash them out over and over again. You got dirt on your white coat, and you had to put up with their backtalk too, complaints about how painful the treatment was and the like. All in all, it was much nicer to stay here in the atelier, even if you only had yourself to contend with all day.

He Googled for some phone numbers and picked up the phone.
'De Wit Camping Goods, good afternoon,' said a voice at the other end.
'Yes, good afternoon, this is Ernst Laupman from Design Studio Laupman.' This time Ernst refrained from blabbing his whole story to the first person to pick up the phone. Instead he needed to speak to someone who could understand his proposals and make important business decisions.
'Could I please speak to whoever is responsible for Research & Development?'
'Er .. what?' replied the voice.
'The head of production then?'
'I'll put you through to Mr. De Bruin,' the voice said. A beeping sound followed.
'De Bruin here,' said a new voice. Ernst could hear factory-like noises in the

background. This was clearly someone you could speak to about production.

'My name is Ernst Laupman, designer. I'd like to speak to you about an idea that for a new kind of tent which could attract a lot of attention and could possibly win industry awards.'

Ernst was careful to say designer rather than artist, because the word artist was all too likely to be associated with a demanding, useless and affected sponger. In other words, it would make a poor first impression. Design, on the other hand, sounded like a profession that earned big money nowadays.

'Our tent designs have already been decided on for the next few years,' said Mr. De Bruin.

'Of course, I understand that,' Ernst replied. 'I'm not talking about a tent that will be part of your normal range of products. It's an experiment, a kind of prototype. The important part is the printing on the tent fabric. Let me explain my idea. I see that your range includes igloo tents. I presume it won't be difficult to make them a bit rounder so that they are roughly hemispherical. Now just imagine that we print the northern hemisphere of the globe on the fabric. I'm thinking of a highly detailed print, with place names and so on. The funny thing is that it could just as well be the southern hemisphere, although maybe there aren't as many camping destinations south of the equator. But Antarctica would look great at the top of the tent.'

'Oh yes, I think I see. Yes, but ...'

'Once you put the tent up on a camp site, you can see where you are and you can plan your route, for example with a felt-tip pen, so there's no need for a map.'

'Hm, yes, but our tent fabrics are made in China and it would be difficult to ... er ...' Ernst heard a dog bark in the background. 'Excuse me, just a moment,' said the voice, then 'Down! Down, Wodan, down!' Ernst was no dog lover, and now he was on the line to someone who had a dog on the shopfloor. At one blow, the company had become unprofessional and untrustworthy.

'Down! Sit!', he heard. Ernst felt uncomfortable with the situation and hung up.

V

Laupvogel's works hung among the other artworks in a large central space in an old school. It must once have been the assembly hall in a technical or domestic science college. All the walls, as well as piping and other irregularities, were smothered with a thick, sloppy layer of white paint, as though a vertical blizzard had taken place. Ernst and Arjan were in the far south of the city in a nationally recognized problem district. Ernst was possibly the only person present to know his way around this neighbourhood. But his work bore no other connection to his home town. He could have made it anywhere, preferably somewhere in complete isolation. A local scene, in as far as it existed, meant nothing to him. If there was a place-to-be, he had never visited it. The local in-crowd of creative celebrities were mere dabblers to him. The only reason he was living in this city was his affinity with the underdog. Anyone with some talent but who was not popular, trendy, slick, speedy or arrived could reckon on his sympathy. Quite a few figures in this city fell into this category. It was not a place with an impressive cultural history, but a working city without pretensions. It was a business and logistics centre but no world metropolis. The city possessed the country's poorest and least educated population. The southern district was often scornfully called the national sewer pit. For days at a time, he would wander through neighbourhoods like this, where over 180 nationalities had settled. Why did he do that? Was it solely to hunt for leftover materials? Or was it a remedy for his elitist navel-gazing? Did he perhaps feel superior to these people on the bottom rung of society? Or was his purpose merely sentimental, to revisit the neighborhood where his parents had once lived? It was a love-hate relationship. He often found the city ugly and dull, but he felt indignant when people from elsewhere said so. After all, he was born here in South – on the same day as Rien Poortvliet.

The exhibition, titled *Passive Aggressive*, was inaugurated with a speech by an official from the borough council. The councillor expressed pleasure with developments in his borough; there was still a long way to go, but the right direction had been taken. The presence of artists in the district was confirmation of an improving trend.

The next speaker was the curator of the exhibition, who was also one of the participating artists. Ernst had his doubts about the correctness of this double role, but no one else seemed to have any objection to it. The curator thanked a whole catalogue of people, but said nothing about why these particular artists had been chosen for the show. The public attending the opening was relatively meagre, some thirty or forty people in Ernst's estimation. But everyone seemed to know everyone else.

Ernst scrutinized the design of the invitation and concluded that it wasn't too bad but hardly world-shaking; a bit of a me-too design, as Arjan would have called it. It complied perfectly with the current 'cultural' design trend. Laupvogel had first been asked to design the invitations, but Ernst felt that there was something morally dubious about the double role of designer and participating artist. So he had politely declined on behalf of Laupvogel. Perhaps no one would have given a damn apart from Arjan and Ernst themselves, and Ernst now wondered what gave rise to his pressing ethical concern to keep these activities separate.

Still wearing his coat and clutching a bottle of Stella Artois, Ernst toured the displayed works. Most of those present at the exhibition opening were chatting with one another. Apparently they had already seen the exhibited work. The air was thick with beer and cigarette fumes. Ernst peered around for some signs of catering but was forced to conclude that free snacks were a forlorn hope.

'It's turning into a bit of a sell-out here,' Arjan joked, gazing at the obscure art objects dotted around the hastily white-slopped interior of the dilapidated school building. 'Yes, it's all rather commercial,' Ernst said, matching Arjan's irony. 'Real mainstream stuff, isn't it?'

Five small panels were clustered on the wall in one corner of the space. At first sight they resembled pasted-up newspaper cuttings. When Ernst came closer, however, he could see that these were meticulously painted pictures of aircraft disasters. He was surprised for a moment; with painterly precision and craftsmanship, the artist had depicted the scattered pieces of the crashed flying machines, their ruptured hulls half buried in the ground from the impact. In some instances flames burst forth from the wreck. Ernst read the title beneath the work: *Planes Hide to Die*, by Sophie de Preille. It was the only participating artist whose name was unfamiliar to him.

Ernst sat at his desk in the studio between washing lines hung with secondhand ladies' clothing. He was replying to his email. The girls from the studio and their female friends had reserved the evening for a clothes swap party, and their preparations were already under way. Between a suspended brassiere and a pair of purple leggings, he observed that Monique was steering a girl of about 25 in his direction. It was obvious to Ernst that she was not from this city. Girls of this kind no longer existed here. Her complexion was far too fresh, possibly indicating that she came from somewhere where the air was less laden with industrial pollution. They shook hands.

'Sorry, I can't recall why we agreed to meet today,' Ernst admitted to the girl.

'I have come to interview you about Dutch Design,' she said. 'You are one of the designers we would like to include in the *life and living* supplement of our magazine.'

'Ah yes, please take a chair,' Ernst said. Dutch Design, eh, he thought. Doesn't that mean the popular crap you see in gift shops? He had seen enough pictures of that kind of thing in glossy magazines in the dentist's waiting room. He studied the girl and took a guess at her bra size. It could be either a 75D or a 75C. A chest measurement 75 was average, but the the cup size depended on the make and style; besides, bras usually included some padding nowadays, so D seemed not impossible. But no, 75C it was.

'I'd like to pose a few questions,' the girl said. 'I'll keep it short because I also have another appointment near here, at Studio "It's Our Pleasure". Do you know them, by the way?'

'No, never heard of them,' Ernst replied although he could already imagine what their output was like. 'Everyone is busy with their own work, of course.'

Ernst felt flattered that the girl seemed to take an interest in him, and that a designer was in her eyes a respectable figure. I wonder if she has a passion for literature, Ernst pondered.

Arjan's face appeared above the protective wall of rockwool slabs that they had erected to give their work area some privacy, behind the back of the girl. He was suggestively stroking a bar of chocolate around inside his mouth in the way a porn actress would do with an erect penis. Damn it, Arjan dragged everything down to a banal level, while he wanted to give serious answers to his visitor's questions. Ernst looked quickly back at the girl to avoid being distracted by Arjan, but it was now hard to concentrate on the interview.

'Did you also study at the Dutch Design Academy?' she asked, switching on her digital voice recorder.

'Er, no, neither of us has an arts training. We come from quite different directions,' Ernst replied.

'Interesting. What kind of background do you have then?' she asked.

The disturbance had made him ill at ease and bad tempered: 'My partner Arjan comes from a farming background, and later studied macroeconomics. I myself have done a variety of things, including physiotherapy and debt collecting.'

Ernst was perspiring slightly, but the girl did not turn a hair at this nonsense. 'What is your working method?' she asked. 'What do you do to generate new ideas, and how do you manage to create something different every time?'

'Well,' said Ernst, 'we usually rent a boat and load it with several crates of beer. One evening we were so plastered that we crashed into a ferryboat. Luckily it was moored at the time. We pushed our boat to the bank and slept it all off in the ferry steering cabin. It was very inspiring. Still, it's just as easy to get a good idea by sitting at a table drinking a cup of tea.'

'I see,' said the girl. 'What does Dutch Design mean to you? Do you consider yourselves Dutch?'

'No, to be honest. We never think about ourselves that way. We work in Holland, of course, so our work is technically speaking Dutch. Apart from that, we aren't really interested in design in general.'

The girl looked disappointed. 'But... you are a design agency, aren't you?'

'True,' said Ernst, 'but it's something we do on the side. For fun. We make our living from art.' He grabbed a stack of sketches he had just made of protest slogans with spelling errors, such as *Fuck the Sytsem*. From under it, he picked up a vacuum-packed object resembling a fox turd. 'Look, these are our products. And we sell them and other things through our web store.' The girl now looked at Ernst with suspicion.

'Wow, you really are an unconventional firm, aren't you?' she exclaimed.

'Yes,' said Ernst, 'although our main activities are not widely known. We sell mainly to major private collectors from abroad. We rejected this one,' he said, pointing to the plastic packages, 'because it turns out that it's been done before.'

After hearing some further bizarrely improvised answers to her questions, the girl decided it was time to go. She already had her coat on when Arjan called out behind her, 'Would you like to take some of our stickers with you?'

'I'd love to,' she replied with diplomatic politeness. 'What a funny company you are.' Ernst had his doubts about that.

Local politicians sometimes cited Laupvogel – to the dismay of Arjan and Ernst – as a shining example of artists who practise creative entrepreneurship. It was a characterization that Ernst considered self-contradictory. The politicians who lauded the creative industry as the best boy in the class were missing one important point: this best boy in the class had all along been copying the work of one of his schoolmates, who now stood in the corner as a punishment for not listening. That fellow pupil had thought up all his questions and answers himself, without prompting from the teacher. There could never have been a creative industry without its alleged practitioners 'borrowing' from the true artistic pioneers. The pioneers had discovered a mine of precious materials but did not exploit it themselves, for they had already set off on the next voyage of discovery. It was the creative industry that exploited the mine; they had the knack of polishing up the raw materials and marketing them to the public at large. The creative industry was nothing but an industrial process based on a division of labour, standardization, planning and the pursuit of profit.

In Ernst's and Arjan's speciality, the resulting output was dominated by stereotypes, cliches and repetition. It was all conformism, adaptation to social relations. How could designers still be authentic and critical if their only function was to boost the economy? What if they were called on to redesign some packaging in order to create new demand for the same product? What if they chose to toil along with the other lackeys in the hedonistic treadmill without throwing a spanner in the works? Looking back once more to twenty years ago, Ernst recalled taking and passing the three-day exam for entry to the Academy of Fine Arts. The work he had made in those days must surely still be stored somewhere in the academy's archives – or might they have thrown it all away long ago? Ernst and Arjan were in the same foundation year. Ernst had been surprised at the outspokenness of his fellow students, including Arjan, a quality which he had never experienced in the schools on his home ground. The past meekness and respectfulness towards the teachers had vanished. Here you could converse and joke with the lecturers almost as equals. It was at the academy that he found his calling. Studying (in as far as you could call it that, for it was more like producing) was no effort to him whatsoever. Not once did he receive a grade lower than the maximum A, except for technical drawing. Arjan had arrived at the academy by a more circuitous route. He had completed a previous study at a graphic crafts school, but now at the academy everything he had previously learned became instantly invalid and useless. Many of their fellow students were far from high-flyers intellectually, and were unable to shake off the brainwashing of their earlier vocational training. Apart from Arjan, none of the students worked on an Apple computer at home. The rest would hang around all day in one of the classrooms, which were empty except for a few computers. It was unclear when the lesson started or ended. Ernst and his classmates killed time together in their classroom, jawing and joking to relieve the boredom. Actually it was the best possible method of study to foster creative development. Ernst always had some A4 sheets of paper in his bag which were preprinted with headings like 'Temporarily Unavailable', 'Wet' and 'Out of Order'. He used these to make fictive announcements for site-specific situations. At the academy, he publicized a variety of fake excursions for different study specialities. The illustration lecturers then had to field questions about a supposed bus trip to the Rien Poortvliet Museum, and the fashion students all arrived at the academy dressed in white as a protest against animals that refused to cooperate with cosmetic testing. The manipulation of amateurish or authoritarian announcements was a game that Ernst was fond of playing. His mucking about with the context had started at the academy, and gave him pleasure for the rest of his life: a graphic mind is a joy forever. As a designer, you could make a political poster look like something from a fashion campaign. He once held a workshop course at a tightly-organized private design college in the USA and instructed his students to distribute fake signs around the campus. They produced among other things a notice styled to look like a message from system management, announcing that one computer terminal would be reserved for browsing internet porn. And a fake advertisement appeared on the notice board offering the car of one of the professors for sale.

The following day, Ernst appeared in the Laupvogel studio wearing a blazer. The long-promised presentation at the Taxation & Customs Museum, with laptop and digital projector, was due in half an hour. But Ernst had nothing ready. All he had produced so far was a succession of ideas that were likely to be adjudged even more Fascist (or perhaps Stalinist) than the first attempt. The lettering was still sharp and angular, and the colours were still black and red. In his attempts to change things to accommodate the inane remarks he had received, he had rotated some of the text blocks by a few degrees. The effect was counter-productive; the communications department of the Nazi Party would surely have bought some additional advertising space.

He zoomed in further using the magnifying-glass tool. Hardly anything could be changed without completely ruining whatever strength the design already had. Monique knocked on the dividing door, which was open:

'Ernst, I had a call yesterday from Freddy's new communications assistant – er, what's her name again?'

'Eveline,' Ernst answered.

'Ah yes, Eveline,' Monique said. 'She asked why nothing arrived yesterday. You promised to send them something for *Strange Insects* or whatever it's called. They are getting desperate.'

'Thanks Monique, I'll call them later today. I didn't get around to it because of all that baloney from the Taxation & Customs Museum,' Ernst said.

'Shall I send Freddy an email to say we're working on it?' Monique asked.

Arjan entered wearing his Prada shower slippers. He threw a glance at the computer screen with the zoomed-in the Taxation & Customs Museum design.

'Is that for that poseur, Freddy Hoonstam?' he asked.

Ernst did not reply, for he was suddenly struck by a flash of inspiration.

'Thanks a bunch Arjan!' Ernst said.

'Why thank me? It looks good. Nice and hard, a bit Austrian with all that black and red. Freddy should be pleased with it. It will go well with all his absurd histrionics,' Arjan said, and began hammering on a heap of pine cones.

Ernst quickly changed the text on the screen from *Reopening of Renovated Tax and Customs Museum* to *Strange Infatuation, by Dance Theatre Spatt!* and vice versa. He emailed the poster design to freddy@spatt!.nl, packed his briefcase and set off towards the museum.

VI

Arjan had grown up in one of the better neighbourhoods of a small provincial town. His father headed the gynaecology department of the hospital. His mother was head of the pediatric psychiatry department and specialized in anxiety disorders. It seemed a matter of course that Arjan would follow them into the medical profession, but things turned out differently. At secondary school, his attention span during the lessons proved to be minimal. He showed little interest for his homework, and instead revealed a passion for subculture sports like skateboarding, snowboarding and surfing. Each of these activities was surrounded by its own expensive fashion fads. All summer long Arjan cycled around the town in his *Snow is Only Frozen Water* T-shirt, a message comprehensible only to other avid board-sporters. What these subcultures had in common was the idea that their sport was a way of life. They could imagine no other future, let alone some purposeful career. Arjan's parents sent him to undergo a succession of psychological tests but to their surprise no trace of a pathological abnormality could be diagnosed. After he had made his way through the secondary school system in unspectacular style, the only option was apparently to send him to the local graphic crafts school. This would keep him occupied for another four years and, who knows, perhaps the company of all those future housewives and graffiti artists would socialize him a bit.

While at the vocational school, Arjan quickly developed into something of an entrepreneur. He accepted design jobs for advertising agencies and other small local businesses. He was sufficiently well equipped to provide small-scale printing services such as restaurant menus and estate agents' folders. By the time he moved on to the Academy of Fine Arts, his income was sufficient to spare him the need to take boring part-time factory jobs, which many other academy students found inescapable. His graphic skills had been honed in the pre-computer days.

Ernst was five years younger than Arjan, and was raised in a small village on an island consisting mainly of farmland. His parents were baby-boomers who little choice but to move out of the overcrowded city and take up residence in a new pedestrian-friendly housing estate, which had sprung up alongside the existing farming community. The original inhabitants of the village, including the neighbours living left and right of Ernst's parental home, were deeply conservative adherents of the Reformed Church. The village had two football clubs, one for the faithful who played on Saturdays only, and another for people who worked for the Post Office and were free to play on Sundays. Life there was relatively carefree, shielded as it was from the more pernicious worldly influences. Ernst's parents, who had first met when volunteers on a children's farm, worked in education. His father taught at a school for children with special needs, and his mother worked with youngsters with physical disabilities.

For a teenager, there was nothing to do in the village. Ernst would hang around the school playground with his friends, most of whom shared his musical tastes for Sebadoh and other indie rock bands, as well as for Ride and the whole shoegaze genre. A larger crowd of youths would gather on Saturday nights for parties at whoever's parents were not home that weekend. All proprieties were thrown to the winds at parties like these, where *A Clockwork Orange* or that lousy Doors film provided the typical backdrop. The thrash would generally end in a bout of what Ernst would now label happy vandalism or postmodern hedonism. Any distinction between high and low culture meant nothing to the young partygoers, for they were all high anyway. Once the teenage party caravan had passed over his home, he would clean everything up just in time for his parents' return; but his father was likely to wonder what in heaven's name had happened to the lawn, and his mother might find a bra in the bathroom – a size 75B, not her own. As the alternative guitar music merged into the rising House scene, everything started becoming more extreme and occult. It grew more menacing towards the end, as had happened with the Flower Children a generation earlier, and several of his friends succumbed to the bad vibes; Underworld's notorious concert at Ahoy Halls was their Altamont.

Lacking other alternatives, Ernst seemed destined to go into teaching. An art academy did not appear on the list of options that the headmaster drew up for career advice sessions. It was not until Ernst was a student at the teacher training college that he became aware of the building across the road, the Academy of Fine Arts, and realized that this was where he really belonged. Ernst was the first person from his village to go to an art academy, as far as he knew. Now whenever he returned to visit his parents, village acquaintances would ask, 'How's it going with the advertising agency, Ernst?' He would nod and let the matter pass.

Ernst was about to be drawn and quartered by four Toyota Starlets, when he awoke abruptly. He pressed his thumbs against his tempels and massaged his scalp back and forth over his skull. He had slumped onto the Kalou sofa and passed out. Apparently, he had also undone his belt and trouser top. As he stood up and started to do up his trousers, the trainee entered without knocking, looked at Ernst and asked, 'Coffee?' 'No thanks,' Ernst replied. He finished zipping up his fly, patted his hair and tucked his shirt in. The girl looked back with disgust into the atelier as she left. He was surrounded by magazines and sheets of paper covered with signatures. Ernst had developed a neurotic tic which involved reproducing the signatures of celebrities. He had quickly mastered the handwriting of Rien

Poortvliet, and that of Andy Warhol proved just as easy. Learning to make an exact copy in a smooth stroke usually took only a few weeks. But the real trick was not to lose the touch. You had to keep practising each signature over and over again, for years on end. In some cases he had perfected his signatures to such an extent that they were actually better than the original – more attractive, and more calligraphic in character. Johan Cruyff was one such celebrity. The original was a scrawl, but in Ernst's version the signature became legendary and classic. He would grab a pen during a telephone conversation or at other idle moments, and compulsively fill a sheet of paper with signatures. When signing any kind of document, he would choose from his stock of alter egos. Invited as an external expert to sign the student diplomas at the academy of Helmond, he began by using the signature of John McEnroe; the student administrators raised objections and insisted on Ernst resigning the certificates. Signing a name felt like an act of power. To sign a name was to take a position. It demythologized a unique person and created the myth of his alter egos.

'Hey, that's very nice, Ernst. But the bottom of the poster is white. What if it gets spattered with mud by passing cars and bicycles? White shows the dirt so easily. Did you consider that, Ernst?' Barbara asked.
Ernst was nonplussed. He had heard some feeble arguments in his time, but this took the biscuit and he was momentarily lost for an answer. The director glanced apologetically at him.
'I think it will sort itself out,' he said turning to Barbara. 'If necessary Ernst could take another look, but on the whole I find it has a chunky appeal. Yes, and it's really cheerful with those bold colours.'
'When I run through the core concepts in our brand profile,' Barbara, 'I must say, it satisfies every one of them!' Barabara exclaimed.
'Brand profile?' the director asked.
'You remember, the consultancy. They drew up a list of core qualities that would bring our brand and our public closer together: open, communicative, wide-ranging, accessible, progressive, fresh, modern, happy and informative.'
'Oh of course, those fellows. Well done, Ernst,' said the director.
'I'm glad you like the design because I admit I'm fairly satisfied with it,' Ernst said, switching off the digital projector. He felt his work was being appreciated at last and calmed down inwardly.
'Unfortunately, we've had to cut into the campaign budget rather heavily, so it won't be more than a small flyer,' Barbara said.
'Only a flyer?' the director asked.
'Well,' said Barbara, 'when I first saw the budget I thought there must be three

naughts missing after the amount. In fact we used to budget everything in thousands in my last job, so it had me fooled for a moment. The cultural sector is a different world, isn't it?'

'But we used to manage a lot more than a flyer on the same kind of budget, didn't we?' Ernst asked.

'Yes, but the cost of the profile study by the consultancy comes out of the same money-pot. So there's only enough left for a small flyer – and on thin paper, too.'

Incredible, thought Ernst, the whole budget has been blown on a sheet of hackneyed slogans mounted on a stupid bit of foamboard. Shouldn't the consultancy have worked for free, considering the museum isn't a commercial customer? After all, firms like that often give free advice to cultural institutes so as to add a bit of cachet to their web portfolio. Including a museum or a theatre company or two raised the status of the firm's pathetic list of clients. It was otherwise all too obvious that their creatively-timid campaigns were mostly for chewing gum, chocolate bars, cable providers and the like. A cultural brand helped mask the emptiness of their otherwise mundane advertising-agency activities.

'But we must have posters and advertisements,' said the director. 'I'll see if I can free up some funds. Barbara, let's have a *tête-à-tête* about this.' Ernst clicked his laptop shut with smug satisfaction.

Still feeling the buzz of his success, Ernst walked into Laupvogel's R&D atelier. 'Telephone for you, Ernst,' cried a voice from the adjacent space. He picked it up. 'Hi Ernst, Freddy here. Thanks man, that's terrific. Your gritty protest style reminds me of when I was young back in the 1980s. Ah, those were the days, when the girls had real pubic hair and not those tonsured Hitler mustaches like today. Not to mention the ladybird tattoos. Anyway, we're going ahead with this. But Eveline wondered how it connects with our target audience.'

'I don't know,' Ernst said, 'Who is your target audience anyway? And shouldn't they connect with you rather than the other way round?'

'Exactly, you put the words into my mouth,' Freddy replied. 'I bet the National Dance Theatre will be green with envy when they see this.'

Freddy may be a fraud, Ernst thought, but his heart's in the right place, and he does have a bit of vision too. The idea of catching the eye of the National Dance Theatre appealed to Ernst. It raised the tempting prospect of making posters for them too some day.

'So that settles the design,' Freddy said. 'You'll go a bit easy on the invoice, won't you?

'Of course,' Ernst replied. 'We know we have a special rates for you.'

Ernst sat down on the Kalou sofa and pressed his thumbs into his temples. The last-minute switch had saved his bacon. He had fulfilled his duty to the studio and to his staff, and with these two commissions the firm would live to fight another day. The studio could work out the proposals in detail, and he could try some new ideas in the atelier with a clear conscience.

Arjan entered. 'Wassup, nigga?' he asked in a farcical attempt at rap jargon.

'All gravy, white boy,' Ernst replied, equally well versed in the hip-hop idiom which had crept into their casual exchanges of late. 'That was a golden tip from you. It's stupid I didn't think of it earlier.' It was not unusual for them to recycle a rejected design for use in some other application, but an instant swap such as this was unique.

After viewing all the work at the *Passive Aggressive* exhibition, Ernst thought about going home and warming up a jar of baby-food for his evening meal. He took a final glance at the pamphlet which accompanied the show. 'The work springs,' it said, 'from the largely artificial context of consumer culture and its institutional framework, its images connoting symbolic, iconic associations with an urgency of reflection and a raw but aesthetic autonomy.' Ernst was not unimpressed by the consummate art-speak of the author of this pamphlet. Whatever it meant, if anything, it seemed to describe his own work in complimentary terms. He could feel some pride at being a participant in the exhibition.

Thinking of the few visitors to the exhibition who had paused to look at his own work made him feel excited and relaxed at the same time. It was as though he had stripped off his bathrobe and lay naked on a table awaiting a massage. The interaction was so much more personal and intense than a poster or advertising campaign which would be seen by hundreds of thousands of people.

As he headed for the exit, Ernst ran into the curator who was also one of the participating artists. 'Thanks for your contribution,' the curator said.

'Glad to take part,' Ernst replied. 'Are you satisfied with the show as a whole?'

'Absolutely,' said the curator. 'and it's marvellous that so many people have come to the vernissage.'

Ernst could not detect the least trace of irony in the curator's over-optimistic assessment. He was about to ask him about the theme and composition of *Passive Aggressive* when a dark-haired woman of a little above average height joined them.

Ernst held out his had: 'Ernst Laupman, may I have the pleasure?'

'Sophie de Preille,' she responded in a distinctly Flemish accent.

Ernst recognized her name from the title card of the miniature air-crash pictures. 'So those were your planes,' he said. 'I like them a lot.'

'And you did the smiley faces on found objects,' she replied. 'Definitely some of the more interesting work here.'

'Thank you,' said Ernst. He guessed that she was a few years older than himself. Her straight-hanging black hair framed a face that radiated optimism and intelligence. She was wearing a black cardigan buttoned over a red T-shirt, together with black jeans and somewhat cartoonish red canvas shoes broadly edged with white rubber. The camera that dangled from her shoulder reminded Ernst of an Italian tourist. She had something gracious and wise about her.

'Do you come from round here,' Ernst asked.

'Now I do. I'm originally from Mechelen, not far from Brussels, and I studied at the fine arts academy there. But I've lived in this neighbourhood for the last two years. I have a studio in an old warehouse in the southern docks. It's a fascinating area, and it's a good city to live in, don't you think? Better than Brussels, at least.' Ernst could not help thinking how totally this lovely, erudite woman contrasted with the stereotype inhabitants of the district. Apart from Salvation Army soldiers and similar evangelists, which outsiders would settle here voluntarily, let alone a Belgian artist like Sophie?

'I'd love to have one of your smiley faces,' Sophie said. Ernst looked at her with pleasure. The relaxing massage had started. Few people reacted so directly to his and Arjan's work.

'Unfortunately, I don't have the funds to buy one. Would you be interested in exchanging a work with one of mine?'

Ernst was delighted. 'What a good idea,' he said. 'I'd be honoured to swap a work with something of yours.'

'How about one of your smiley faces for one of my planes?'

'That is exactly what I would like,' said Ernst. He offered his hand to shake on the deal.

She took his hand and kissed him on both cheeks, pausing halfway to say, 'Thank you so much. This makes me very happy.'

'Me too,' Ernst replied. 'Shall we celebrate our deal with a drink?'

'Not now, thank you. I really must get an early night. I have a part-time job as a receptionist at a bank in the city centre. It's not bad work. All I have to do is dress up smart and be nice to the customers.' Ernst was surprised. It had never occurred to him that an employee of a conservative bank might actually be leading a double life.

'We all have to make a living somehow, don't we?' Sophie continued.

'Who doesn't?' replied Ernst. He went back to take a another look at her miniatures in the corner of the gallery. What a privilege to be able to choose one of these! He could have stretched the moment for hours, but a decision was needed. He chose the second picture from the right, the one with the explosion on the runway. Of all the miniatures, the image was so unexpected in this format.

As he walked alone back to the metro, what had seemed like a miserable slum was now a cosmopolitan paradise. Forget the jar of baby-food, he decided. He would treat himself to a meal at the restaurant which his studio staff had often mentioned and where he had never eaten. And then... whatever the future would bring, but in any case he was looking forward to a new day tomorrow in the Secret Annex.

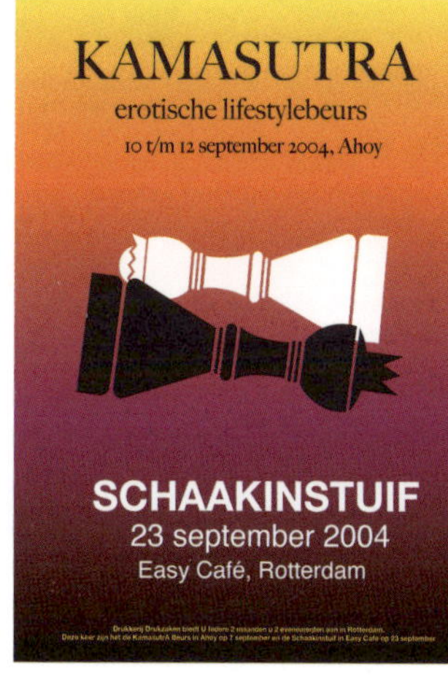

International Film Festival Rotterdam, poster, 2009

Drukzaken, poster series combined events, 2004

Nederlands Fotomuseum, logo ZWART/WIT, 2010

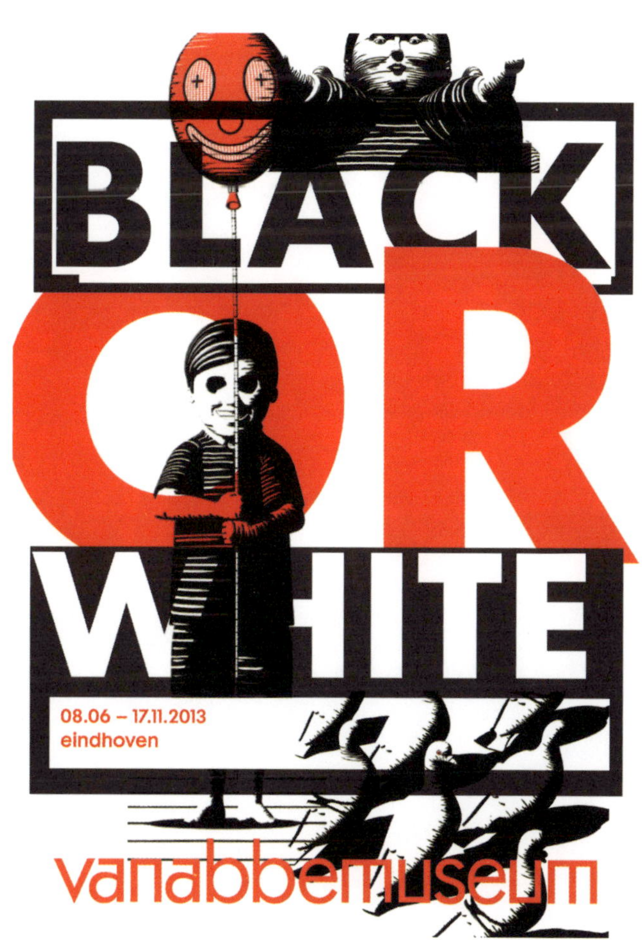

Van Abbemuseum, poster Black or White, 2013

LantarenVenster, routeing, 2010

Remote City, 2011 – Installation, LED, remotes, water, 104 x 87 x 102 cm

Unesco IHE, sketches for visual identity, 2012

Museum Boijmans Van Beuningen, poster *Keith Haring, Heaven and Hell*, 2010

Photo, 2006

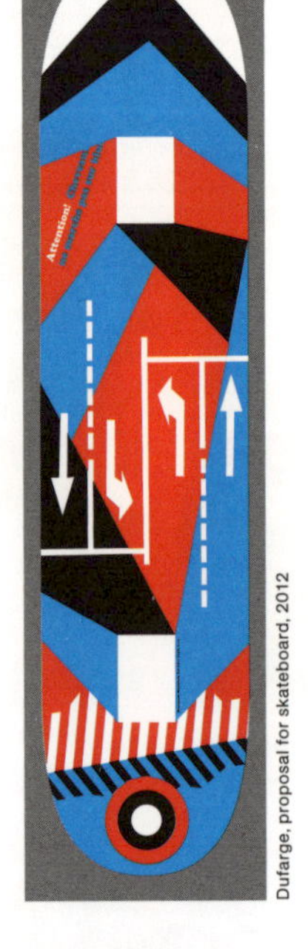

Dufarge, proposal for skateboard, 2012

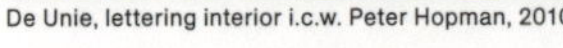

De Unie, lettering interior i.c.w. Peter Hopman, 2010

LantarenVenster, posters, 2010/2011

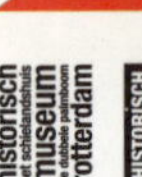

Historisch Museum Rotterdam, sketches for visual identity, 2006

SAT 08 DEC
CAT
WALK
NOW&WOW

Now & Wow, posters, 2001–2013

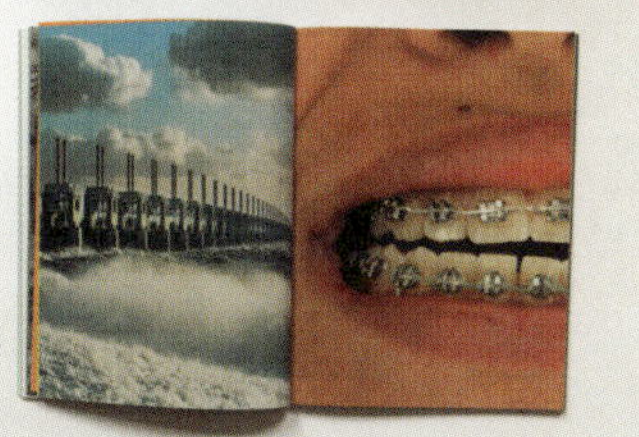

Zeeuws Museum, publication *Kunst moet je voelen*, 2007

Boomerang Freecards, 2001

Now & Wow, ad for *Kissy Kissy Bang Bang*, 2006

Same Mistake Twice, 2011 – Ink on paper, 70 x 50 cm

Taste in Men, 2011 – Ink on paper, 70 x 50 cm

Arab Spring and Aaron Winter, Naioio Publishers - 39.50 eur
eng/ned editie - ISBN 978-94-6208-040-9 - hardcover - 264 p

DANCE WORKS ROTTERDAM/ ANDRÉ GINGRAS

Dance Works Rotterdam / André Gingras, logo, 2010

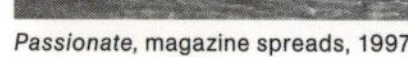

Passionate, magazine spreads, 1997

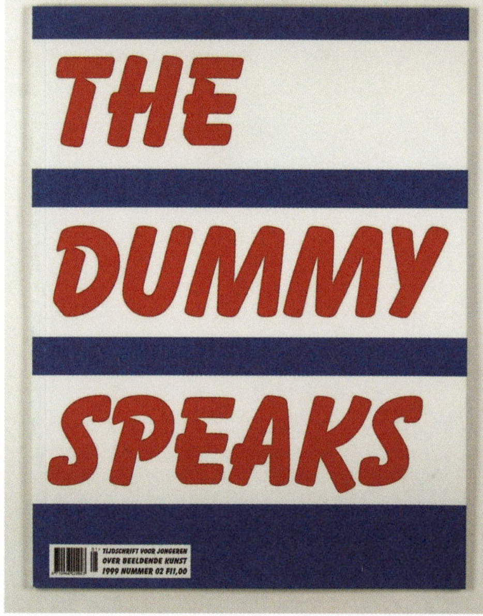

The Dummy Speaks, magazine cover, 1999

Fairy Tale Religions I, 2010

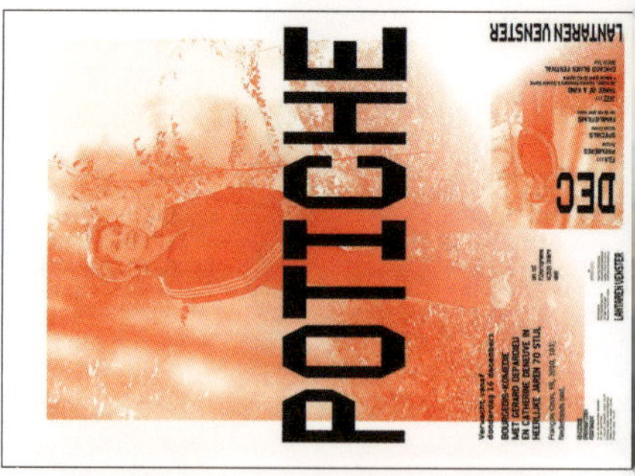

Poetry International Festival, posters, 2004

Mister Motley, magazine covers, 2002–2004

Ro Theater, poster *BOE!*, 2009

The Netherlands Foundation for Visual Arts, Design and Architecture/De Balie, invitation debate, 2003

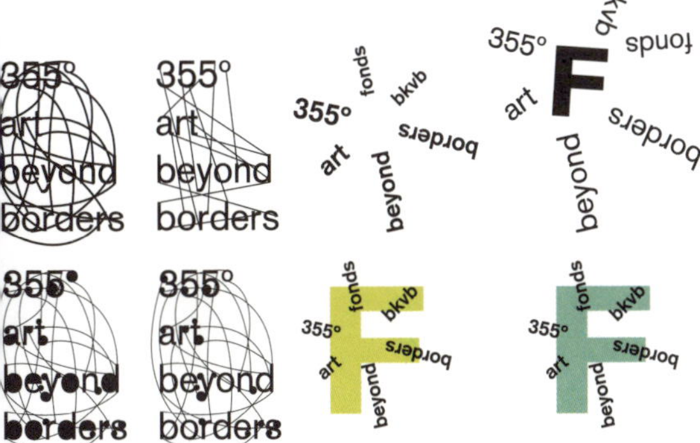

The Netherlands Foundation for Visual Arts, Design and Architecture – *355° Art Beyond Borders*, sketches for logo, 2010

Schuilen In Het Rijks (manifesto for the preservation of culture), facade banner *Boijmans Bezet*, 2010

Tronies (TENT, Rotterdam), 2011 – Overview (part 1)

Museum Boijmans Van Beuningen, sketch for *Keith Haring – Heaven and Hell*, 2007

Anoeska with *Burning Love*, 2000

Bud RIP with *Burning Love*

Boomerang Freecards, *Burning Love*, 1998

120

Nederlands Fotomuseum, poster *Chance*, Christian Boltanski, 2012

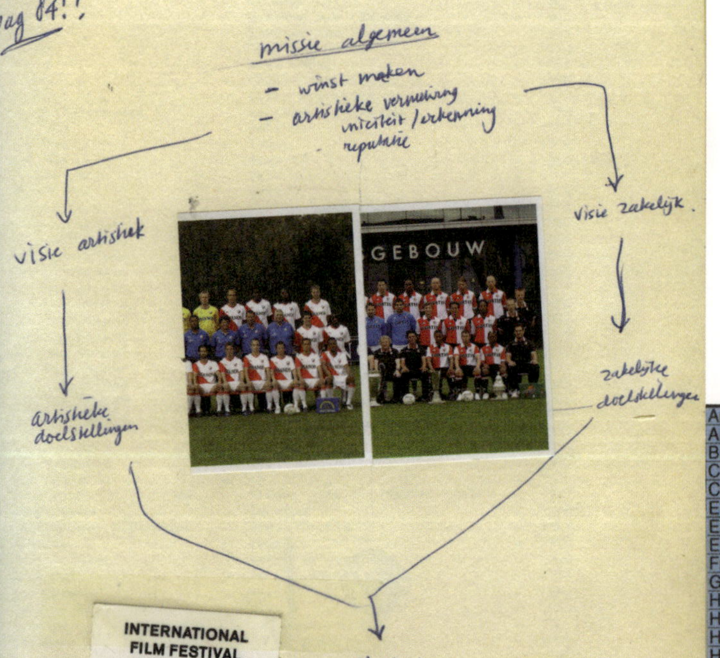

André	24	Johan	21
Ariane/Paul	27	kantine	37
Bram/ Fern	31	Kirsten	28
Chiel/Paul C	25	Paula	30
Chris	17	Receptie	40
Elroy/Matt	22	Rene	35
Els	39	Rene F.	54
Erik	53	Richard	32
Fred	59	Robin	38
Gammy	29	Rob-Jan	52
Han	14	Rosana	15
Han verg	16	Steve	51
Heleen/Sop	12	Walter	49
Helma	41	Wil /Jacq	13
Henk	20	Willem	26
Jeroen	36	Zen	19

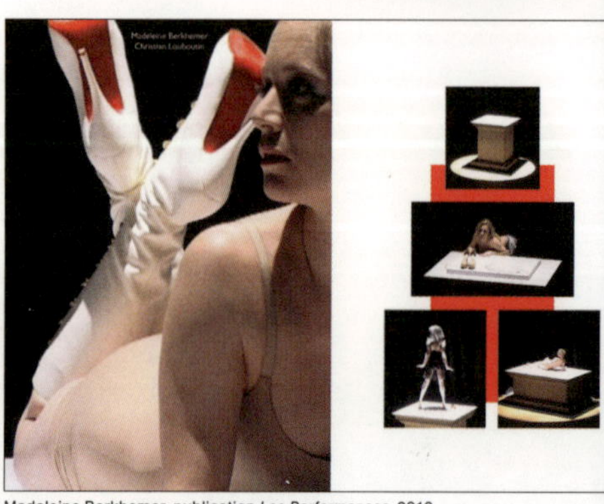

Madeleine Berkhemer, publication *Les Performances*, 2010

Sculpture International Rotterdam, sketch for *50 years*, 2011

International Film Festival Rotterdam, art poster, 2012

TNT Post, stamps, 2009

121

Historisch Museum Rotterdam, clean graffiti *Nice 'N Fresh*, 2009

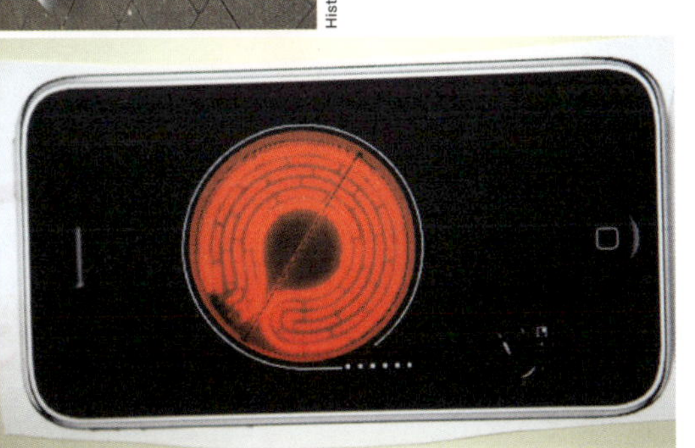

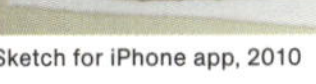

Sketch for iPhone app, 2010

Museum Boijmans Van Beuningen, *Aesthetic Terrorism*, 2000

Foundation of Reality I, 2010 – Newspaper pictures on paper, 70 x 100 cm

Foundation of Reality III, 2010 — Newspaper pictures on paper, 70 x 50 cm

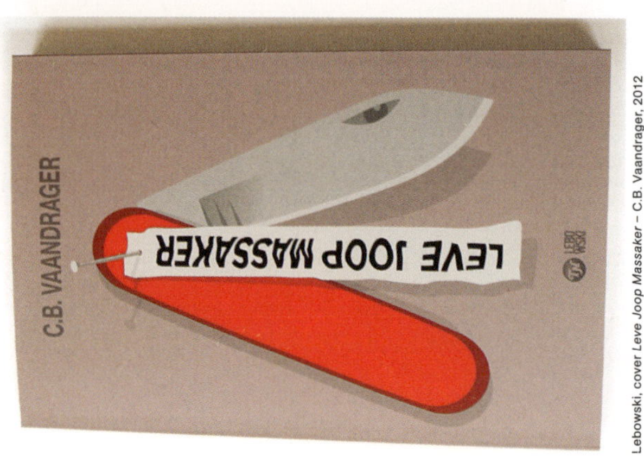

Lebowski, cover Leve Joop Massaker – C.B. Vaandrager, 2012

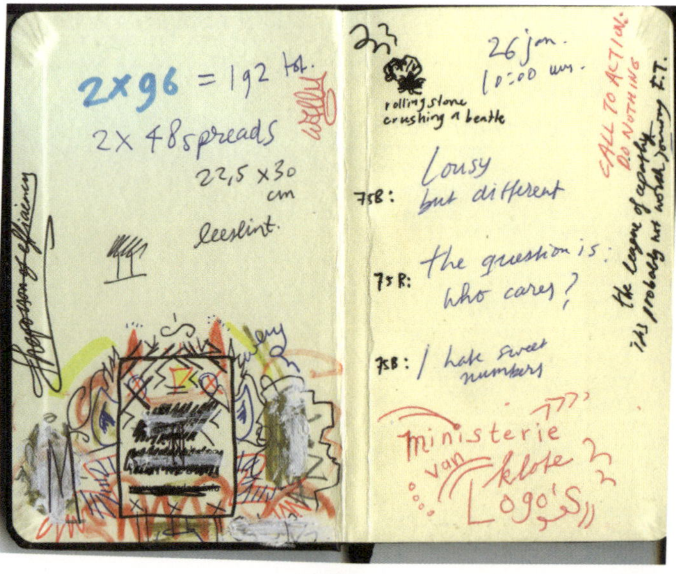

R2001 (Rotterdam Cultural Capital 2001), catalogue contributions, 2001

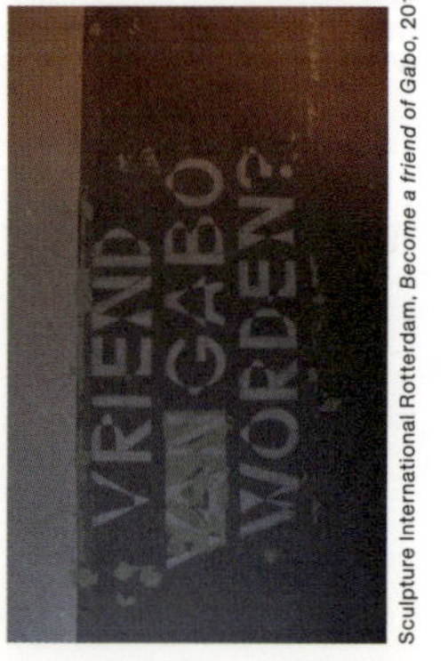

Sculpture International Rotterdam, Become a friend of Gabo, 201

Logo interpretation R2001, 2001

Poster for flea market, 2006

...d Other Sizes, ladies clothing exchange, 2011

Flyers 1996–2000

...oijmans Van Beuningen, poster Caldic Collection, 2002

Van Abbemuseum, publication *Plug In to Play*, 200E

The Master Of Them All, 2006

Photo, 2003

Lighthouse, 2010 – Photo print, 100 x 65 cm

Midget Hotel (Schiedam), 2003 – Plastic foil on transformer kiosk

GMW Advocates, logo, 2012

Designprize Rotterdam 2007, ad, 2007

020 Publishers, publication *Marenka Gabeler. Posing*, 2001

Photo, 2006

Poetry International Rotterdam, poster, 2004

Survey, 2011

Photo, 2006

International Film Festival Rotterdam, sketches for campaign 41st edition, 2011

Van Abbemuseum, poster *Zidane*, 2009

Photo, Adcom studio, 1996

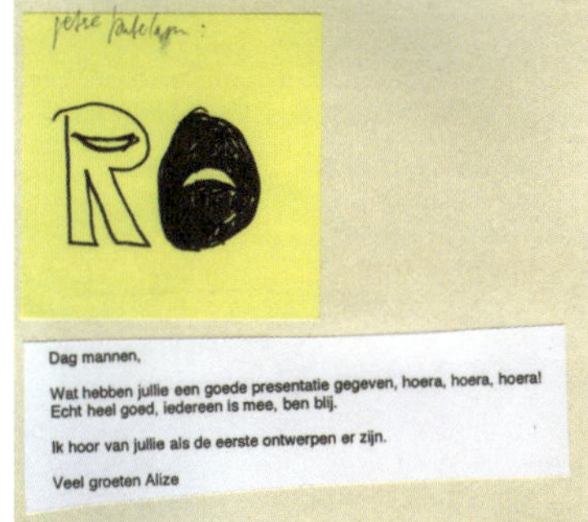

LantarenVenster, ticket, 2011

Dag mannen,

Wat hebben jullie een goede presentatie gegeven, hoera, hoera, hoera!
Echt heel goed, iedereen is mee, ben blij.

Ik hoor van jullie als de eerste ontwerpen er zijn.

Veel groeten Alize

(Hello Men,
What a great presentation you did, hurray, hurray,
hurray! Really good, everyone is in, I am happy.

I'll hear from you when the first designs are there.

Many greetings Alize)

Pain, 2011

Egbert, 2001

Photo, 2007

129

Van Abbemuseum, poster Be(com)ing Dutch, 2008

len. Dit is hun commentaar:

Ministerie van Defensie

Ministerie van Binnenlandse zaken

Ministerie van Buitenlandse zaken

Ministerie van Financiën

Ministerie van Justitie

Ministerie van Landbouw, Natuurbeheer en Visserij

Ministerie van Volksgezondheid, Welzijn en Sport

Ministerie van Verkeer en Waterstaat

Ministerie van Algemene zaken

Ministerie van Sociale zaken en werkgelegenheid

Ministerie van Volkshuisvesting, Ruimtelijke ordening en Milieubeheer

Ministerie van Economische zaken

Ministerie van Onderwijs, Cultuur en Wetenschappen

Interview Adformatie, government logos, 1998

Boomerang Freecards, *Love of the man goes through the stomach*, 1999

Nike, sketches for *Nike Ladies Run*, 1998

Vitruvian Dancer (Los Angeles), 2006 – Installation

Institut Néerlandais, sketches for visual identity, 2011

Van Abbemuseum, poster *René Daniëls*, 2012

Strabrechtse heide, 2012

Showroom MAMA, campaign
Keine Angst Gratis Haarschnitt, 1997

Beyond Graffiti, 2013

LantarenVenster, facade design, 2010

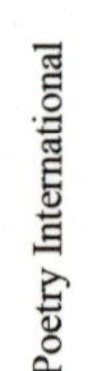

Poetry International

Poetry International
Rotterdam
Mediteranée.

Met Gerrit Komrij,
Jules LaFontaine
Rien Vroegindewij

Veertien juni
tot en met
éénentwintig juni,
tweeduizend-drie

De Rotterdamse schouwburg.   #34

Poetry International Rotterdam, scketch for poster, 2003

Codarts, website, 2009

Be Happy, type design i.c.w. Peter Hopman, 2011

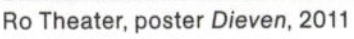

Ro Theater, poster *Dieven*, 2011

Mobile Homelessness, 2006

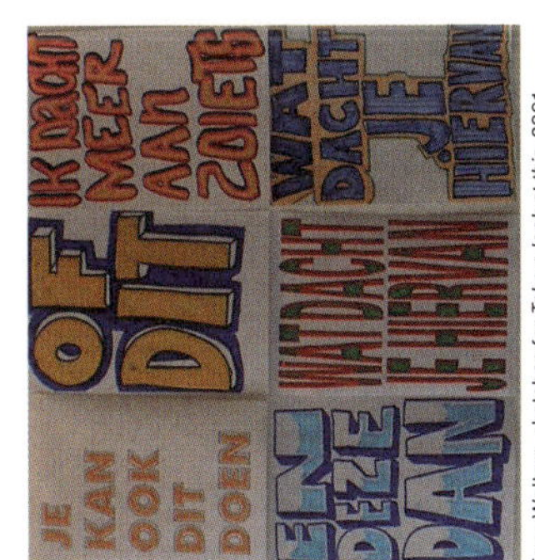

Fons Welters, sketches for *Take a look at this*, 2001

Delta Metropole Association / Artgineering, poster *South Pole*, 2012

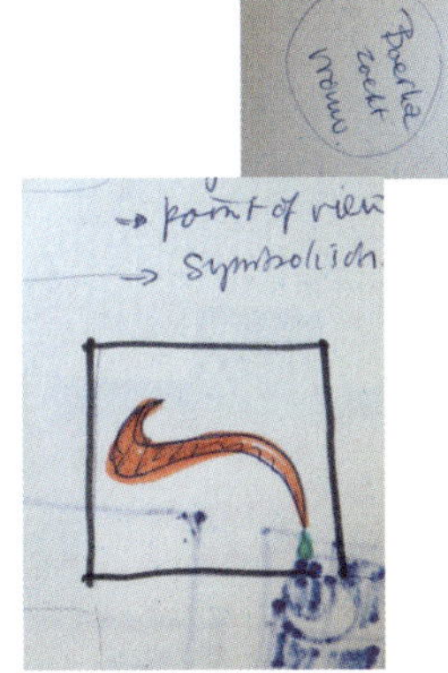

Van Abbemuseum, installation *Heartland*, 2012

Metal Detector Award, 2010 – Coin, diameter 25 mm

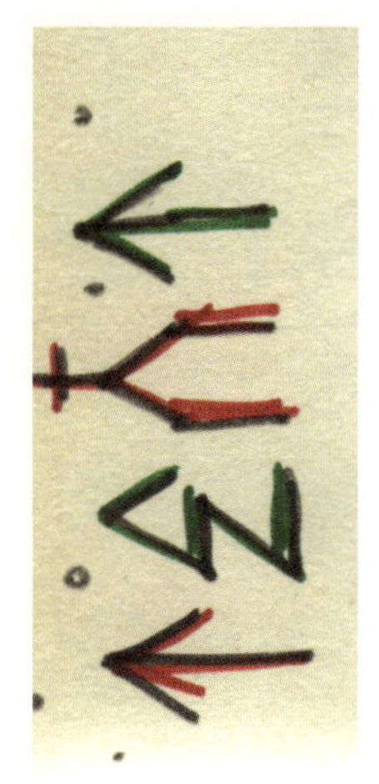

Les oiseaux de champagnes, 2011

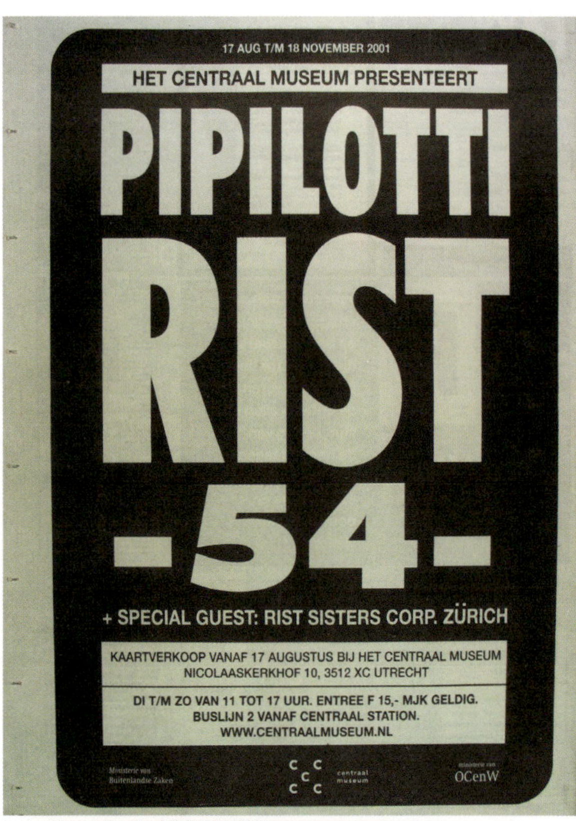

Centraal Museum Utrecht, ad *Pipilotti Rist*, 2001

International Film Festival Rotterdam, Daily Tigers, 2012

Kunstgebouw, page of annual report, 2007

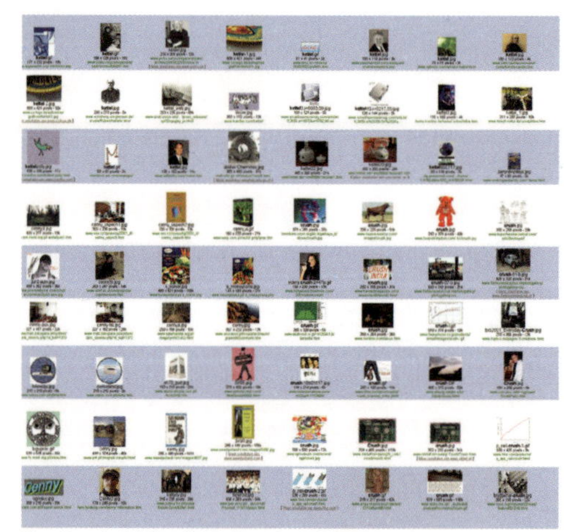

Clone Records, 12' Album Kettel, *Cenny Crush*, 2002

TENT, logo, 2010

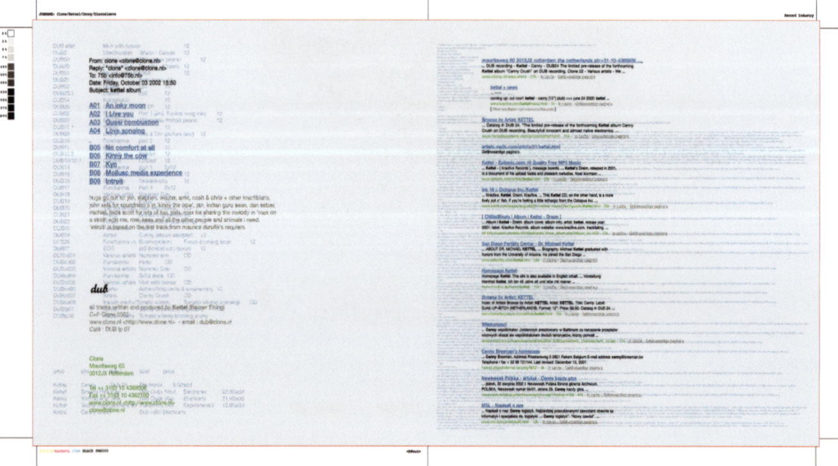

Clone Records, CD Album Kettel, *Cenny Crush*, 2002

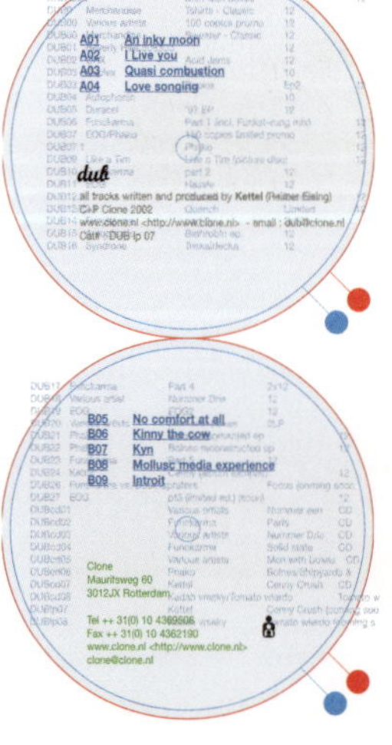

KPN Telecom, ticker, 2000

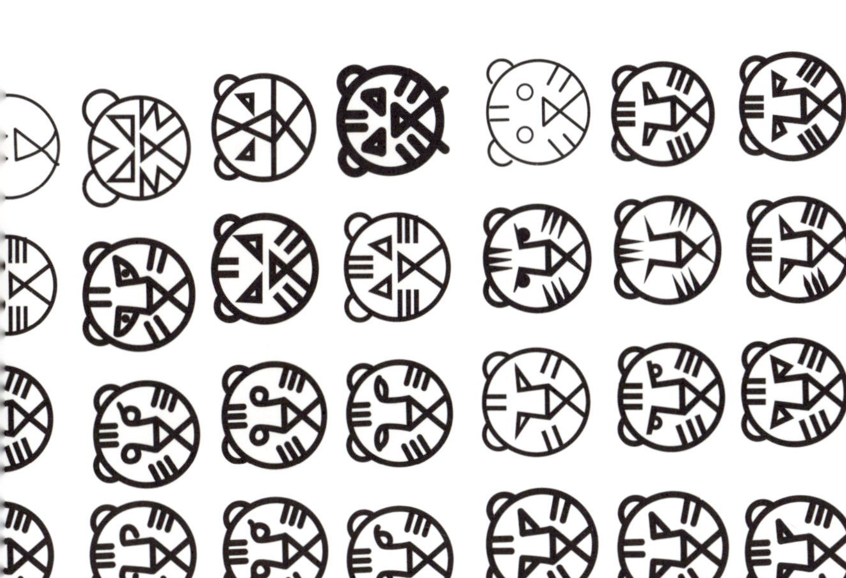

Ro Theater, truck, 2010

...rring Partners, 2002

Delta Metropool Association / Artgineering, *South Pole*, brochure, 2012

Dance Works Rotterdam / André Gingras, tram, 2011

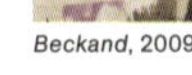

Beckand, 2009

Branden (2010) – Silkscreen (#1/3, edition of 200), 1189 x 841 mm

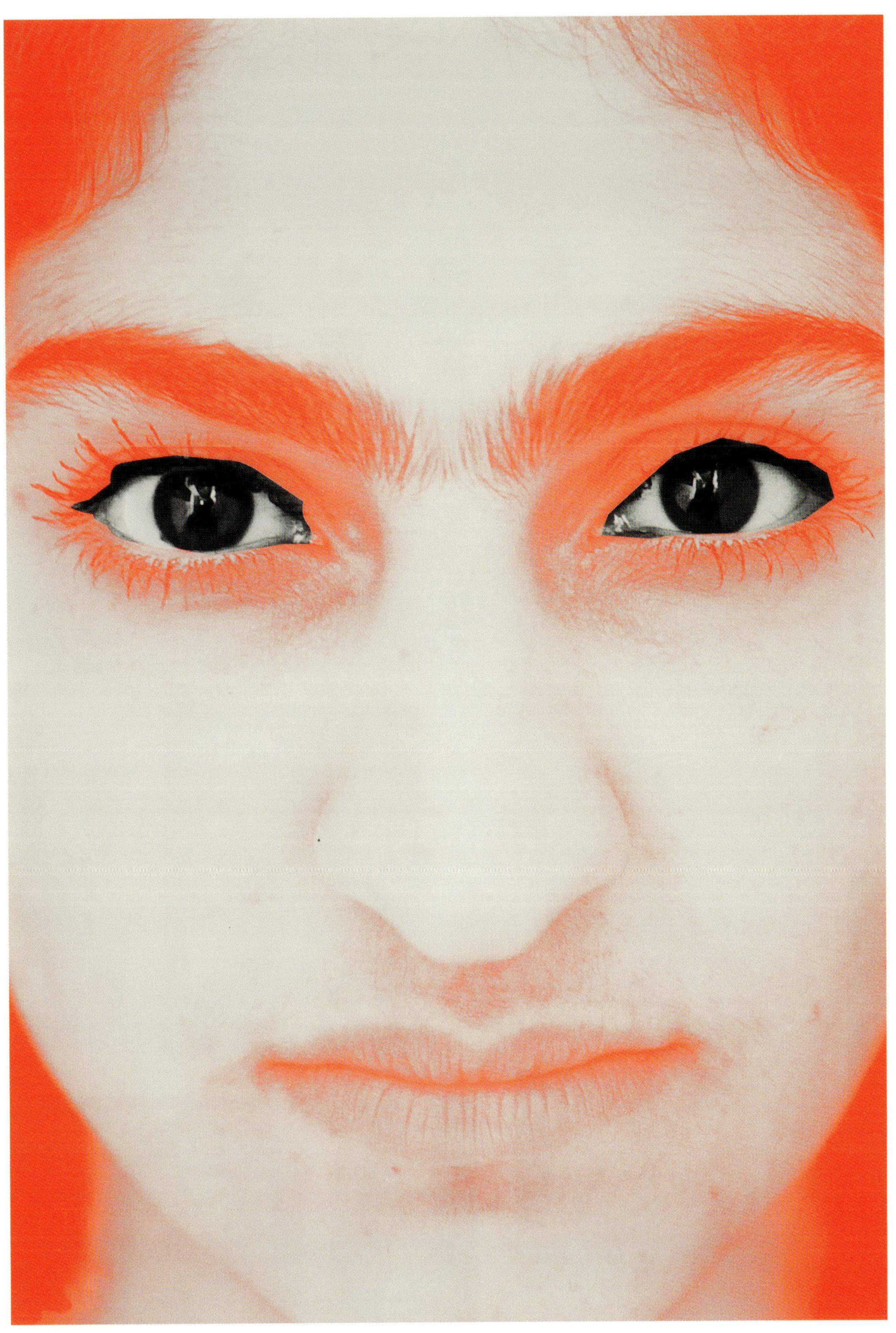

Branden (2010) – Silkscreen (#2/3, edition of 200), 1189 x 841 mm

Now & Wow, poster *Now & Wow Fest II*, 2012

Arling & Cameron, *We Are A&C*, 2001

Boomerang Freecards, *For Sinterklaas*, 1998

Clone Records. 12" *Kettel – Cenny Crush*, 2002

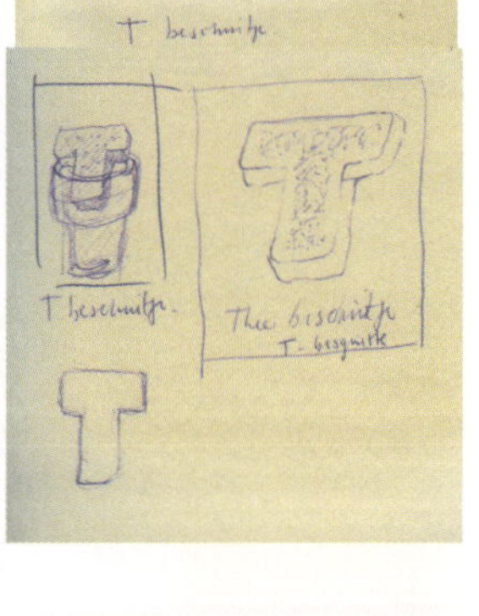

Buro Michelle Wilderom, visual identity, 2011

Institut Néerlandais, campaign, 2013

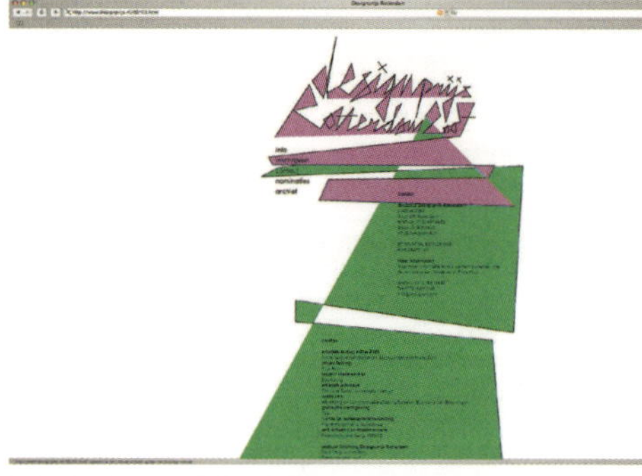

Design Prize Rotterdam 2007, ad, 2007

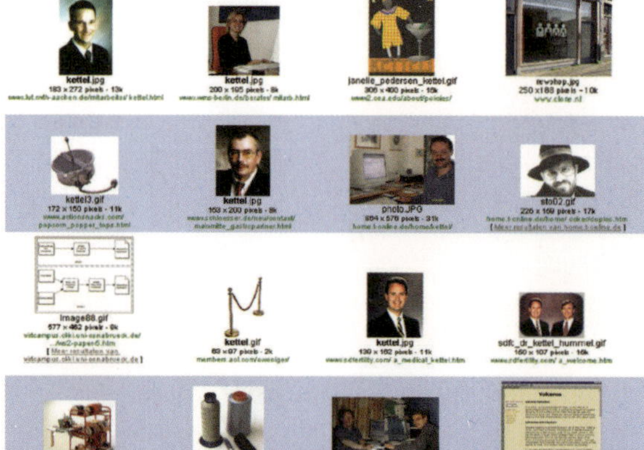

Sculpture International Rotterdam, template, 2010

Strange
Messenger

The Work of
Patti Smith
21 08 04 - 21 11 04

Museum Boijmans Van Beuningen, invitation, *Strange
Messenger, The Work of Patti Smith*, 2004

Nederlands Fotomuseum,
poster *ZWART/WIT*, 2013

Zeeuws Museum, campaign proposal, 2009

Van Abbemuseum, poster *Deimantas Narkevičius, The Unanimous Life*, 2009

Van Abbemuseum, posters *Deimantas Narkevičius, The Unanimous Life*, 2009

The Netherlands Foundation for Visual Arts, Design and Architecture, T-shirt introduction visual identity, 2001

Meekers, poster *Helaas pindakaas*, 2012

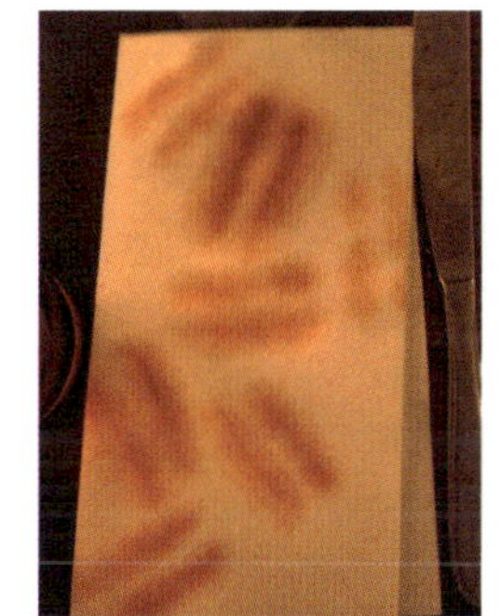

Photo, 2013

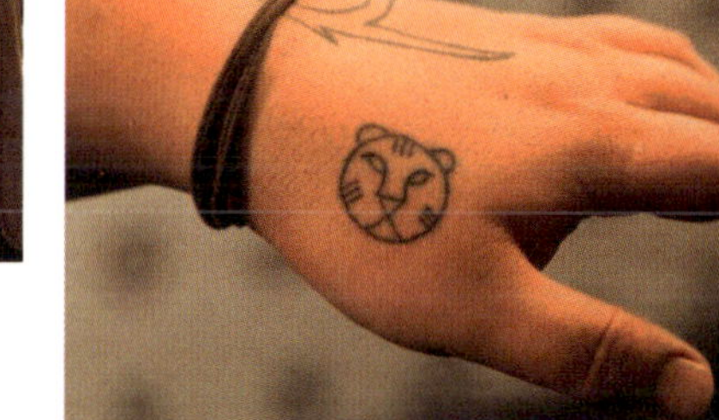

Tattoo on the hand of Raul Augusta, 2011

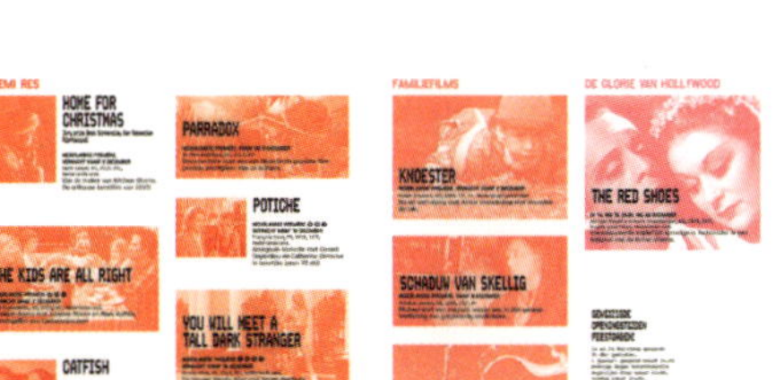

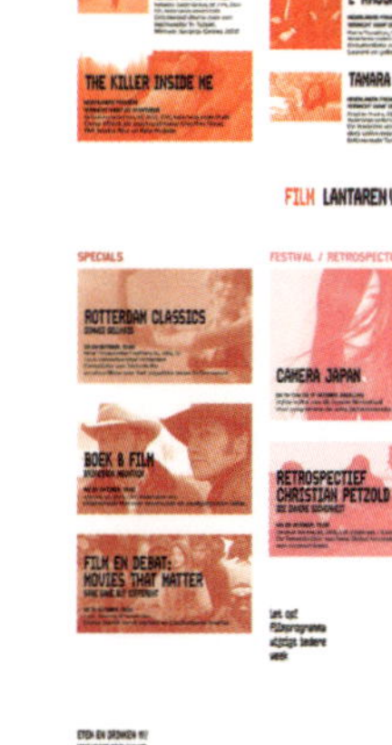

LantarenVenster, monthly posters, 2011

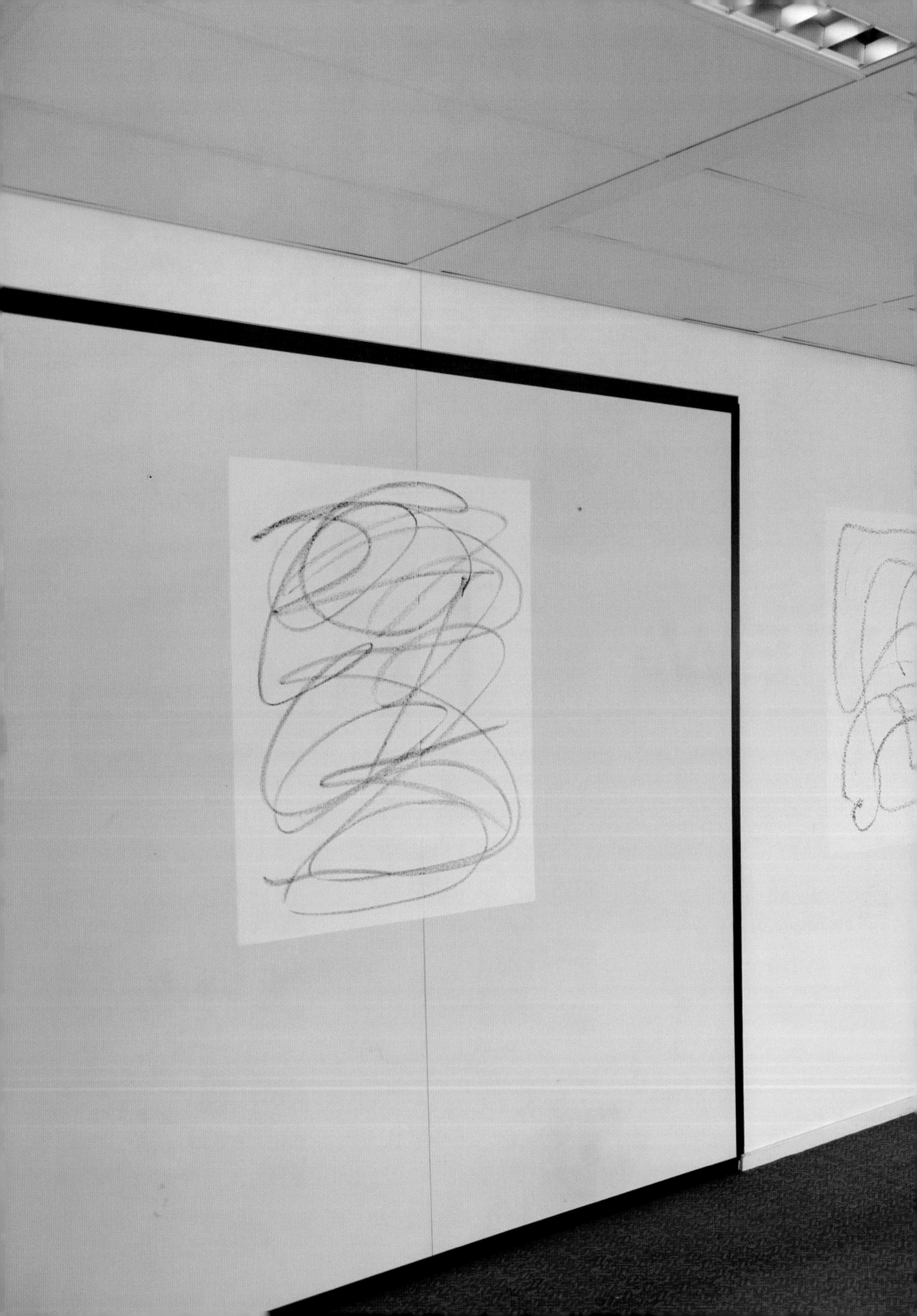

Untitled I, II, III (Re: Rotterdam), 2012 — Oil pastel and latex on wall

(Foundation for lunatics and weirdasses)

Ro Theater, campaign introduction visual identity, 2010

NAi Publishers, title page publication *Marc Bijl, In Case You Didn't Feel Like Showing Up*, 2009

Flaming Volvo; Filling up at the Arroyo Seco Parkway, 2006

Flaming Volvo; Parading at Bob's Big Boy – Friday's Classic Car night, 2006

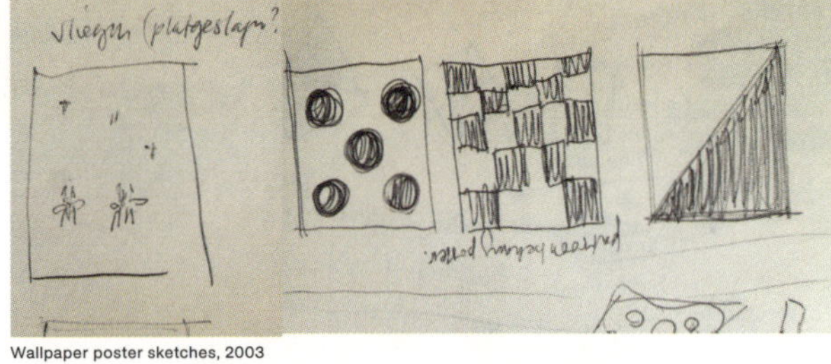

Wallpaper poster sketches, 2003

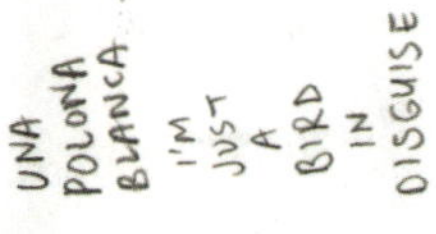

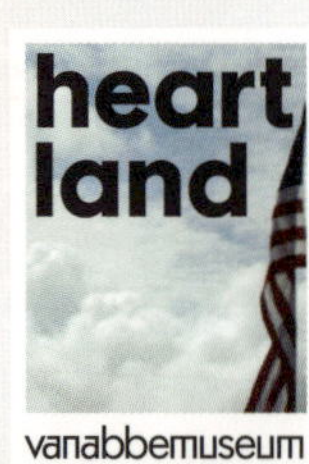

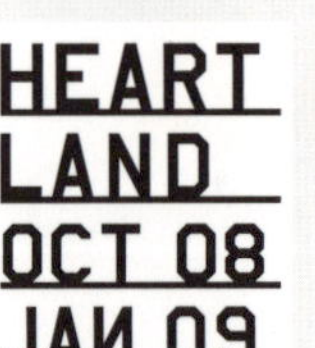

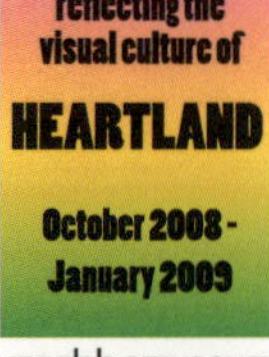

Van Abbemuseum, campaign sketches *Heartland*, 2008

Rothschild&Bach / Spunk Boeken, cover *Renske de Greef & Jan Hoek JA/NEE*, 2002

145

Off Corso, facade poster, 2000 (tonight: free entrance for all Amsterdam visitors)

Now & Wow, flyer, 2006–2007

Ro Theater, website, 2009

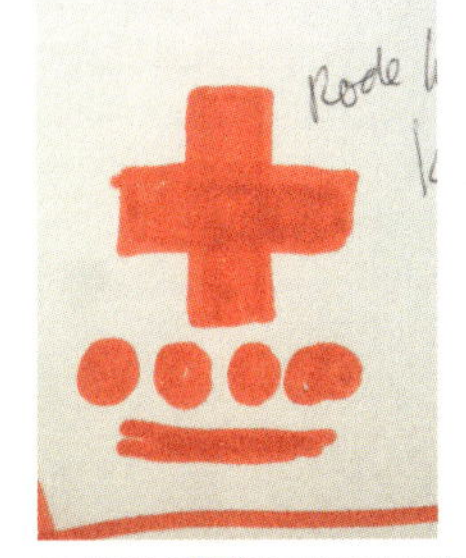
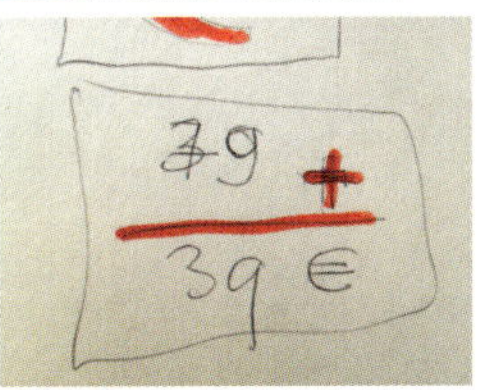

...er, 2011

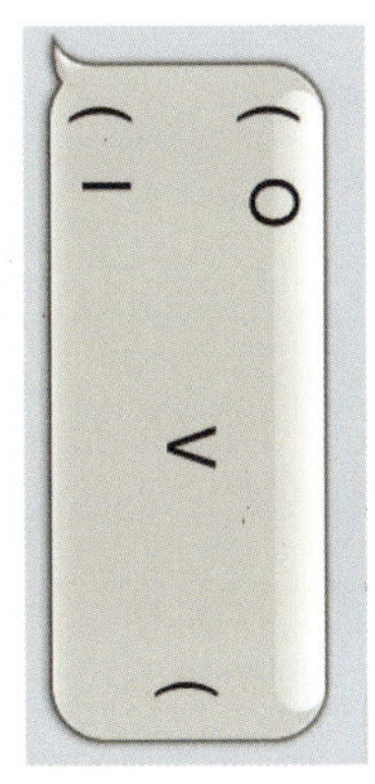
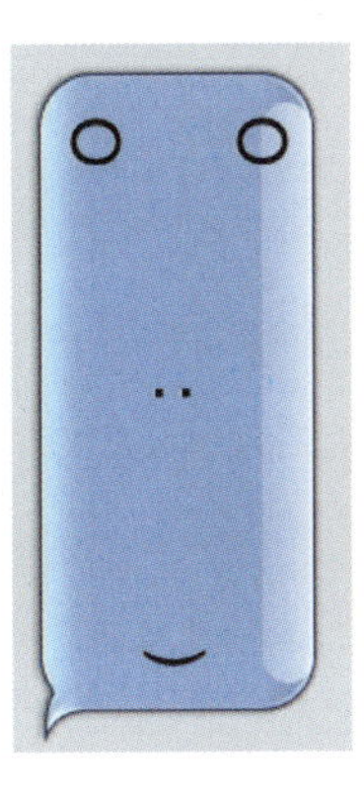

Lot Angeles, 2006 — Paint on inkjet print, 70 x 100 cm

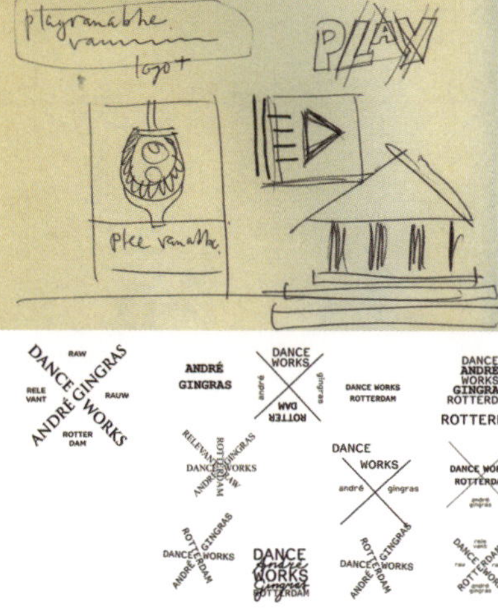

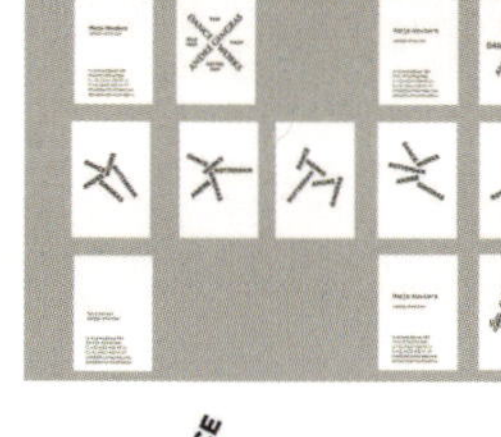

148

Dance Works Rotterdam / André Gingras, sketches for visual identity, 2010

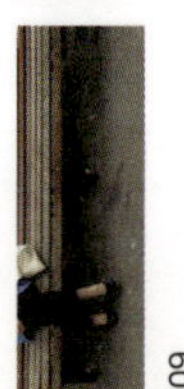

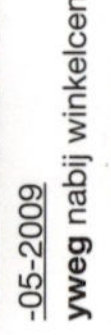

RAAM, flyers villa Escamp Literary, 2010

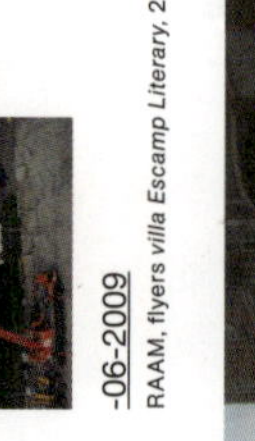

(fake sign: *no window prostitution in our street*)

Ro Theater, poster series *Branden*, 2012

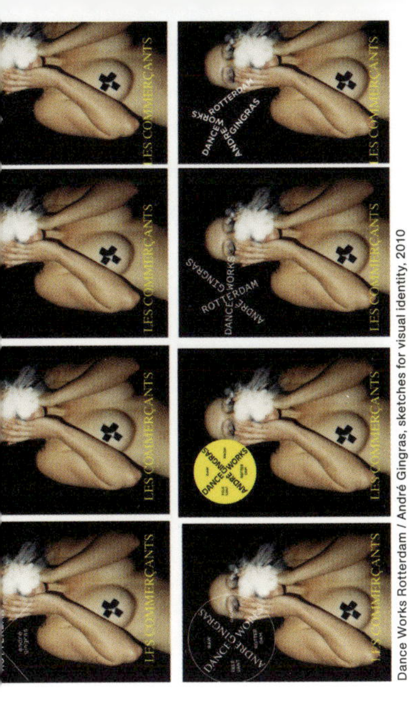

Dance Works Rotterdam / André Gingras, sketches for visual identity, 2010

De Unie, monthly flyer, 2010

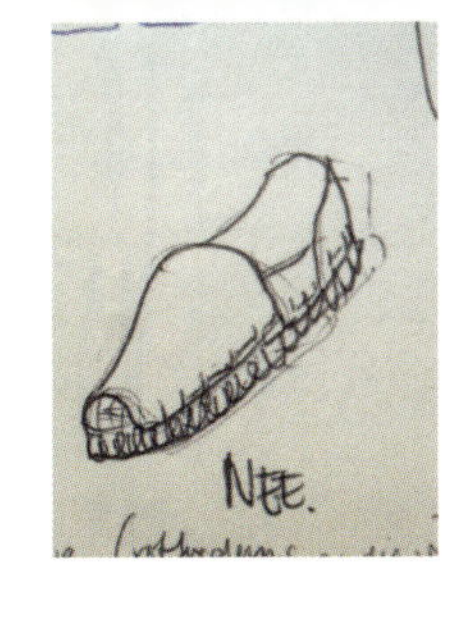

Rothschild&Bach / Spunk Books, cover *Renske de Greef, Seks in Afrika*, 2006

...ater, poster series *Branden*, 2012

Kunstgebouw, annual report covers, 2006/2007/2008/2009

Floodlight 3000 (MGH2O, Rotterdam), 2009 – Installation

Digital Archive (Vedute Collection), 2010 – PowerMac, 44 x 32 x 7 cm

Camouflage Commercial, 2006

Sculpture International Rotterdam, visual identity, 2009

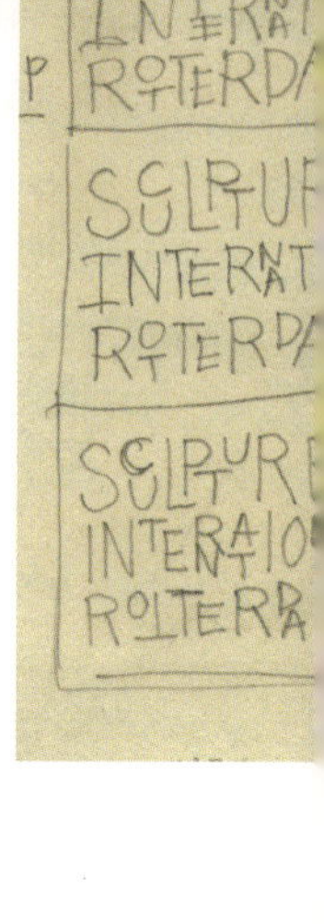

Mister Motley, poster, 2006

Van Abbemuseum, Sheela Gowda, *Open Eye Policy*, 2013

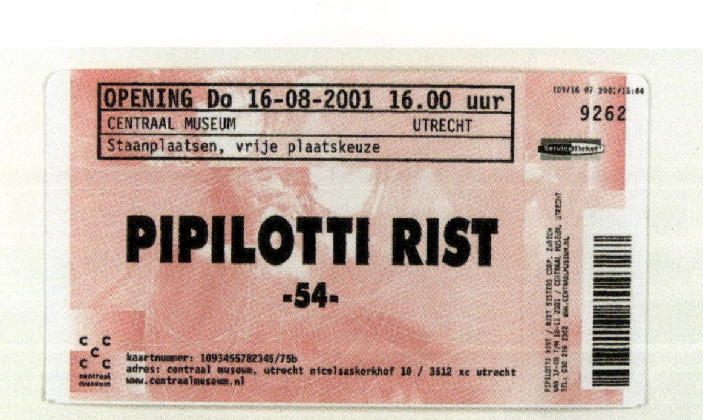

Centraal Museum Utrecht, ticket *Pipilotti Rist -54-*, 2001

Art Center College of Design, Pasadena,
lecture poster, 2006

ZUS, campaign *Vote for Luchtsingel*, 2011

Photos, 2006/2007/2008

Museum Boijmans Van Beuningen, sketches for *Aesthetic Terrorism*, 2000

Fake Ads for Coca Cola, 2003

153

De Unie, posters, 2010

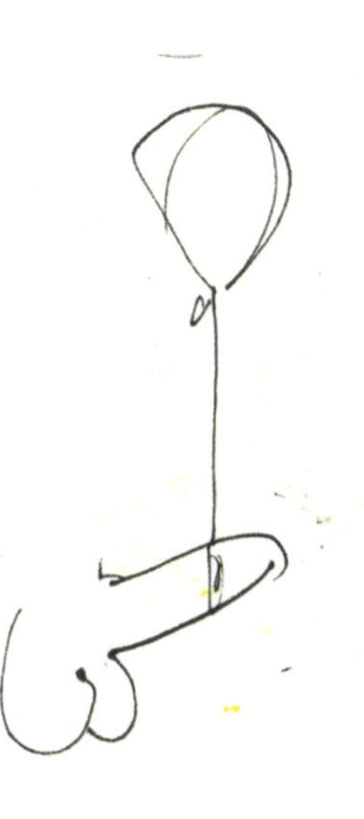

Ro Theater, poster *Ro Festival*, 2011

Paintarget I, 2011 – Paint on paper, 170 x 125 cm

Paintarget II, 2011 — Paint on paper, 170 x 125 cm

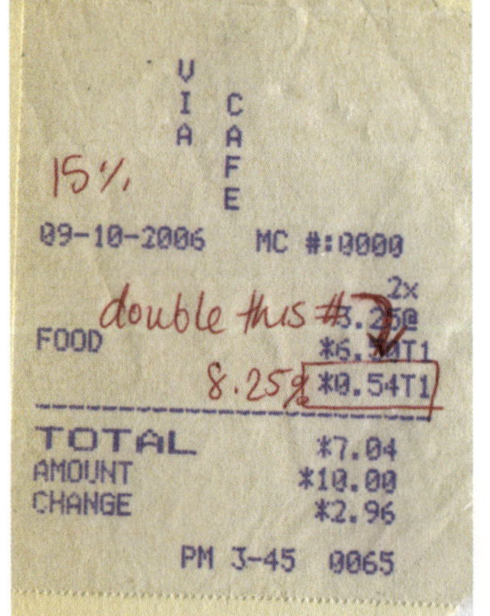

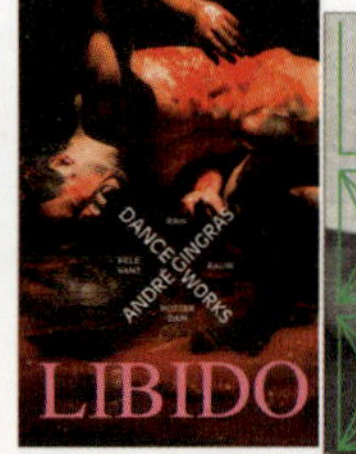

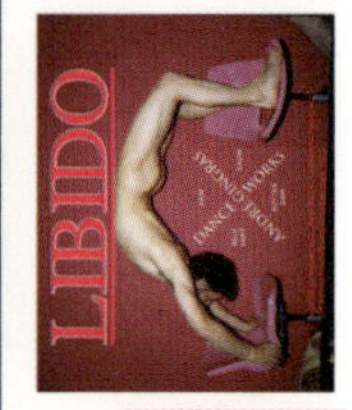

Dance Works Rotterdam / André Gingras, sketches for
visual identity, 2010

Metropolis M, magazine cover, 2012

Sculpture International Rotterdam, window stickers for
When the Lightness of Poetry, 2010

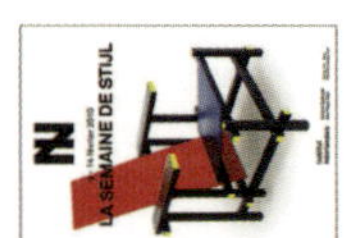

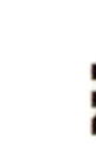

Institut Néerlandais, sketches for visual identity, 2011

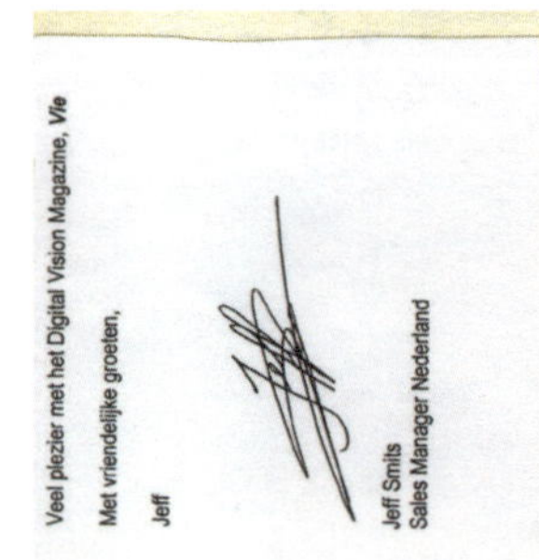

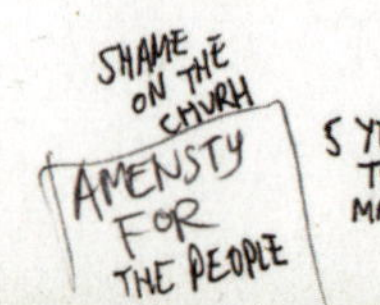

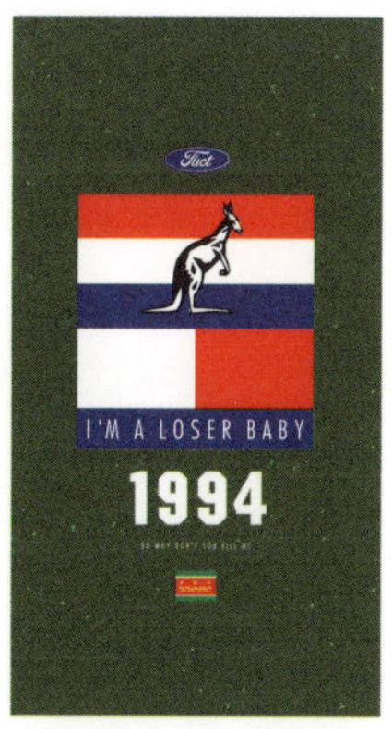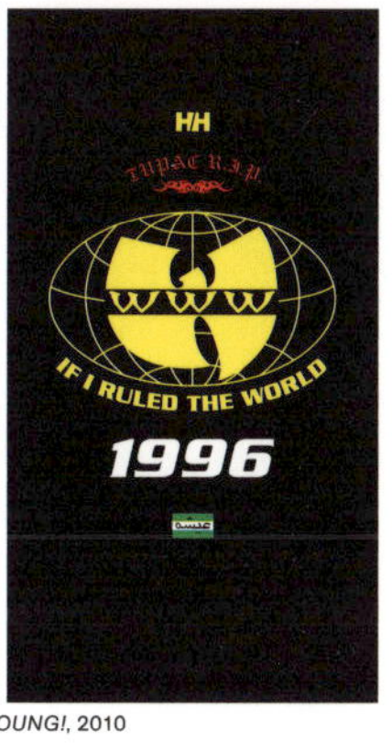

Historisch Museum Rotterdam, panels *YOUNG!*, 2010

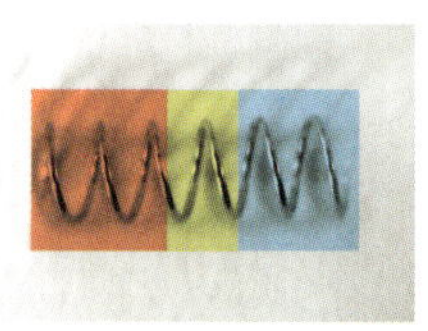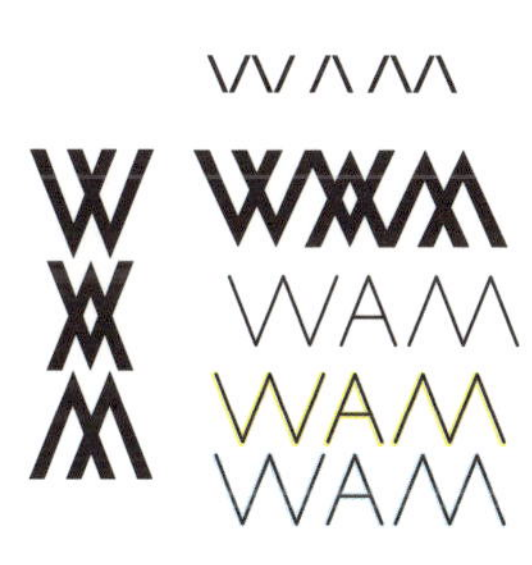

WAM Architects, sketches for visual identity, 2009

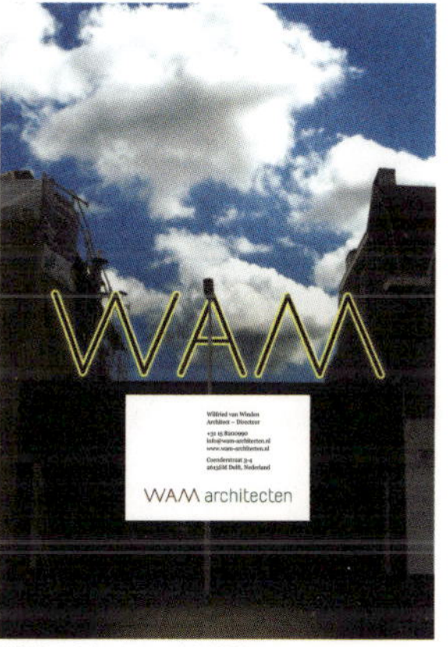

WAM architecten, card, 2009

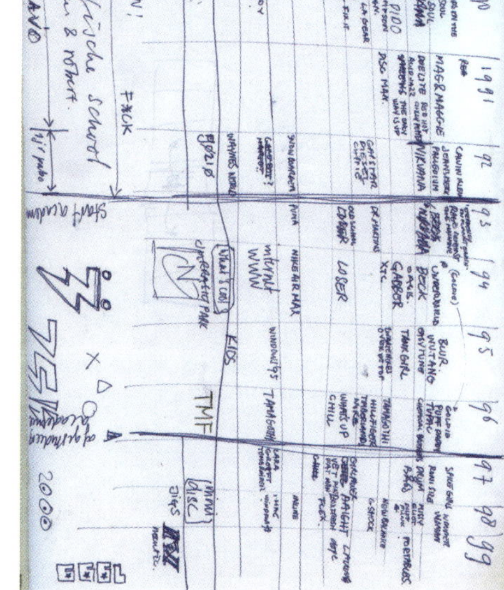

Theater, poster *Death of a Salesman*, 2011

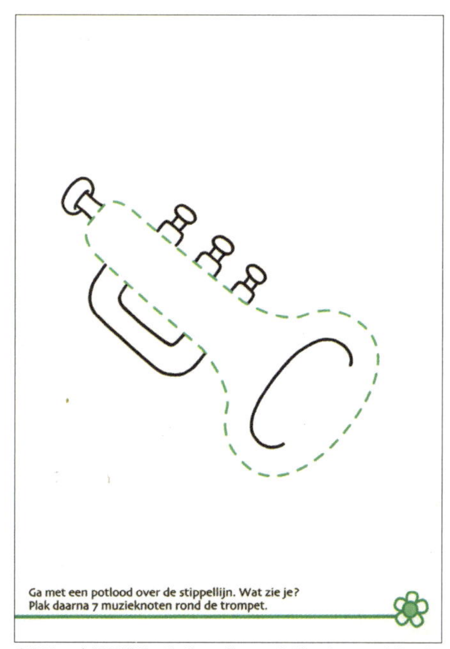
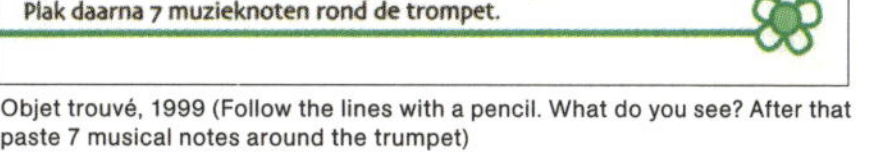

Objet trouvé, 1999 (Follow the lines with a pencil. What do you see? After that paste 7 musical notes around the trumpet)

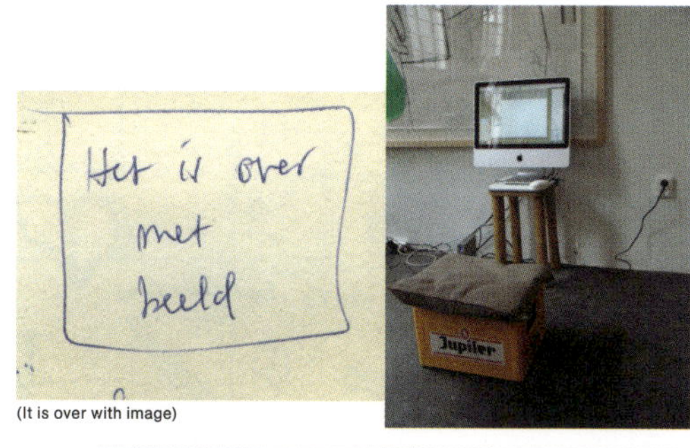

(It is over with image)

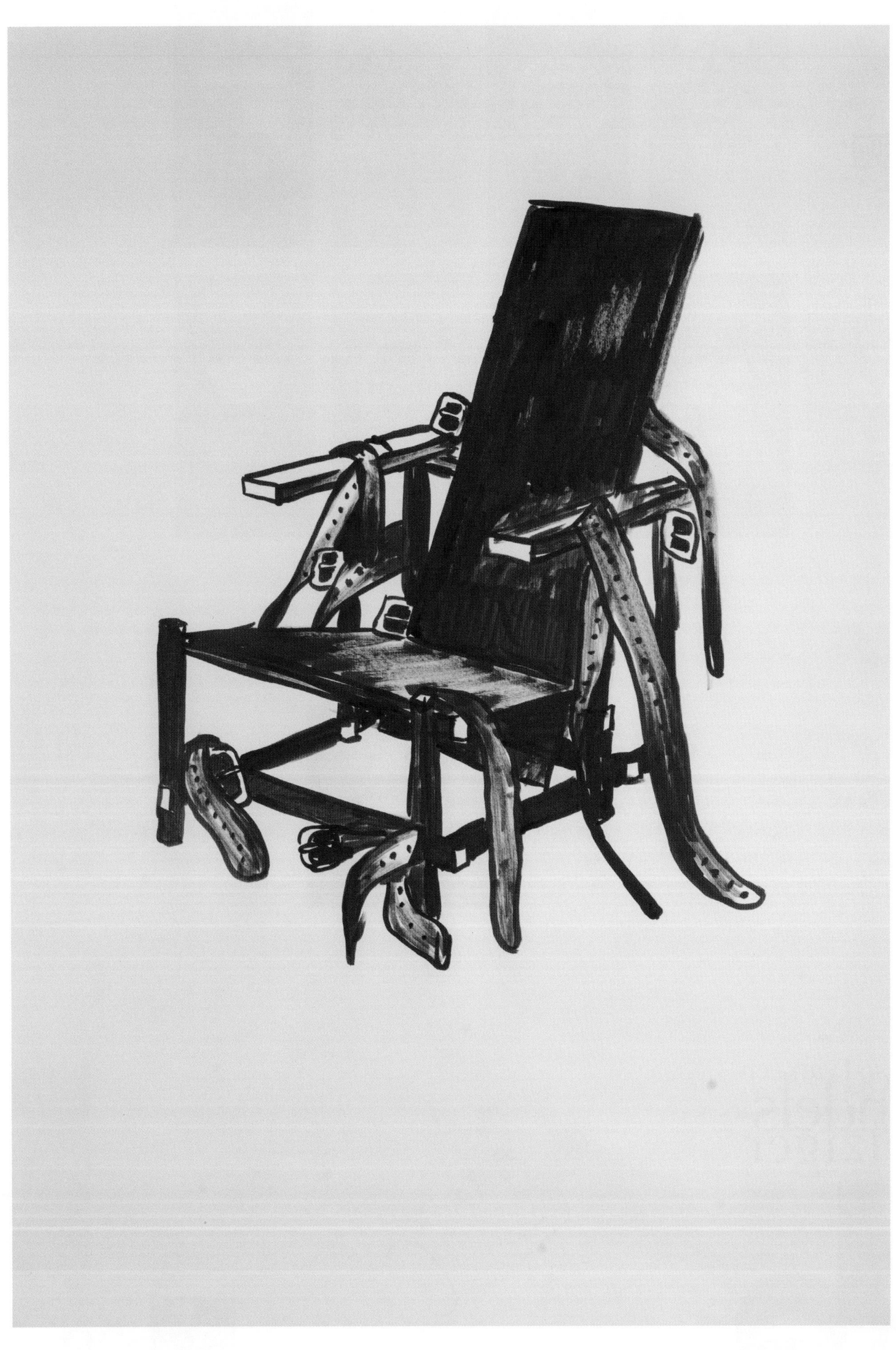

Stylish Execution, 2006 – Ink on paper, 100 x 70 cm

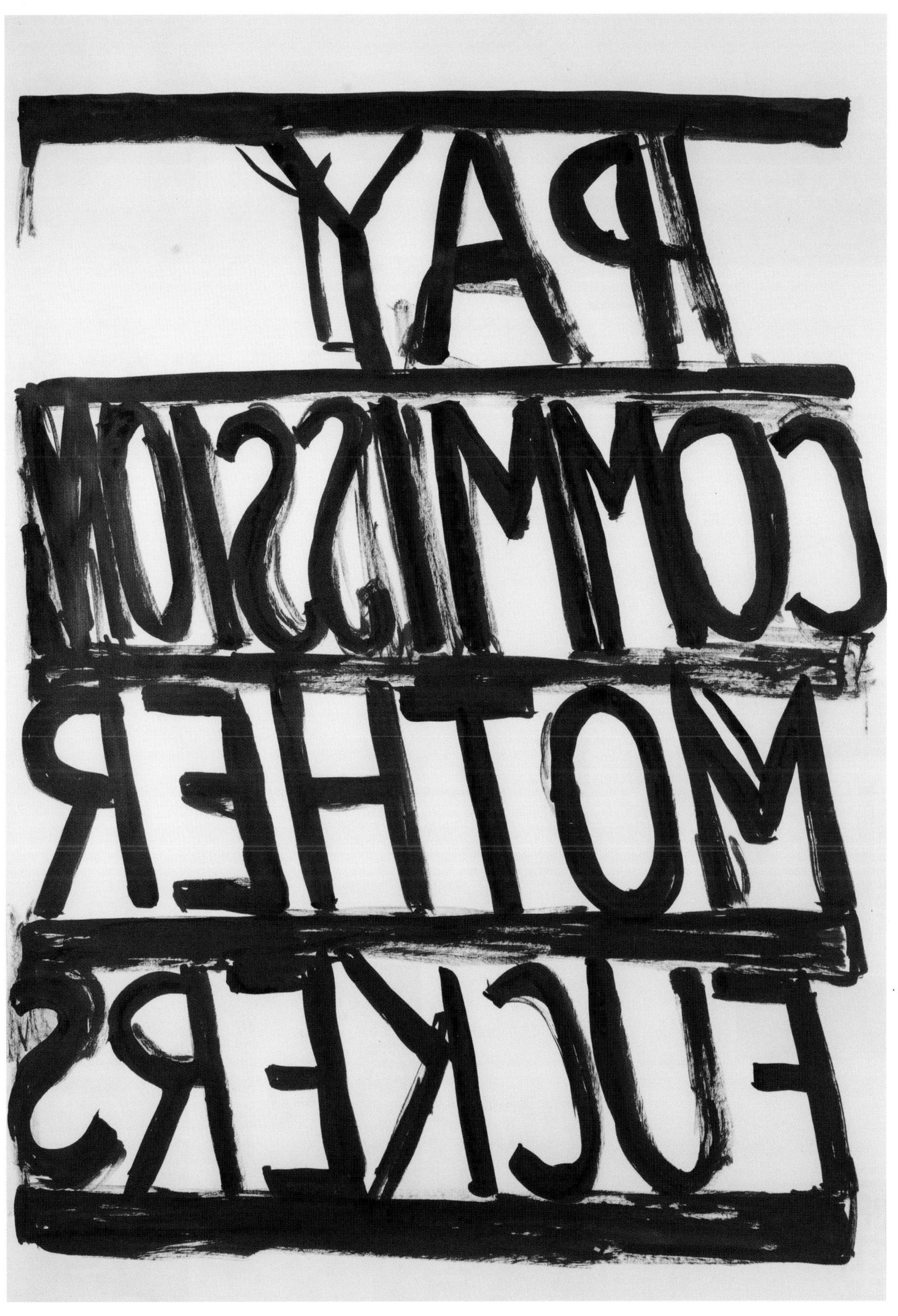

Please Pay Please, 2006 – Ink on paper, 100 x 70 cm

Van Abbemuseum, poster exhibition, 2011

Fake Johan Cruijff autograph, 2002

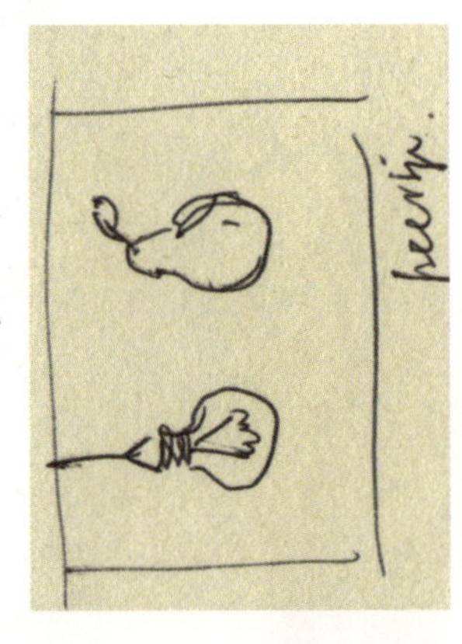

Dance Works Rotterdam / André Gingras, font, 2010

Dance Works Rotterdam / André Gingras, sketches for visual identity, 2010

International Film Festival Rotterdam, logo Cinema Sandwich, 2011

de Volkskrant, Volksheld Skateboards, 2001

Hubert Bals Fonds, publication True Variety, 2003

Historisch Museum Rotterdam, campaign ANNO, 2007

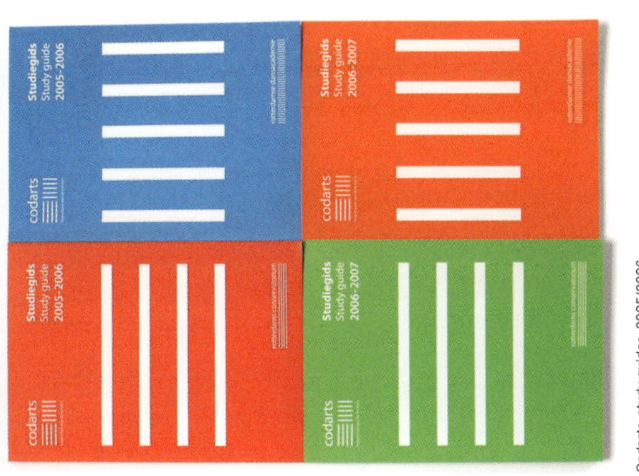

Codarts, study guides, 2005/2006

Het lichaam van

Shelter, 2012

International Film Festival Rotterdam, campaign 41st edition, 2012

Parking Space, 2006

TENT, sketches for visual identity, 2011

Feminine Presence, 2011 – Paint on tile, 40 x 20 cm

Structuring the Office of Anti-Public Relations, 2012 – Ink on paper, 100 x 70 cm

Van Abbemuseum, campaign *Heartland*, 2009

(TENT theme night. Will there be nice art to enjoy in let's say the coming century?

in conversation with Jetse Batelaan, Pieter Vos and Rens Muis)

Arts, a farce in two acts (TENT, Rotterdam), 2012 – Performance i.c.w. Jetse Batelaan.

Het bestuur van de Stichting Dolf Henkes nodigt u van harte uit voor de uitreiking van de Dolf Henkes Prijs 2006 op vrijdag 24 november om 16.30 uur in Arminius, Museumpark 3 (tegenover Museum Boijmans Van Beuningen), Rotterdam.

Dolf Henkes werd in 1903 in Rotterdam geboren. Vanaf zijn dertigste wijdde hij zich geheel aan de beeldende kunst. Na zijn overlijden in 1989 liet hij een omvangrijk oeuvre na van ruim 5000 kunstwerken. Een deel van de nalatenschap van Dolf Henkes wordt op zijn verzoek om de twee jaar bestemd voor een stimuleringsprijs voor jonge kunstenaars.

De Dolf Henkes Prijs gaat in 2006 naar de Rotterdamse kunstenaar Erik van Lieshout. Met zijn scherpe waarnemingsgave analyseert Van Lieshout de alledaagse realiteit in onze huidige verwarrende tijd. In een duizelingwekkend spel van politiek correct en incorrect voorziet hij de sociaal-culturele werkelijkheid van vlijmscherpe commentaren.

Programma
16.00 uur Inloop
16.30 uur Welkom door de voorzitter van de Stichting Dolf Henkes, Erik Hammerstein
16.35 uur Juryrapport door Arno van Roosmalen
16.45 uur Lezing door Xander Karskens, conservator hedendaagse kunst Frans Halsmuseum/De Hallen
16.55 uur Prijsuitreiking door wethouder Participatie en Cultuur, Orhan Kaya
17.05 uur Dankwoord door Erik van Lieshout
17.15 uur Optreden van Mike Redman, Eni-Less en Deformer
17.35 uur Sluiting door Erik Hammerstein

Bij het verlaten van de kerk krijgen de aanwezigen een gesigneerd werk in oplage van Erik van Lieshout als 'aandenken' van de Dolf Henkes Prijs 2006 (zolang de voorraad strekt). Aansluitend wordt om 18.00 uur in Museum Boijmans Van Beuningen de tentoonstelling 'This can't go on (Stay with me)' van Erik van Lieshout geopend. Deze tentoonstelling is te zien tot en met 4 februari 2007.

Deze kaart is uw toegangsbewijs voor de prijsuitreiking en is geldig voor twee personen. Met dank aan: Arminius en Museum Boijmans Van Beuningen

Dolf Henkes Prize, invitation, 2006

RoXY, programme magazine, *Red&Blue*, 1999

(i thoroughly enjoyed your exhibition, and took it at a leisurely pace. my favourite piece was Migratory Birds. it's been a long-cherished dream of mine to get that kind of movement on the stage. i've made enough embarrassing attempts already, with mimes flapping about the place. you guys have got a lot closer. and that you came across 'the last day' in the street i find disturbing and reassuring in equal measure. that was point 1, point 2 is that i have an appointments problem this wednesday. i have to get a move on with my stage sets for We are happy (Wij zijn blij) and i only really have that morning to do it. do you two still have a presentation that afternoon? i think i'll only be able to get to you by 13.00, if that, and leave at 16.45 as then i have a meeting about Boijmans TV but i'll be staying in Rotterdam as i'm going to see 'Man of Moods' by the OT Theatre. so the early evening is another option.
Sorry about this, I hope we can find another way. Regards, Jetse)

ik heb op mijn dooie gemakje genoten van jullie tentoonstelling. persoonlijke favoriet vormen de Trekvogels. is een lang gekoesterde droom om die beweging ooit op het toneel te kunnen zetten. heeft al veel genante momenten opgeleverd, met mime spelers die wat door de ruimte fladderden. jullie zijn een stuk dichterbij gekomen.

en dat jullie zo maar op straat 'de laatste dag' zijn tegen gekomen, vond ik verontrustend en gerustellend op het zelfde moment.

dit ten eerste,
maar ik heb aanstaande woensdag een agenda probleem. ik moet stappen zetten met mijn decor voor Wij Zijn Blij, en dat kan eigenlijk alleen maar die ochtend. hebben jullie nog steeds een presentatie die middag? ik denk dat ik

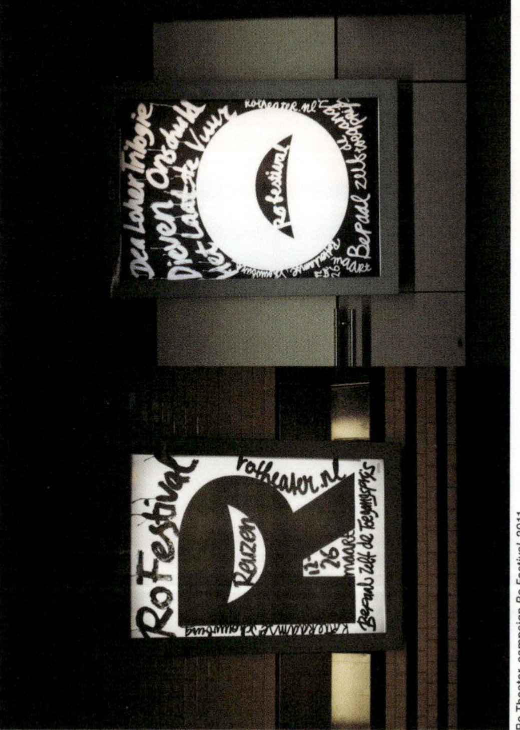

Ro Theater, campaign *Ro Festival*, 2011

Van Abbemuseum, poster *Piero Gilardi – samen werken* (Collaborative Effects), 2012

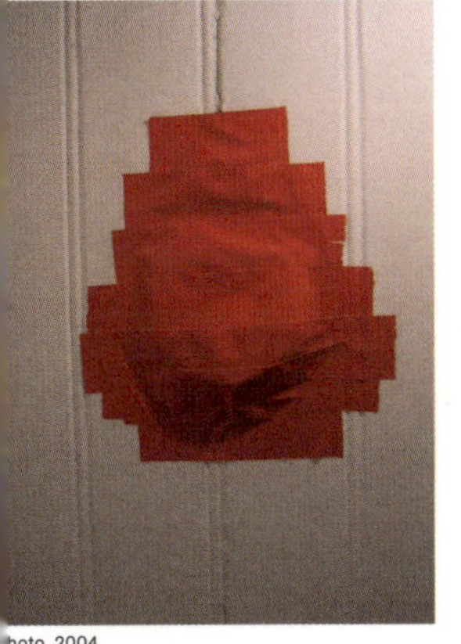

Arling & Cameron, sketch for *Music for Imaginary Films*, 2000

photo, 2004

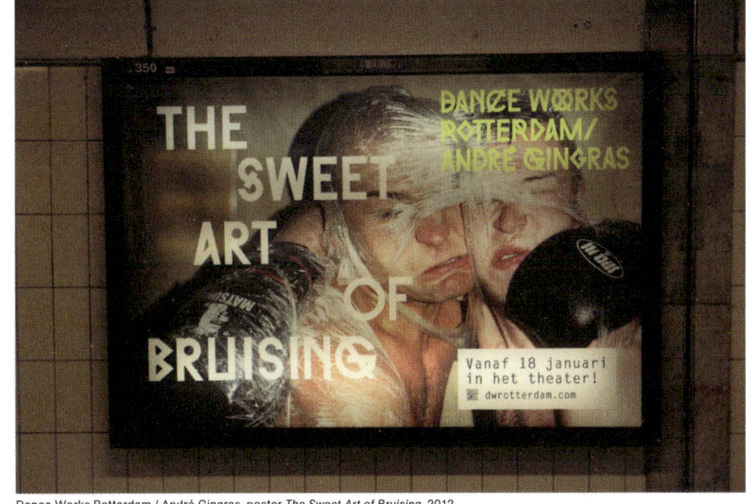

Dance Works Rotterdam / André Gingras, poster *The Sweet Art of Bruising*, 2012

(salt cubes)

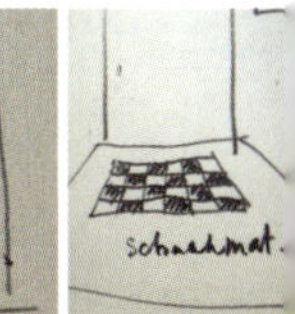

Botox Gonna Work It Out, 2005

Institut Néerlandais, poster *Surréalistes de Rotterdam*, 2012

Museum Boijmans Van Beuningen, exhibition wall *It's All Dali*, 2005

165

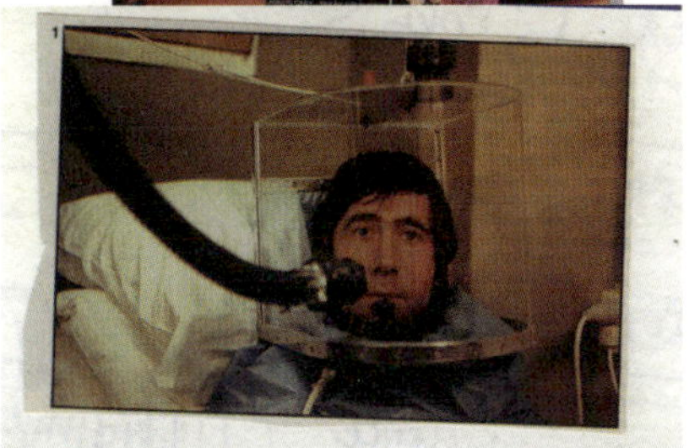

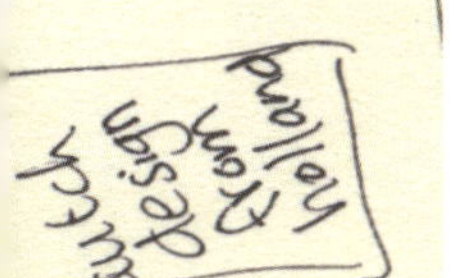

Nederlands Fotomuseum, sketches for campaign *ZWART/WIT*, 2010

Untitled, 2011 – Ink on paper, 80 x 80 cm

Untitled, 2011 – Ink on paper, 80 x 80 cm

Boomerang Freecards, *Cucumber Time*, 2000

Now & Wow, sketches, 2000

sleutels
een straat-collage
staandrager

uitgeverij passage

Passage publishers, cover, 2012

168

Van Abbemuseum, posters *René Daniëls*, 2012

Now & Wow, flyer, 2000

Now & Wow, ticket première, 2000

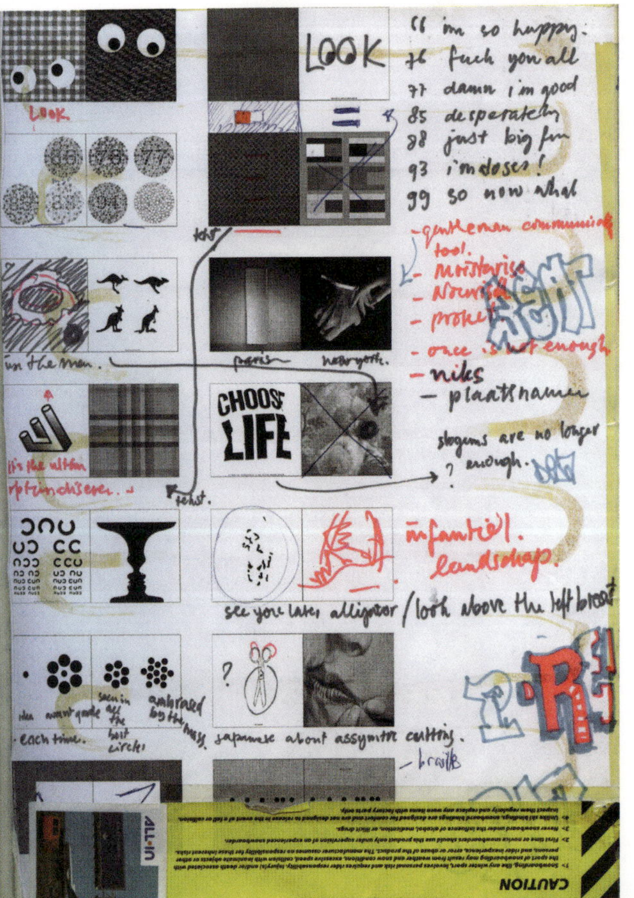

(Dear people of Specker,

For Easter next year it struck us as a
idea to have the statues on Easter Is
reproduced in chocolate. (you know
ones, those huge stone heads) With
Marzipan filling, perhaps

Does this idea appeal to you? if it do
could we make an appointment to m
and discuss it?)

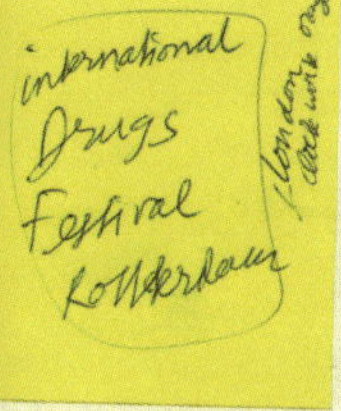

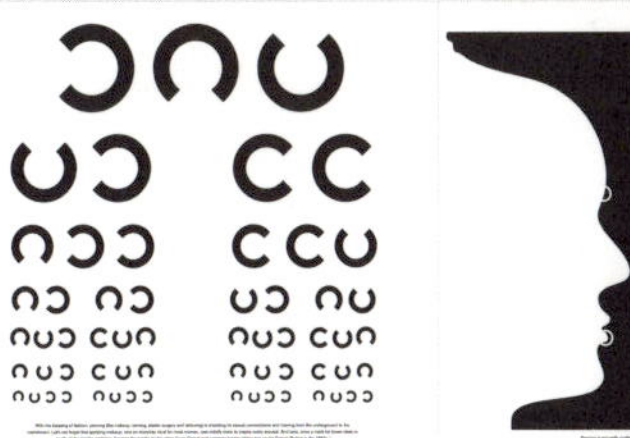

"Gerrit Rietflat" Academie oplossing Ruimteprobleem.

Gerrit Rietflat Academy, sketch for lack of space solution, 2012

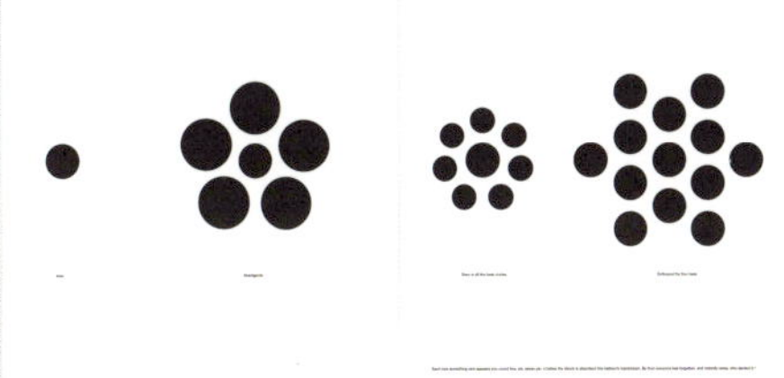

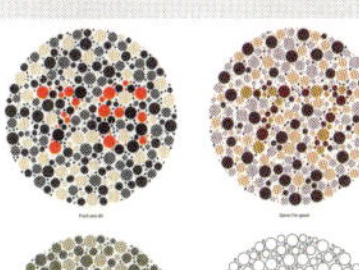
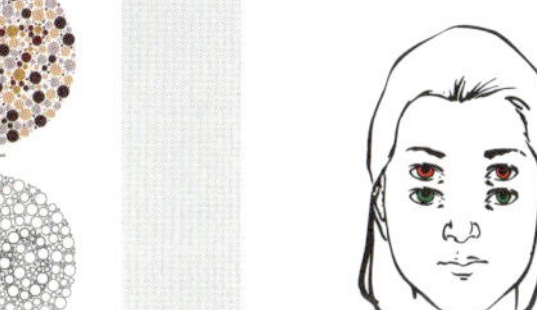
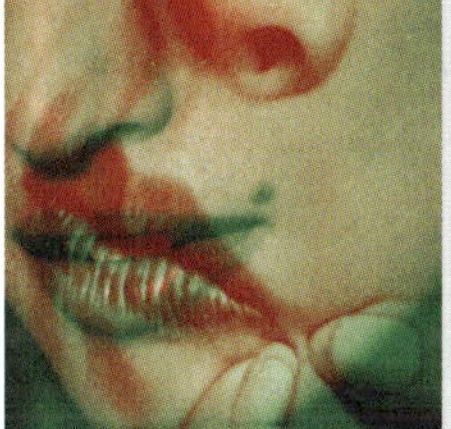

BIS Publishers / André Platteel, spreads *Look (Symbol Soup; 8)*, i.c.w. Peter Jeroense, 2002

...er, facade banner *Ro Nu*, 2011

Sketch, *Silicon Valley*, 2010

...heater, poster *King Lear*, 2011

Van Dale schrapt
'neger' niet

ROTTERDAM, 7 MEI. Het woord neger behoort tot de Nederlandse taal en hoort daarom thuis in de Dikke Van Dale, het Groot woordenboek der Nederlandse taal.
• *Pagina 10*

Now & Wow, poster *Negerzoenen & blanke vla*, 2004

KARMA
SHARMA
MOSH

Framing Nature (Maassilo, Rotterdam), 2012 — White latex on wall

Sketch for Theo van Gogh monument, 2011

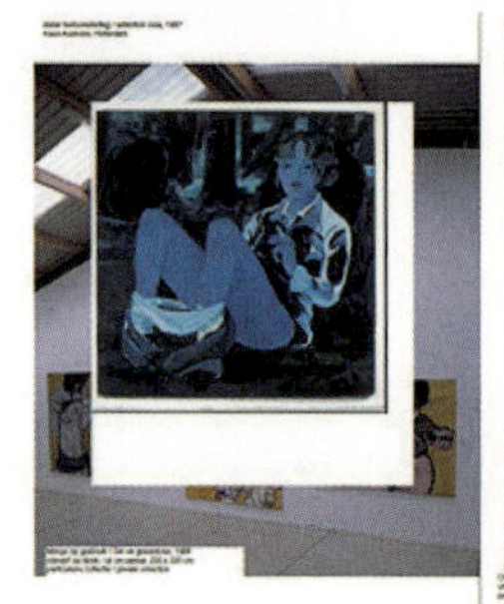

NAi Publishers, publication Erik van Lieshout *Naughty by Nature*, 2002

Remote City, 2011

Ro Theater, poster *Bonte avond van bodybuilders*, 2011

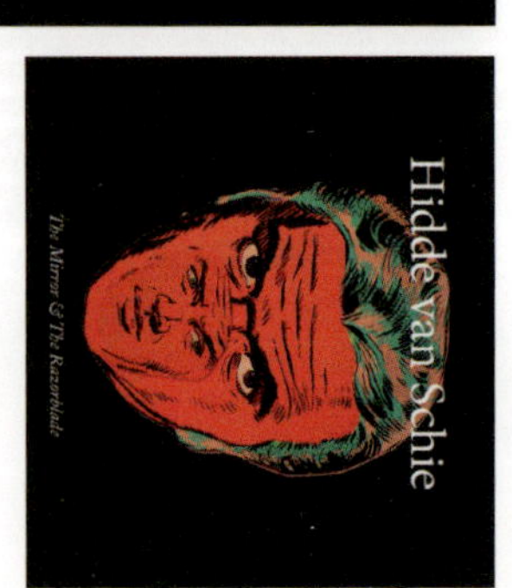

Hidde van Schie, *Dusty Diamond Eyes*, *The Mirror & The Razorblade*, CD, LP and publication, 2013

Photo, 2012

Netherlands Foundation for Visual Arts, Design and Architecture, flag, 2009

Alphabet Street

Pieter Vos

Airport Hotel

So here I was and I knew it was going to suck. I had come by bike – the bike I had ridden yesterday to the ski run for the umpteenth time with my snowboard across the handlebars. Now there were two hockey sticks there instead and I was wearing my hockey stuff under my clothes. There was nowhere to park my bike, since your average Airport Hotel doesn't have a bike shelter. Everything there is geared toward cars and motorists and that didn't include me. The others were okay. They came by car. The ones who didn't have a car were smart enough to organize a lift. Not me. My mind was elsewhere yesterday as I had been snowboarding and then skateboarding in the city with Daan and Maarten. I'd arrived home at two in the morning completely wrecked and now I was here. I knew it for sure – this would be my last hockey match. As I parked my bike in the car park against a dumpster, some of my teammates got out of their car. I felt nauseous right away. Those guys thought they were so cool, real he-men in an over-the-top way and that really pissed me off. They smoked cigarettes and wore suede cowboy boots. The dirty parking lot was paved with those cheesy fake bricks. Willem-Jan came by car too, a small red lightweight Citroën AX Sport. A smart car, I had to admit. I'd wanted a lift in it to Barendrecht one time and I'd been clever enough to put my hockey things in it in advance. And he was a nice guy, although I'd only known him a few weeks. The others were already inside by then but I just wasn't interested. Still, now that I was a little older, I found myself on men's hockey teams where they only wanted to drink beer, smoke, talk about girls and listen to music. That last one was fine with me, except that I only listened to hip hop and only idiots did that in those days. In other words, it wasn't my music blasting out of the stereo tower alongside the field.

I saw that the buffet included half a can of orange juice that had had a packet of supermarket squash emptied into it. This is where we ate brunch. Before away games we decided among ourselves how much money had to go into the beer kitty and how to organize a trailer to carry the boxes. This was the sort of thing we had to get together to discuss: buffet, brunch, beer kitty, boxes. Jesus, I thought, what next?

Brush

There it is again! The new dish brush. That gives hope. Then the kitchen looks as good as new and it shines like new. All thoughts of that eternal pool of cold water around the tap and the old dish brush have faded away. I'm no longer irritated by the kitchen cupboards whose upper edges still need finishing and even the brown stains on the gas stove look great. The sink unit, on reflection, is a thing of wonder, at least if you manage to keep it clean!

I really fancy cleaning the drain and before I know it I'm clutching the dish brush. Well this is good, a bit of soap and water and that brown drain looks nice and shiny and everything seems to work. But now the dish brush is wet and I don't want to leave it on the kitchen counter like that. I open the door to the kitchen balcony and bang the brush on the handrail as if I were drying lettuce. Back in the kitchen I see that I've spilt water on the floor. Quick, a cloth to clean it up, but there's no cloth to be seen. The tea towel will have to do. Okay, the floor is dry but I'm left with a dirty tea towel. So I leave it on the stairs on its way to the laundry basket. Now, where was I? That was it, the drain. It's nice and clean now, although it has some filthy cracks along the edges where the water has worn it down. All sorts of stuff gets stuck in there, but let's just say this is something you get with a concrete sink. Now I *could* decide to make a wooden top but of course nobody would advise it, for what should be obvious reasons.

I retrieve the tea towel from the stairs and dry the sink with it. When it's all over, I take a new dishcloth and place it next to the dish brush. The new cloth looks lovely and clean. I glance at the new brush and realize that this is an illusion. Tomorrow the brush will look as disgusting as ever.

'Wow', I hear, 'that looks great!' My wife Mary has just come in. She's as happy as I am about it and I tell her how excited I am whenever there's a new dish brush. 'That brush isn't new,' she says. 'Yes it is,' I counter. 'No it's not, it's just come out of the dish washer,' she says.

Copyright

It's difficult to define what falls under copyright and what doesn't, even when it's clear that something has been copied. To give an example: It seems clear to me that Samsung has copied the Apple iPhone and iPad, but were they entirely created by Apple to begin with? This is the subject of some serious lawsuits right now. Apple looks closely at existing designs too. The most recent example is the Swiss station clock designed in 1944 by Hans Hilfiker. Apple had incorporated this clock in its iPad without permission. Now it has to pay the Swiss railways compensation for every iPad sold. Apple has also looked closely at Braun and Sony and this is logical enough if you're doing research into solutions for a product of your own. I myself look at graphic design, art, architecture, fashion and film. So there's no way anyone can claim that what they're doing is completely original. I'm influenced by things I like, whether I want to be or not. Everything is related in some way to what came before. 'It's all been done before' is said often enough, but that conversation-stopper simply isn't true. Every era has its own variations on the same recurring themes. This always results in something unique, something that relates to the here and now. Anything made at another time can't do this, as it has history written all over it. That's why contemporary art is so relevant. It sees the same recurring subjects with new eyes. You can see straight away if a thing has been copied. This is what makes *Antiques Roadshow* fun to watch.

Dormobile

I'd been moaning for years about getting a racing bike and now finally I'd got
one for my birthday. It was a white Batavus with mudguards and all the other
extras. It was a godawful bike, but somehow I was so happy to have it I was
willing to overlook this. After all, I'd studied the brochures of many racing
bikes and so I knew deep down this wasn't a good one. To cap it all off, I had
discovered a chrome BMX 'cross' bike in the Raleigh brochure. I was so taken by
it that I forgot all about all those silly racing bikes, like the one I owned. During
a subsequent cycling holiday I soon discovered that my Batavus was getting
the best of me. While my sister pedalled on merrily on her metallic purple
chopper, having the holiday of her life, I was really sweating it – which only
made things worse. We had with us a lightweight tent made by Slee, a company
whose reputation spoke for itself. For some time I had had difficulty accepting
my parents' holier-than-thou, pseudo-dynamic-organic trip. The whole grain
pancakes, the ancient carrots that were 'still perfectly edible' and the buckwheat
cooked in sour milk (quick fried and polished off with syrup!) – it just made me
uncomfortable. It was okay as food goes, but it was getting to the point when I
yearned to down some Coca-Cola. Something my kids are now proud to tell me.
'Dad, we were at a party at Grandma's and had Coke to drink.' And the look as
they say it – coked up, you might say.
But all that went out of the window when I met Mary. I told her in graphic
detail why Slee tents were the best and all other tents were crap. We even went
camping in my parents' old tent near Santandèr on the north coast of Spain. We
had set it up for one night at a locals-only campsite, where we felt like aliens
stranded on the wrong planet.
It was September 11, 2001, and the towers of the World Trade Center were in
the process of collapsing. Mary had just left the restaurant. We sat on the terrace.
She told me that the restaurant TV had just shown two beautiful buildings
collapsing and I thought it most odd that they'd do that to such big beautiful
buildings... I actually only heard half of what she'd said. Later we realized we'd
just ordered rabbit, accidentally, because we didn't understand the language. Back
at the tent, we listened to Radio Netherlands Worldwide on my dad's transistor.
The first thing we heard was 'They're jumping out of the windows right now.'
The next morning we were woken by a flurry of activity in Spanish. I unzipped
the tent and found myself peering into a gigantic Dormobile. Luckily we hadn't
camped on their regular pitch, otherwise we would have been under it.

E&E

Thanks for your help, love and patience. I'll pass it on.

Focus

When I was about fourteen I used to make my own skateboards and
snowboards. The prints I made for them were abstract graphic grids and
textures reminiscent of Jackson Pollock. I also made a collage of the Tower of
Babel with skaters riding it. *The Tower of Babel* by Pieter Bruegel the Elder is
my all-time favourite painting. Ever since I was four, we regularly went to look
at it in the Rotterdam Boijmans Van Beuningen Museum. The story of the
Tower of Babel expresses universal values. Its construction symbolizes man's
desire to reach for the sky. Man is creative and ambitious. He has blind faith
in his capabilities and in the endless possibilities of technology. The tower
also symbolizes man's arrogance for which he is punished by God. This is a
quality I recognize in myself. I want to have control over everything and make
it perfect. My focus is so extreme that it backfires on me – every time, but I've
never wanted to avoid it. It's when you feel you've lost control of something
that you learn the most and move forward. As Leonard Cohen sang: 'There is a
crack in everything. That's how the light gets in.'
I can focus finely on things others often consider utterly incomprehensible.
As a result, I regularly get compared to Larry David in *Curb Your Enthusiasm*.
This TV series is a fictionalized version of Larry's daily life. There are no
scripts as such, the actors only being given a framework within which they
may improvise. The whole thing is shot using hand-held cameras. Larry David
and Larry Charles, who has directed many of the series' episodes, had earlier
worked together on *Seinfeld*. I regard Charles as extremely focused. I mean
just look at his shoes on Wikipedia. Can't beat those New Yorkers. I live there
too, as it happens. It's that focus on the everyday that I find so compelling. It
all began with Woody Allen's films. Woody by contrast is regularly way out of
focus, particularly in *Deconstructing Harry*, but even that's sheer genius.

Google

'What? Say it again? Goggle?? Not another search engine?! Like Yahoo.
Google? What the fuck. Okay, I'll take a look... http, right? And then
slash slash colon? www.google.com. Got it! What now? Just type
anything? Will do… Rotterdam. Yeah, it works, hey, not bad. Better than
Yahoo! Thanks man, wow.'

'Yes, hi. Have you seen what Google can do now? You can search using
images! Really! Take a look. Just type a word and then click on Images.
Nothing happening yet? O god, wait, you have to go to google.com.
The Dutch version isn't up yet. Right. Yeah. Got it now? And then
Images. Bizarre, isn't it? Right now we're working on an LP cover. I
was just searching for the artist on the record, since he lives up north in
Groningen. Give him a google! Kettel's the name. Yes, Kettel. With a
K. I didn't know him either. His stuff's pretty sick. Sounds a bit like a
less zonked Aphex Twin. What? Nothing? Are there no images of him?
How do you know, you don't even know him! Now I can see it too, the
guy with the 'tache. It's not him. What's that? What's the cover going to
be like? This, I think. The thing you're looking at in Google Images! The
ones with the light-blue horizontal stripes and that dark-blue and light
grey type. On the LP and on the CD. What do you think? Exactly, that's
what I thought. I like it, only now we have to see what Kettel and Clone
Records think of it. Yeah right, okay… later!'

Hi

‘Hi.’

Hi

I

I Love NY
Who was it again who designed that, Merel?
Milton Glaser.

Jimmy

My life as a graphic designer began in the third year of primary school. I drew
Donald Duck. Not his image but the letters D-O-N-A-L-D-D-U-C-K.
I made my first skimboard (a board for surfing on the thin wash of previous
waves) when I was eleven. It was to be my Donald Duck skimboard.
One day a boy came to visit us at the house. I really wanted to see his work
and I still remember his name was Job. He had a bunch of graphic stuff with
him and I remember being most excited by it all. On asking around later, it
transpired that it had been Job Meihuizen, these days programme manager
at Premsela, the design and fashion institute. No one remembers exactly why
he had visited my parents but it probably had something to do with the local
drawing society (Teekengenootschap Pictura) or puppet centre (Stichting
Poppenspel). My parents were friends with his parents through the puppet
centre. My uncle, Charles Thiels, who had been curator of the Historical
Museum of Rotterdam, was also involved. From then on I knew for sure that
I wanted to be a graphic designer. Edwin Nikkels, son of graphic designer
Walter Nikkels, was a fellow pupil at the primary school. Once we took a look
in his father's workplace. That was pretty awesome.
It was then, around 1982, that the first branded clothing arrived in the class.
My school friend Jimmy turned up one day in Nikes and faded jeans by Crums
or Heavy. This was uncharted territory for me, but I noticed straight off that it
was super cool. This was mainly because of the way the girls reacted to it. All
at once Jimmy was the centre of attention and that took some getting used to.
Before then, being able to run fast, winning at marbles and playing football
had been more than adequate and these were areas in which I excelled. All
American products were cool. What attracted me to them the most was the
graphic design. I spent the whole day drawing the logos of Nike and New
Balance. I even made entire working drawings for NB. This brought the
attention back to me, since oddly enough the girls thought my drawings were
cool as well. I myself was blissfully unaware that buying or drawing these
articles could give you an element of coolness. I just wasn't interested.

Killing clays

The girls were having a hen party and were off to shoot clay pigeons. I had to hurry as the ladies were already outside the door. Quickly I asked Mary what those pigeons look like. Well, sort of reddish, she said, a bit like the pigeons you see around town. And they were off!

Los Angeles

I'm in a photography shop with my daughter Veere. She's going to be two
next month. As the insurance hasn't been arranged yet, we can't use the car
and walking in L.A. is out of the question. Luckily we're able to fax the
car insurance company. On giving the Triple A a ring, I'm relieved to hear
Dorina say: 'You can drive safe now!' And now we're in the Volvo heading to
Santa Monica via the 110 and Highway 10. We park it on Ocean Boulevard.
Double espressos in Los Angeles are more like half espressos. They serve
them in huge cups. It's a strange city. If I'd asked for just an espresso, I'd have
had to scrape it out. Lots of fit-looking babes drinking ice coffee. Regular,
sugar-free, soy and low-fat. The folks behind the counter are fat and black,
those in front of it slim and blonde. We drive back by way of Beverly Hills.
We eat a burrito in a parking lot opposite the Nature Market on Hillhurst
2080. The tastiest burrito ever.
In the supermarket, there's this woman on the phone. She's dressed in tight-
fitting shiny black ultra-short pants and a fitted see-through black lace blouse
with short puff sleeves. The blouse is shorter on the sides than at the front
and back. This gives you a view of her body and tattoos. She's wearing tall
platform pumps and has a tattoo of two swords on the back of her legs. These
begin just below her buttocks and go all the way down to her heels, with a
break at her knee pits, as if they've briefly penetrated her flesh. Two children
run up to her. She tells her girlfriend on the phone: 'that freak wound up in
rehab again' and that she'd 'like to stab him'. I trail her to catch a little more.
Without looking at me, she makes a show of what a bitchin' person she is by
giving her kids the candy she herself used to be given when she was a kid.
When she hangs up she looks at me attentively and laughs. I don't. Veere
runs through those long passageways as if she were six.
I wake up and take an Alka-Seltzer. 'Kiss head,' says Veere as she approaches
me. Am I hearing that right? 'Kiss head,' she says again. She points at my
head and kisses it. Then she says 'Ameyica.'

Muppets

If I've learnt anything from Jim Henson, the creator of *The Muppet Show*, it's the concept of working together. Rens and I sometimes call ourselves Statler and Waldorf, after the two old fogeys who heckle the action on stage from their balcony in the theatre. We often do the same thing from our studio. It could be a hit format on TV, no doubt about that. We confer on all matters before verbally demolishing them with relish. Extremely unhealthy of course, but great fun and afterwards we reassess everything as brilliant and extraordinary.

It's easy to criticize a thing as being bad. It's much harder to consider a thing to be good and then defend it. To say nothing of explaining the difference between good and bad. That's quite impossible. Why is a thing bad and why is a thing good? That's an argument we might do well to abandon.

In working together, we can pick up on each other's properties and qualities and make use of them. We can also try out and expand on each other's ideas, and that makes for effective processes. That sense of mutual responsibility, and anything the other adds, is good for the momentum. We first got into collaborating at the Willem de Kooning Academy, as and when the occasion arose. In the second year we really wanted to make things for the real world. We worked for De Vlerk (a pop/rock venue, later called Waterfront), *Passionate* (a literary magazine), Hardcore Skatestore, Club RoXY, Showroom MAMA and MTC Party. These jobs were unpaid, but we did get creative freedom. This way, we could keep on experimenting. This brought us more commissions and we gradually found ourselves in a position to ask to be paid. By then we had people working for us and that was a huge step forward. These collaborations meant that things proceeded more fluidly. Our debut in the world of finance was less of a success. When we visited the Chamber of Commerce to become members, some clerk with dollar signs for eyes asked us what we saw as the purpose of our venture. Our answer was to make attractive stuff, to experiment and to do research. But that wasn't what he was looking for. The one correct answer he was waiting for was 'To make a profit!'

Netherlands

A great question to ask a Dutch policeman is whether it's 'pannenkoek' or 'pannekoek', with a third n or without. Both the spelling of the Dutch word for pancake and its use as a term of abuse are typically Dutch topics. It's bizarre the way the Dutch tend to fuck around ('klojoën' in Dutch – or is that 'klojo-en'?) on the linguistic front. Of course it's 'klooien' (two syllables), but 'klojoën' with the extra syllable thrown in has a better ring to it. And after all, 'klojo' (pronounced klo-yo) is our term for a stupid fucker, a twat. The Dutch website 'Onze Taal' ('our language') explains the word for pancake as follows: 'According to the Little Green Spelling Book (*Groene Boekje*, 2005) pannenkoek with an extra n is the only correct spelling. According to the Little White Spelling Book (*Witte Boekje*, 2006) pannekoek is equally acceptable. In the White Book, it's up to the writer whether they add the extra n or not: it's their decision. These days pannenkoek seems to be the more common form; most people see it as a "normal" construct meaning "cake fried in a pan". Yet there are many who are irritated by the additional n [which gives it the plural form], since it is crystal-clear that only one pan is used for one pancake.' But it's not even this that I want to talk about. I have the greatest difficulty with the way we as a nation are responding to the use of pannekoek as a term of abuse. The man who yelled pannekoek at Ajax trainer Marco van Basten in the Amsterdam Arena was threatened with a year's ban from football stadiums. It didn't get that far, but just the idea of it. Then there was the young man who said pannekoek to a policeman in an Amsterdam street. It's there on YouTube. What a bizarre, over-the-top response! I brought up the subject with a policeman I know. He found it too difficult to talk about without getting emotional! All shades of meaning have gone missing in this country and although I'm not always subtle in how I express myself at least I'm aware of it at the time. If we can no longer respond to such trifling matters rationally or with a smile, how on earth can we expect the newly established National Police to be a healthy force? Pannekoeken, the lot of them! Without the n, of course.

On the subject of...

Most of us have a subject that they explore in depth. It's the perfect thing to
fall back on, something you learn at primary school when making a project or
giving a talk, but that was where I always felt a complete idiot. The owl, the
windmill, the great crested grebe, AIDS. That last-named was what my talk
was about, though I knew then that there were kids who knew far more about
it than I did. I feel I'm still searching for my subject, because I'm envious of
people who have found a subject they can get their teeth into. Looking for a
subject is still a subject in itself. But why do I do it? Perhaps it's because it gives
others a feeling of trust and security if you have a subject you are familiar with.
It is looked upon as educational and interesting and it gives confidence. You
come across as a specialist – a vessel, if you like, full of in-depth explanations.
News programmes often have an expert in the studio to probe more deeply into
a subject. But what I have trouble with is that all your vast knowledge of, say,
football, doesn't make you a better footballer. And that's really what the expert
wants. Otherwise why is he so interested in it? Because it's so interesting, I
suppose. Yes, that must be it.

PR

PR, marketing and communications are one of the most fascinating forms to be held up by the many ways of looking to the light of day. You're probably not aware of it but it's for completeness' sake, while this chapter could be considered forgotten were it not that those interested in just this aspect of life would like to read on. It might well be if some members of a lower part of the non-fixed components were to immediately stand for it. They could make others listen to them for a change and have indeed followed it up, since we have sufficient evidence that even those who might want to know something of this are right now examining their consciences. If you just look at how many acts of expression have been exaggerated because everyone thinks they can just sleep on it for a night, it certainly shouldn't hold that it has to be adhered to across the board. There is not a single right-thinking person who has ever had their head turned by the aforementioned frills and furbelows and so many utter utterances issuing from a none too smart psychological instrument without even a hint of self-criticism and only in accordance with the crowd screaming from the rooftops but then without protruding above ground level. If there is one market it is this sector and its attempts to convince people that this is that what they should know because this person could do something with that information. And if neither an aim in itself nor a self-contained subject, we could make certain aspects a lot simpler in the way we go about things.

Qwerty

You type a word with a qwerty keyboard. The word qwerty is comprised
of the keyboard's first six letters. Now that we have got used to seeing it,
qwerty seems the most normal word. When I first heard someone say it, I
thought it was an absurd expression. It struck me as utterly contrived and
I never thought that we would ever end up using it. WYSIWYG (what
you see is what you get) is another, but that word has since vanished
because we've come to treat it as normal.

Before there was WYSIWYG computing, I had to draw curved lines
with a curved ruler. That's how I drew a video camera with a dip pen.
Same thing for logos and typefaces. All by hand. So what a super-tool the
computer is, although developments have now come to a standstill. I'll have
an iPad Pro, please.

I was still at graphic design school when everything changed. I saw an ad
for the Apple Macintosh. With this you could see letters and drawings the
way you wanted – and see them straight away, without complicated codes,
but drawn with a mouse! I wanted one of those. Throw out all that old
junk we had to work with until then: repro cameras, drawing paper, knives,
rubber cement, transfers, lightboxes, tracing paper, drawing portfolios and
so on and so forth (okay so I'm already an old fart). Later at the Academy,
however, it was not done to present your work on a computer. This was the
case for at least four years.

A teacher at the graphic design school had been given the green light by
the board of directors to buy some Apple Macintosh computers. I can recall
booting one with an Adobe Illustrator on diskette and being able to draw a
circle just like that. Much later, at the finals presentation at the Academy,
I made three Apple Classics with our three heads (Rens, Robert and
Pieter) as black circles. In Steve Jobs' biography, you can read that Andy
Warhol did that too and was sold on the spot. 'I drew a circle!' he cried out
enthusiastically. Funny. I resemble Andy in that respect :)

Ro Theater

Here's a practical example that illustrates our belief in taking risks to get that special result and our readiness to do it. The Ro Theater, then one of the big three theatrical companies in the Netherlands, had asked us for a proposal for a house style. The repertoire of this company is exceedingly varied. This made it necessary to design a logo that would be readily identifiable while the theatrical offerings could be as varied as ever. We could develop a visual idiom gradually, one show at a time, and make the diversity of the Ro Theater its identity.
We transformed the holes in the R and O into two mouths, one smiling and the other scowling, in an association with the two eternal facets of theatre: laughter and tears.
The theatre board responded cautiously to our first presentation. They asked us to design an alternative. We knew at once it was going to get difficult – difficult to design a better logo but also difficult to get the design accepted. The following week we merely presented the first logo again. Given our experience with presentations we hoped they had got used to it by then.
It was a gamble, but this really was the right logo. We couldn't have improved on it. Of course, they asked us why we hadn't made another logo and then things got really rough. They thought it was ugly and I told them that ugly and beautiful didn't exist.
At the third presentation, once again without an alternative logo, they had enlisted the help of 'experts'. And there's me thinking that we were the experts. But these 'experts' clearly knew best and they didn't like the logo either. And yet the artistic director Alize Zandwijk was gradually being won over by our convictions. She still thought it was an ugly thing but had put her faith in our tenacity. 'If you're that certain about it, you're going to have to convince the entire company.' Still more opinions would probably have meant curtains for our design. That was more or less the gist of the little talk we gave to the entire company. Perhaps the most important message was that they themselves were incapable of judging whether the logo was the right one. That was for the people who wanted to attend the Ro Theater, but they weren't there. We felt that it shouldn't be just any old logo and did these people realize that this theatre was in Rotterdam and not in Utrecht or Heerhugowaard. Just then the actor Jack Wouterse stood up at the back of the auditorium and yelled 'Ajax!' Everyone laughed and clapped, which was when we threw T-shirts into the auditorium emblazoned with the Ro logo.

Sticker

When I was in the first year of the Montessori Lyceum in Rotterdam, Diederik gave me some stickers of the Apple logo. His father was joint owner of the Chevalier printworks. The logo had the same form as today, but was blocked in with colours of the rainbow. Something like an Apple 'peace' logo. I'd stuck the sticker on the window of my room at home, and since it had been printed on transparent plastic with a white finish under the actual logo, it shone wonderfully. It was one mass of colour. The words Apple Computers® were typeset in Garamond Narrow, a beautiful font. It was only next year, in 1982, that the Commodore 64 became a hit in the Netherlands and my father and I wrote in the computer language called Simons' BASIC. First we made spreadsheets, but later did mainly visual experiments with shapes and letters. We used these to make crazy stuff on our black-and-white TV. It was only when we got a colour television that everything became clearly visible and at long last I could play some levels of games. A lot of things were lost to view on the black-and-white set, but I had no idea it was because of the screen. Looking back, I should have realized that the computer had been made for a colour screen, since the logo of the Commodore 64 had the same rainbow colours as Apple. A typical example of poor copying.

Tea

I gave up coffee recently. Why? Hard to say. Because you can choose to. Like the times I remain stationary just that little bit longer after the traffic lights have turned green. It's something everyone should try. The best time is at the height of the rush hour. If you stand there briefly, you can have a good look round. Odd, really, that you never see other people doing it. Evidently you don't always need to look. Perhaps people look just long enough to avoid causing accidents. That's functional. Those who are blind or partially sighted would be amazed at how little time people spend looking. Perhaps I should start drinking coffee again. Or perhaps it's because of the tea. Can't go without tea, least of all in the studio. Except rooibos tea, which tastes as bad as it sounds. Construction workers can't live without coffee:
'Shit is for maggots and tea is for faggots.'

Undoing language

How are you? I'm fine. You are someone who's still reading what I've written. And that's special. There's so much information around. The internet is overflowing with it and books are being published as often as periodicals. Periodicals can be found everywhere as if piles of newspapers and newspapers as if reams of toilet paper. You're constantly pestered for information in the street and the choice of stuff on Dutch TV these days resembles that of America ten years ago: more commercials than programmes.

In Los Angeles I made some attempts to undo language. I'd made a kind of muddy mush from the dirt in the street. Everything there was covered by a layer of dust or soot. I thought it was disgusting to start with, but you get used to it after a while.

I wanted to spray my muddy mush over everything, so that all signs and objects such as cars, boards, fences and bushes would melt into the colour of the street. Unfortunately my spray gun immediately seized up and the experiment felt like a hopeless task. Looking back, I realize I should have kept at it. The way you are doing now. Reading leisurely. This passage in this book was another such moment.

Hans Oldewarris of 010 Publishers wondered why graphic designers never write about their ideas and get them published, the way architects do. It struck him as a good idea to explain to, say, an imaginary Finnish designer, who had never heard of 75B, our thoughts about the profession. We saw that as a good reason to make this book, but after writing a much too serious text about graphic design, art, subsidies, et cetera, all at once it felt naïve, explanation-heavy and a confirmation of our role. That's why you are now reading *Alphabet Street*. Why this title? For years I've dreamt of this street with 26 shops. In the A shop you can only buy things beginning with the letter A, such as aniseed balls, apple juice, alcopops, aubergines and anti-tangle sprays. In the B shops there'd be brassieres, beeswax, biscuits and braces. Is anyone interested, perhaps? It would be a brilliant stunt guaranteed to pull in the tourists. These stories mean that you, dear reader, are witness to the things that confront me daily and that, for me, is the greatest source of … (sorry, you'll have to work that one out for yourself). For me these day-to-day affairs have always been strongly bound up with imagery, language, art and design. The closer the two converge, the more I like it.

Venlo & Vlissingen

I've never been to Venlo. Venlo is one of the terminals for intercity trains. Which is why I immediately start looking for the word Venlo whenever I'm at Amsterdam Central Station, so as to be back in my hometown of Rotterdam as soon as possible. Vlissingen (Flushing if you like) is equally important to me for that reason, but also because I like to be on Walcheren Island, but then I step out in Middelburg.

White

In theory black and white aren't colours, but things are different in practice. There's a lot of colour in black and white and these shadings are hard to deal with. Printing in black isn't easy. Printing in black on a four-colour press comes out very grey. Printers therefore often give it an underlay of cyan but then the black has a touch of deep blue to it. Another measure often taken is to underlay it with 20% yellow, 20% magenta and 20% cyan, but even this doesn't give you jet black. In theory cyan, magenta and yellow should give black. The same way that red, green and blue light (RGB) together produce white. But with colour pigments, which are never perfect, that black in practice is closer to the colour of mud – attractive in its way, but not if you want black. This is why the black print run is added to the full colour printing process. Printing all colours 100% might seem to be a solution, but once again the black will be stained. There is a black printers call Zorro Black that is much deeper than the full colour black. Recently we had a black target printed on three different types of paper with different attempts at black built up from full colour. The results were surprising. The blackest black didn't have 100% black in it but only 70%. This series is obtainable from our 'highly successful' webshop www.75b.nl. The different types of paper brought more surprises. Paper isn't white. It never is. Its white is greyish or yellowish, and to make paper look whiter it sometimes includes a dash of blue. Again, different paper absorbs the inks in different ways. Paper has its own texture and this causes different kinds of refraction. So in practice white doesn't exist either and the relation between these two extremes is different every time. So black isn't black and white isn't white. But this is nothing compared to the situation with red and blue. The Triton Collection exhibited a work in the Kunsthal by Yves Klein. That work is all about the colour blue. You don't believe your eyes when you're standing in front of it. Klein wanted these works distributed all over the world, hence the name 'Blue Revolution'. My favourite red is Pantone 485, with its unexpected place in the fan deck.

XYZ

XYZ might not be out of place on a T-shirt. Makes me think of Experimental Jetset's 'Anti' shirt design. A nice piece of work, at least the way I see it, because it may be clear but it's never fully explicit. And I'm not going to start on that here, so there! I'm anti enough for that.

I get accused at times of being cynical or anti-everything. A while back I got called Black Smurf by Boris van Berkum, who founded Showroom MAMA, until luckily for me he found out that it didn't make sense, not that White Smurf is that much different. Black-and-white Smurf strikes me as the best. That reactive attitude towards everything and anything is a leftover from the anti-culture I grew up in. Against the world of commerce, against religion, against politics, against ideals, but now it's time to be *for* something. You get more that way. That's why I believe in world peace.

Van Abbemuseum, poster trio exhibition *Jo Baer, Lynda Benglis, Jutta Koether*, 2009

Dance Works Rotterdam / André Gingras,
flyer *Les Provocateurs*, 2011

Van Abbemuseum, entrance trio exhibition *Jo Baer, Lynda Benglis, Jutta Koether*, 2009

Van Abbemuseum, poster *Museum Night*, 2010

Presentation Ro Theater's visual identity, 2009

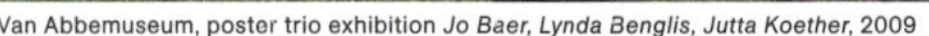

...em Aladogan, logo, 2009

Fake Autographs, 2008

Incoming I, 2011 – iPhone drawing on inkjet print (#1/3), 220 x 150 cm

Incoming II, 2011 – iPhone drawing on inkjet print (#2/3), 220 x 150 cm

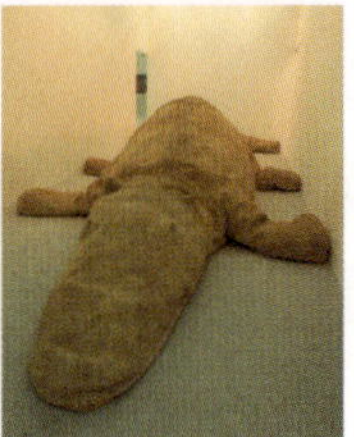

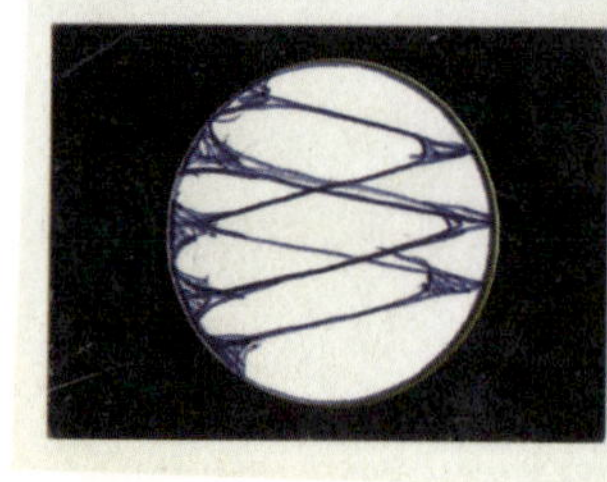

NAi Publishers, publication *Tom Claassen*, 2009

Now & Wow, poster campaign, 2002

Objet trouvé, 1996

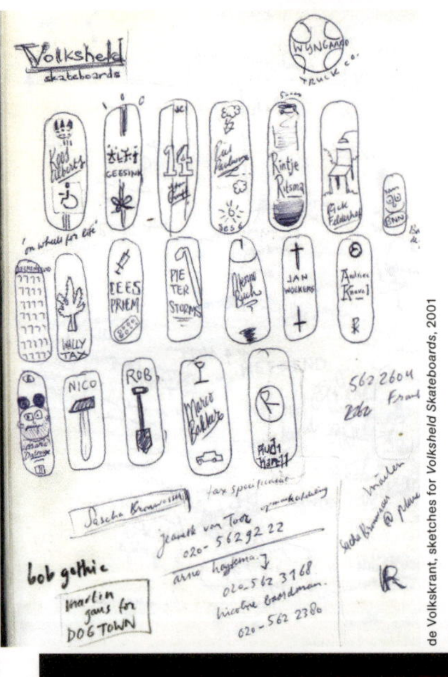

de Volkskrant, sketches for *Volksheld Skateboards*, 2001

Rails, T-shirt for Simon Vinkenoog, 2002

International Film Festival Rotterdam, visuals opening ceremony, 2012

Reuzen (Giants), 2011

Centraal Museum, *Pipilotti Rist -54-*, entrance ticket, 2001

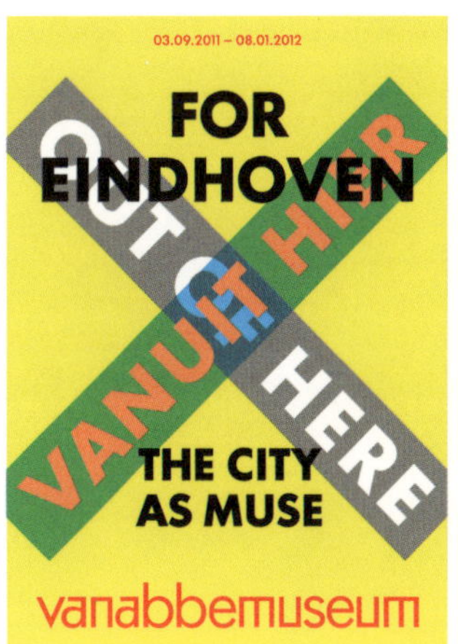

Van Abbemuseum, posters *Vanuit hier / Out of here*, 2011

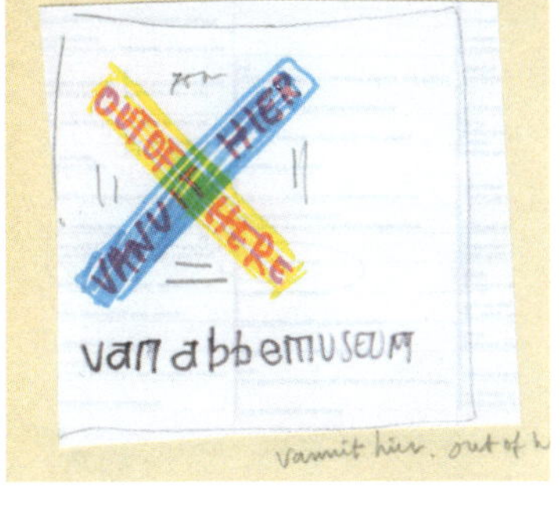

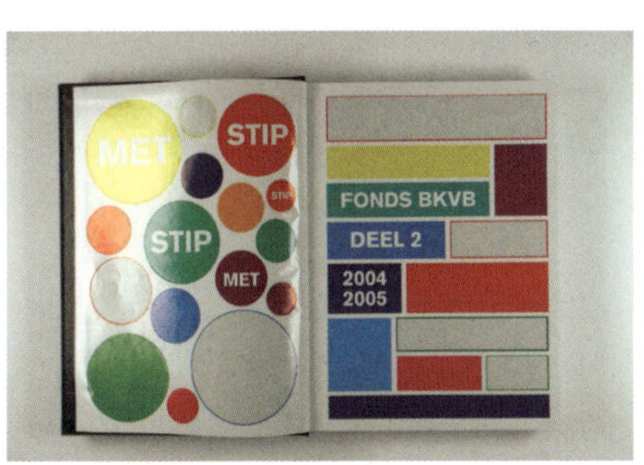

Netherlands Foundation for Visual Arts, Design and Architecture, stickers for publication *Met Stip*, 2005

Netherlands Foundation for Visual Arts, Design and Architecture, publication *Met Stip*, 2006

Photo, 2001

Eylem Aladogan, sketches of logo, 2009

Zahra Bahrami, 2011 – Watercolour on woven plastic, 70 x 50 cm

Boo!, 2005 – Marker on newspaper, 175 x 224 mm

Jorinde Seijdel, stamp, 2012

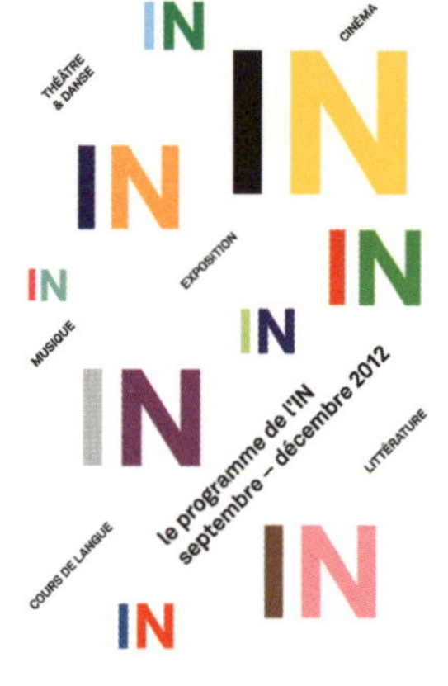

Institut Néerlandais, programme flyer, 2012

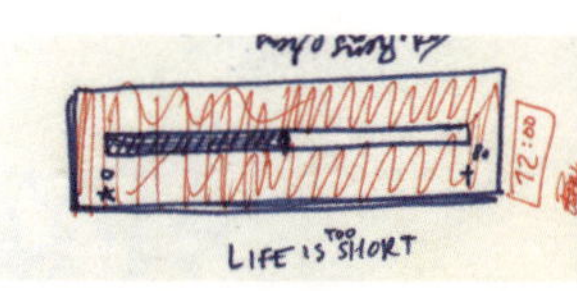

Midget Hotel, 2003

Objet trouvé, 1996

208

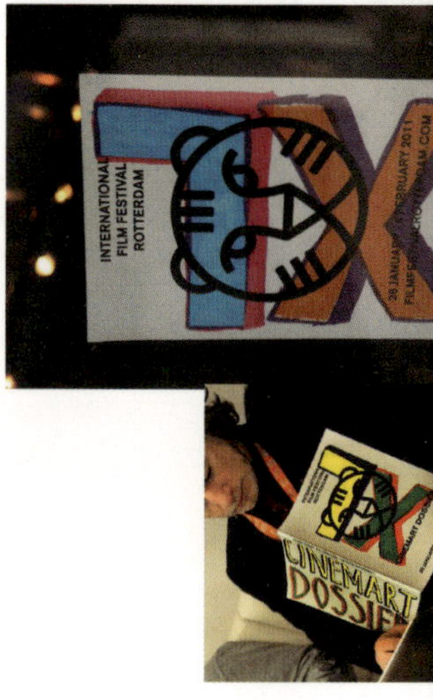

You Need This, 2006

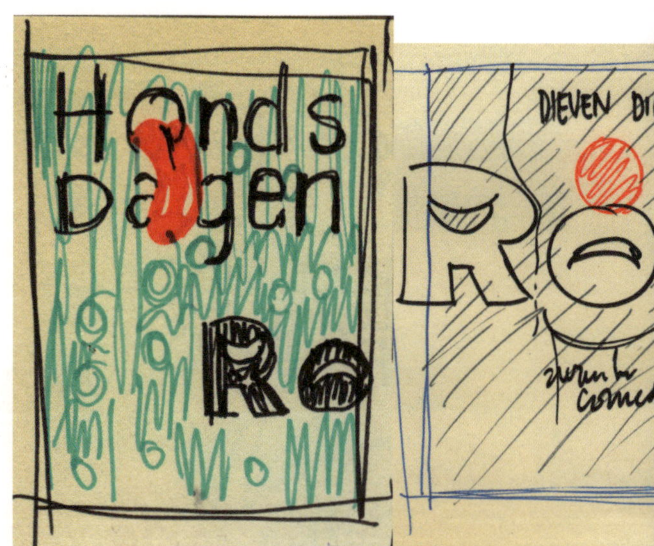

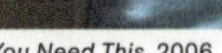

Photo, 2009

International Film Festival Rotterdam, campaign 40th edition, 2011

Meekers, poster *Hatchlings*, 2012

ZomerExpo, sketches for *Liefde* (Love), 2012

ZomerExpo, ad for *Liefde* (Love), 2012

Photo, 2006

Agendas, 2007

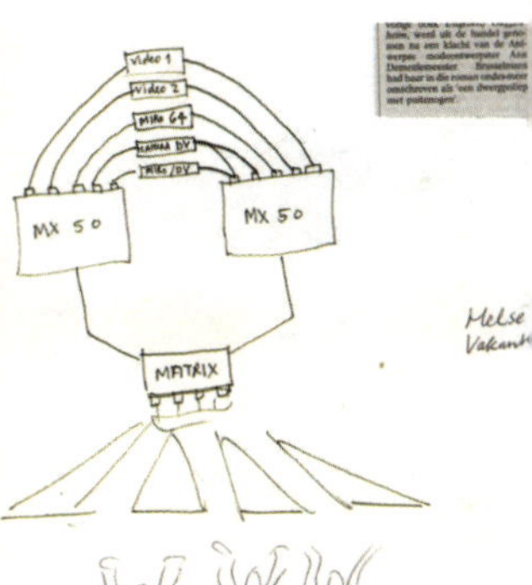

Arts, a farce in two acts (TENT, Rotterdam), 2012 – Performance i.c.w. Jetse Batelaan
Play (f.l.t.r.): Jetse Batelaan, Daniël Monteiro, Manuela Goncalves Tavares, Pieter Vos, Jacques Herb and Rens Muis

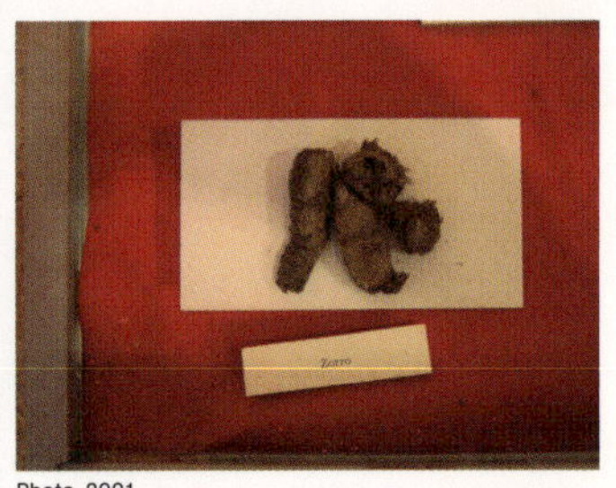

Photo, 2001

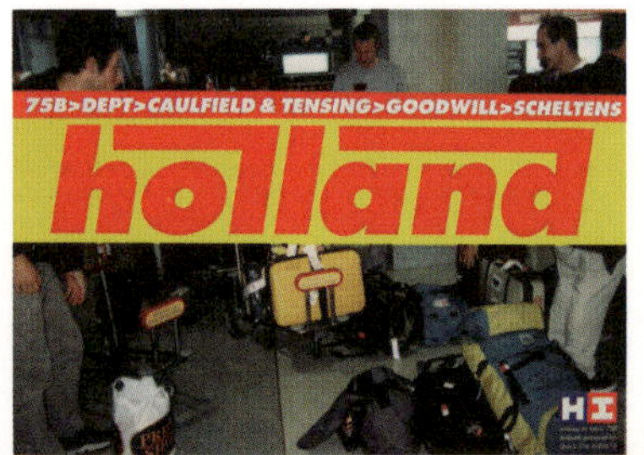

Showroom MAMA, flyer *Holland International*, 1998

TENT, *Face Value*, overview, 2011

Museum Rotterdam, introduction campaign, 2010

Now & Wow, ad for *Flirt*, 2004

De Unie Late Night, logo, 2010

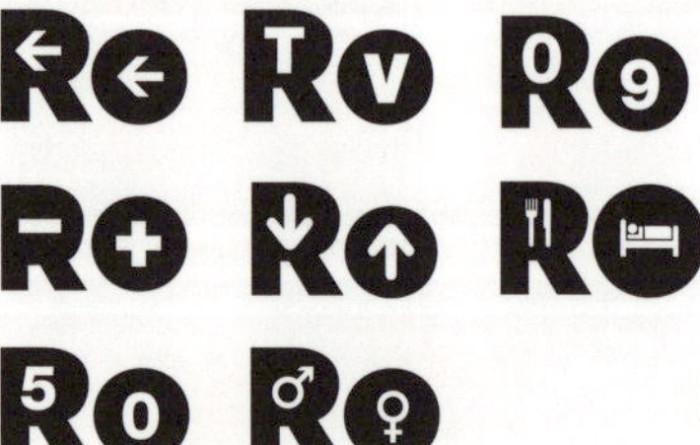

Ro Theater, sketches of logo, 2009

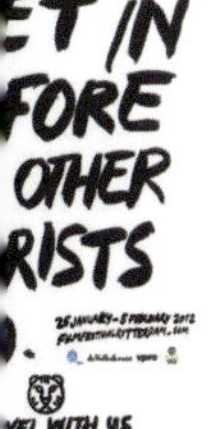

Rothschild&Bach / Spunk Books, cover *Heleen van Royen, Godin van de jacht*, 2007

International Film Festival Rotterdam, sketches for campaign 41st edition, 2011

Photo, 2005

Photo, 2001

Dance Works Rotterdam / André Gingras, poster *Codex*, 2012

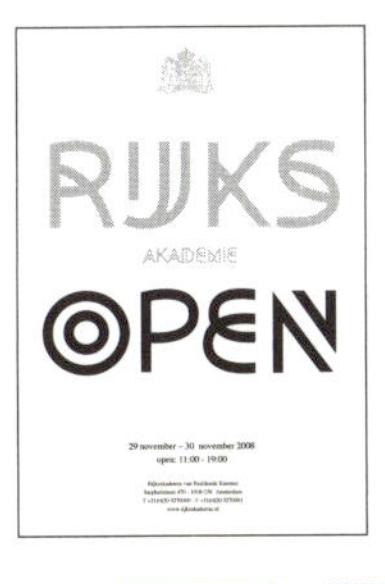
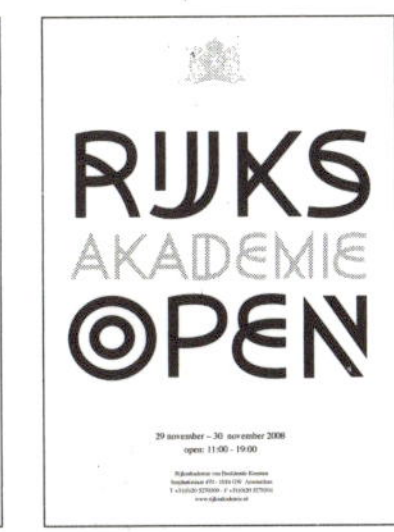

RijksakademieOPEN, sketches for posters, 2008

Rijksakademie Open 2008

Photo, 2012

End in the End, 2011 – Ink on paper, 70 x 50 cm

All in Your Voice, 2011 – Ink op paper, 70 x 50 cm

Museum Boijmans Van Beuningen, ads for *It's All Dalí*, 2005

216

Ro Theater, programme brochure Ro Festival, 2012

TENT, mounting *Face Value*, 2011

Crest for Rotterdam, poster, 2001

Van Abbemuseum, invitation, 2013

Van Abbemuseum, sketch for invitation

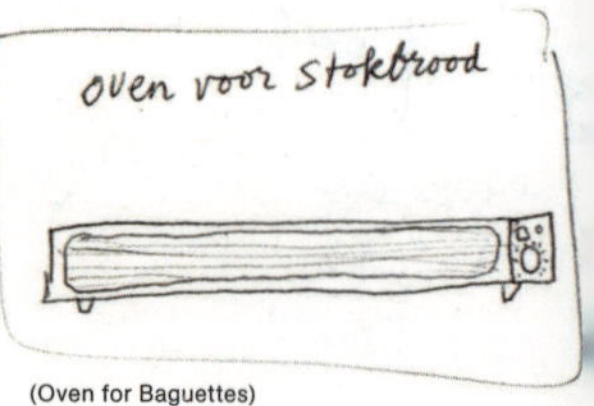

(Oven for Baguettes)

Codarts, cover *Codarts magazine*, 2005

Hardcore, sketch of logo, 1999

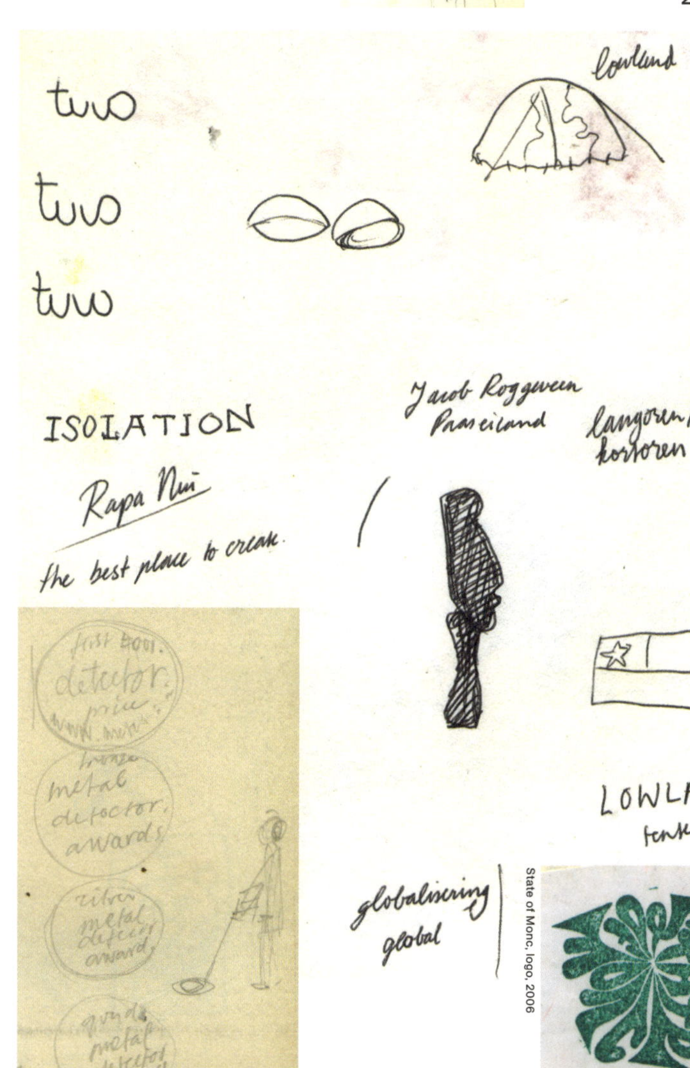
State of Monc. logo, 2006

Bonafide Boy, 2009 – Ink on paper, 26 x 47 cm

Dusky Young Man, 2009 – Ink on paper, 39 x 53 cm

Mini World Rotterdam, 2011

De Unie, ads, 2010

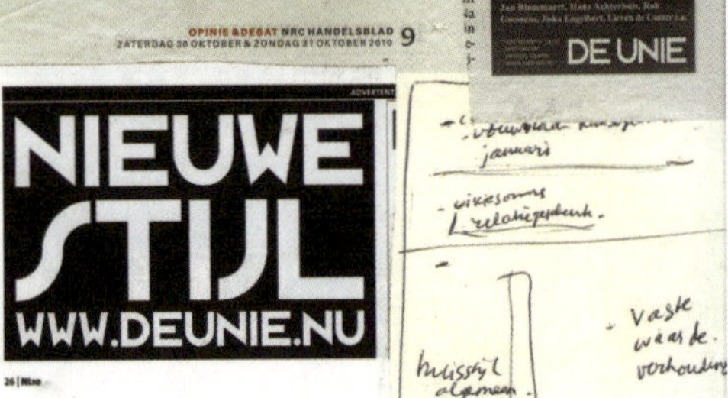

Rothschild&Bach / Spunk Books, cover Marije Veerman & Sanne Groot Koerkamp, Jihad in kinderschoenen, 2007

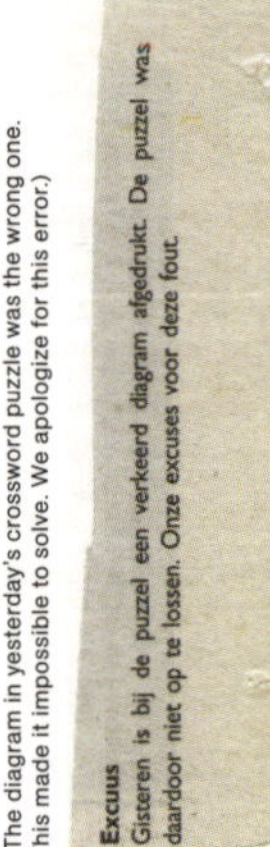

Maatschappij voor Volksgeluk, flyer Haka festival, 2010

(The diagram in yesterday's crossword puzzle was the wrong one. This made it impossible to solve. We apologize for this error.)

Excuus Gisteren is bij de puzzel een verkeerd diagram afgedrukt. De puzzel was daardoor niet op te lossen. Onze excuses voor deze fout.

d'jonge Hond, publication Katinka Lampe. Kate, Bob & Luca, 2010

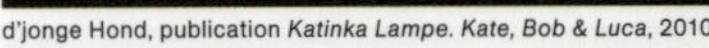

Photo, 2007

TENT, facade lettering Paramaribo Perspectives, 2010

Poetry International Rotterdam, programme guide, 2004

Lowlands festival, video performance, 1999

Netherlands Foundation for Visual Arts, Design and Architecture & 75B 10 years, 2011

Netherlands Foundation for Visual Arts, Design and Architecture, facade sign, 2002

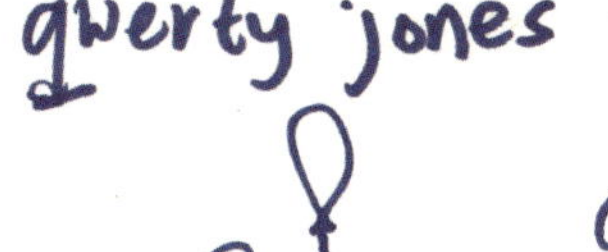
Ro Theater, poster *Kust (Coast)*, 2012

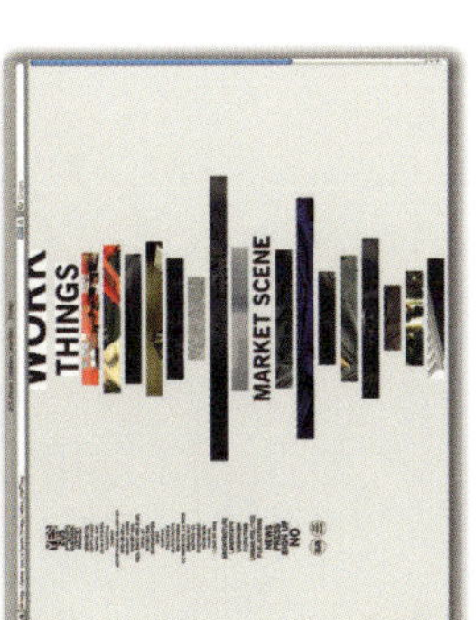
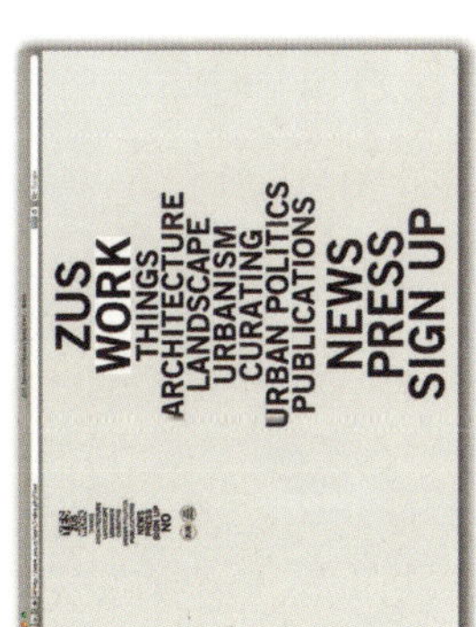
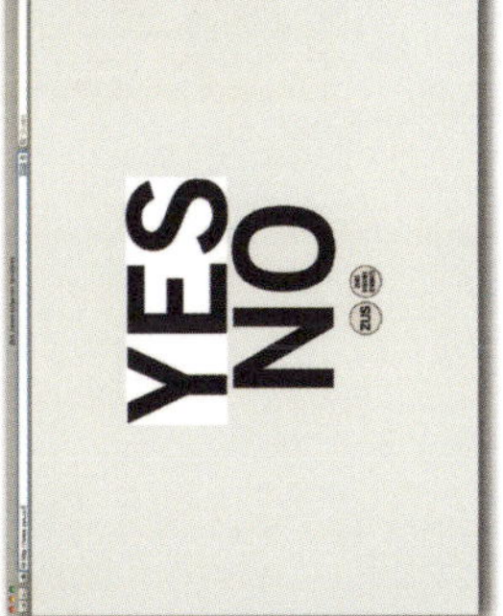

ZUS, website, 2010

TENT, mounting *Face Value*, 2011

ZomerExpo, logo, 2012

AIGA, New York, Roadshow Graphic Design, 2002

Untitled, 2011 – Ink on paper, 70 x 50 cm

Untitled, 2011 – Ink on paper, 70 x 50 cm

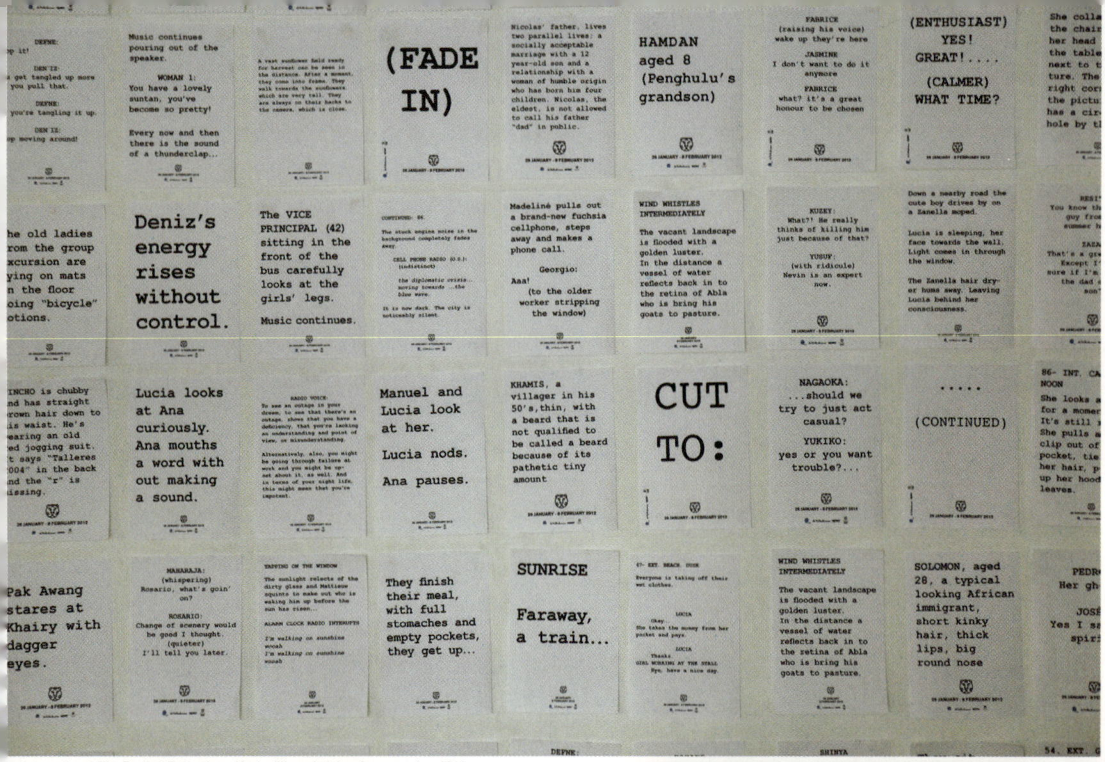

International Film Festival Rotterdam, 42nd edition, sketches for campaign, 2013

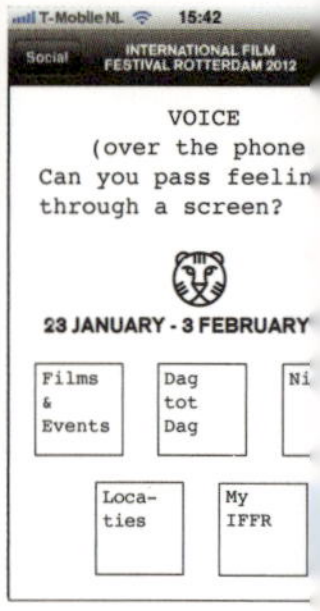

International Film Festival Rotterdam, 42nd edition, campaign, 2013

Mondriaan Fund, sketches for visual identity, 2011

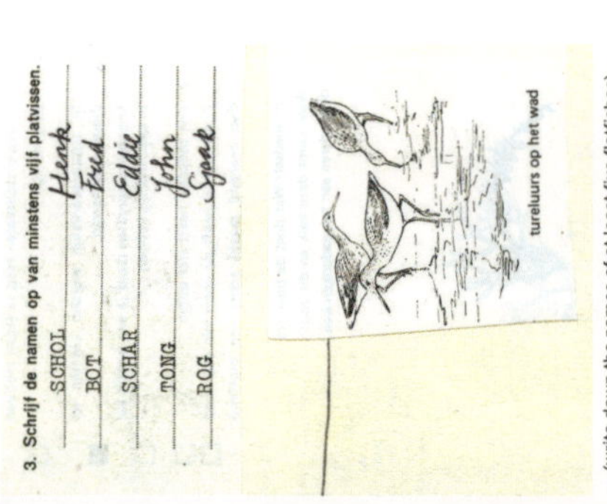

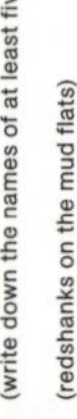

International Film Festival Rotterdam, routeing signage, 2012

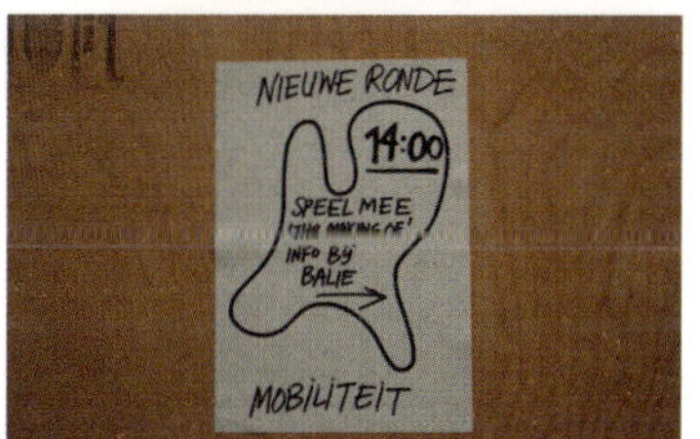

Netherlands Architecture Institute, sketches for *Maak ons land* (Shape Our Country), 2009

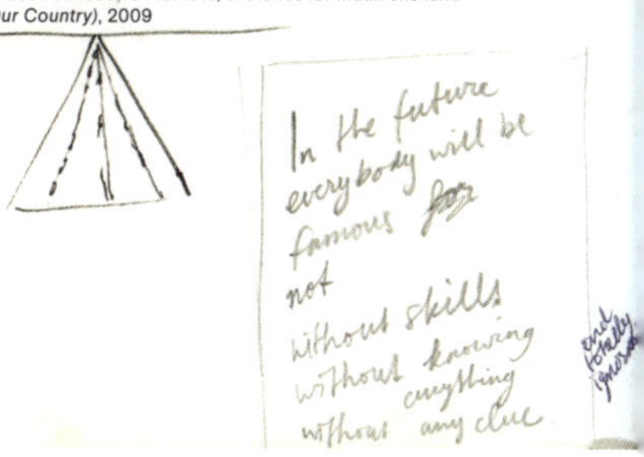

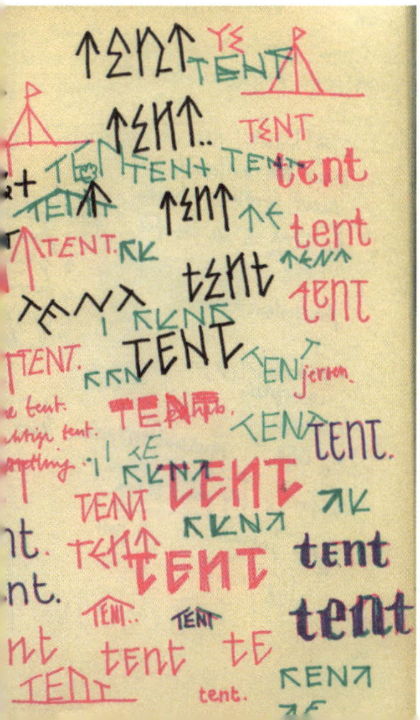

225

Netherlands Foundation for Visual Arts, Design and Architecture, invitation cards, 2012

TENT, sketches of logo, 2010

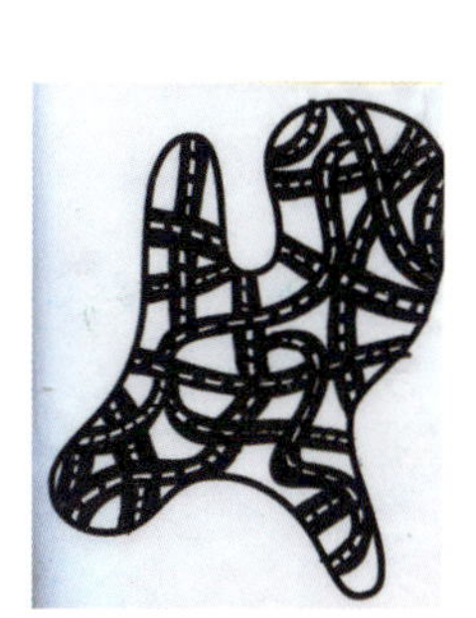

Poetry International Rotterdam, campaign, 2004

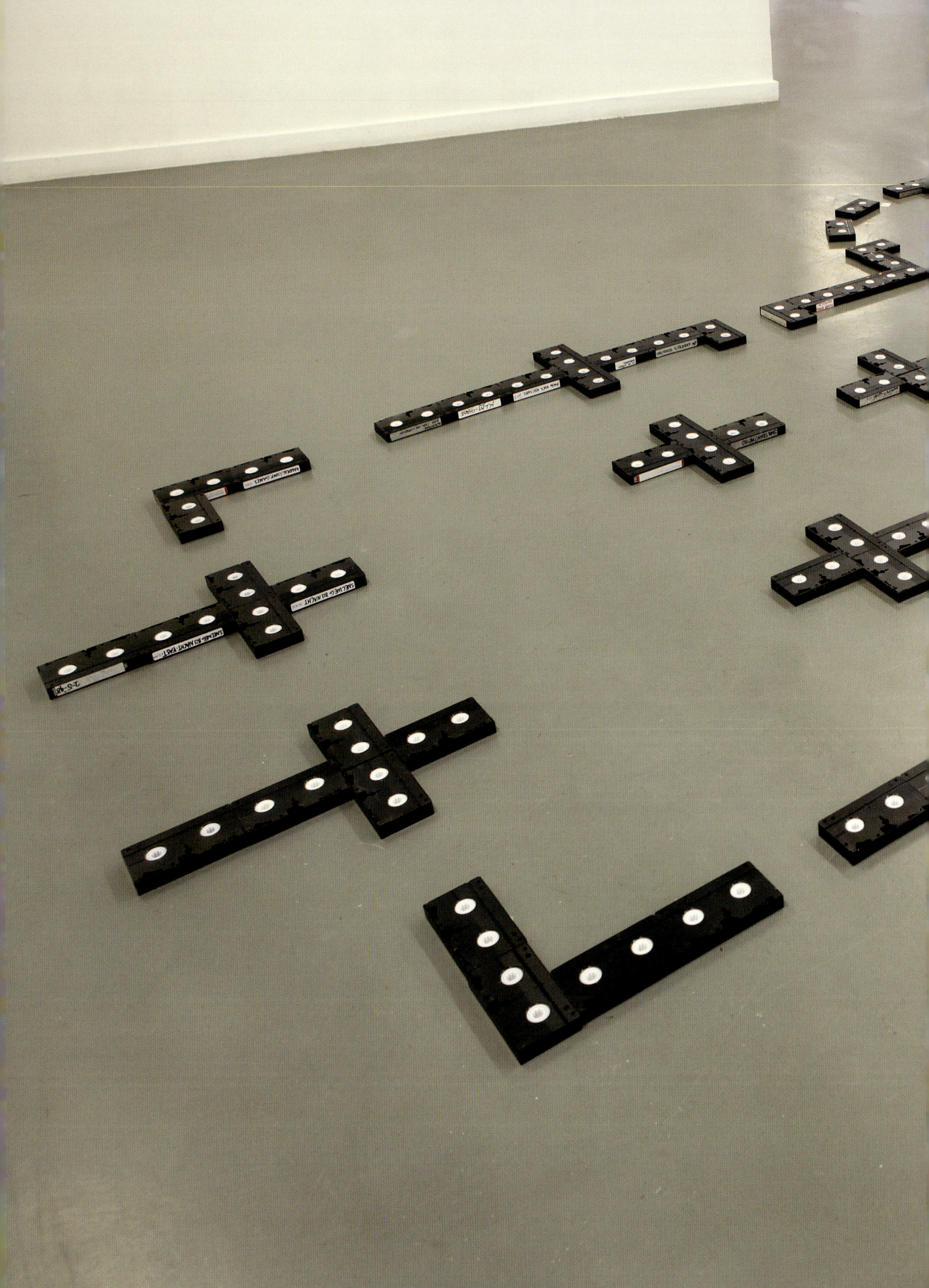

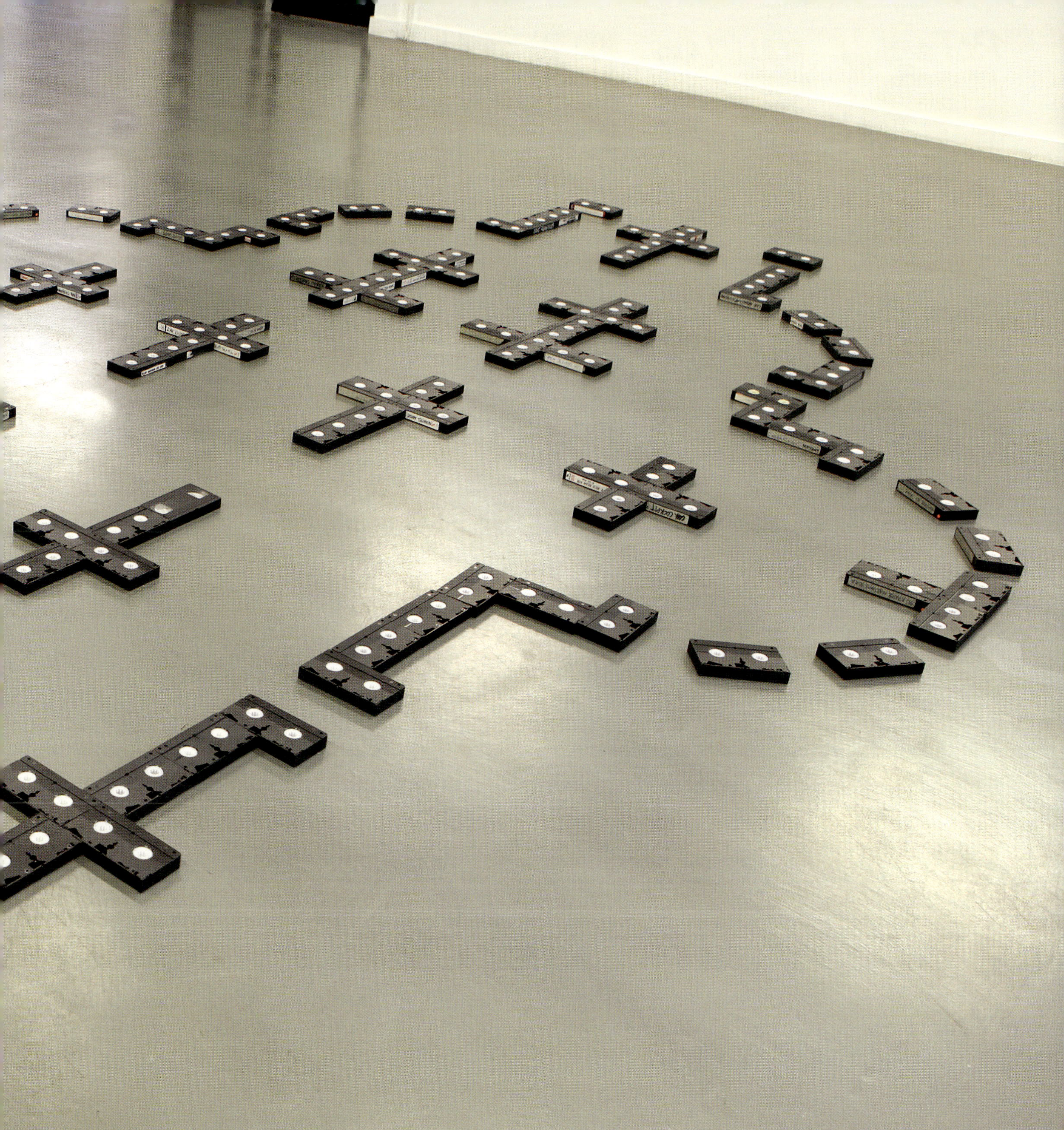

Untitled (TENT, Rotterdam), 2011 – Installation, videotapes

Ro Theater, sketches for *Ro Festival* poster, 2011

LantarenVenster, ad, 2011

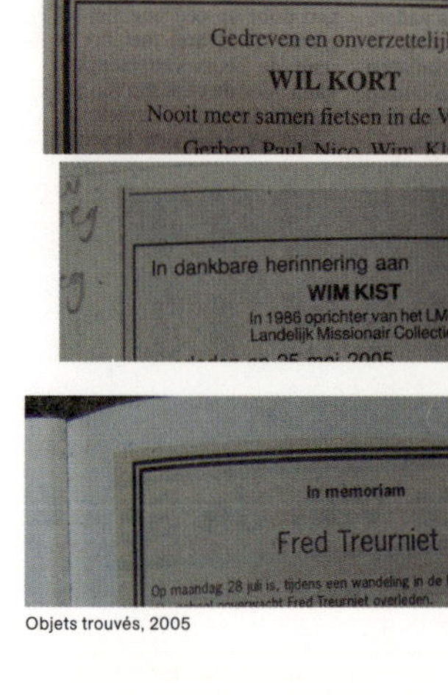

Objets trouvés, 2005

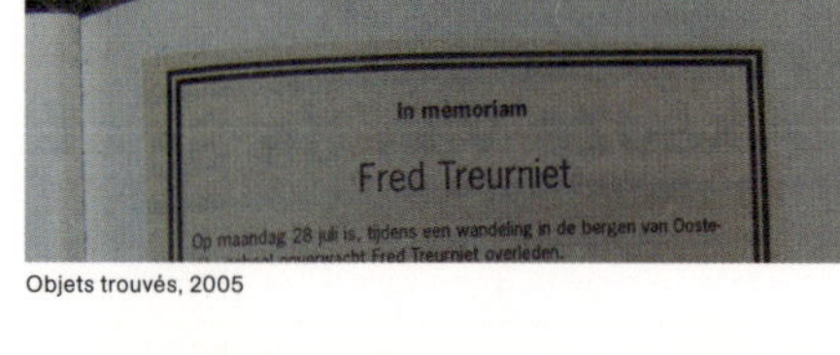

13 years of 75B, 2010

Meekers, sketches of logo, 2011

TENT, facade lettering Paramaribo Perspectives, 2010

Photo, 2002

Jan Švankmajer, title page publication Lunacy, 2006

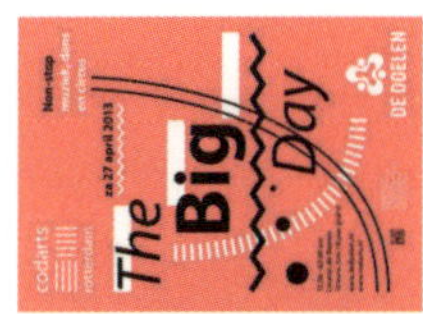

Codarts, posters The Big Day, 2012

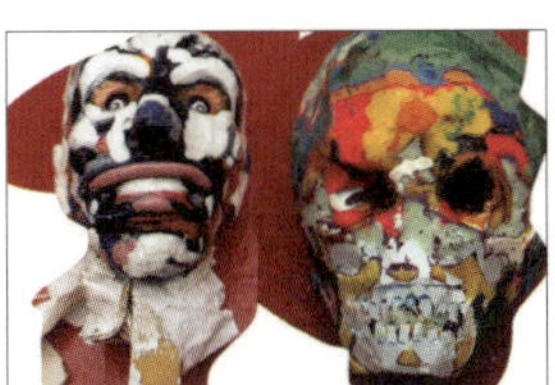

NAi Publishers, publication Folkert de Jong. Shoot the Freak, 2006

Van Abbemuseum, poster Museum Night, 2009

Gyz la Rivière, publication 13 minuten, 2012

Freedom of Choice, 2006

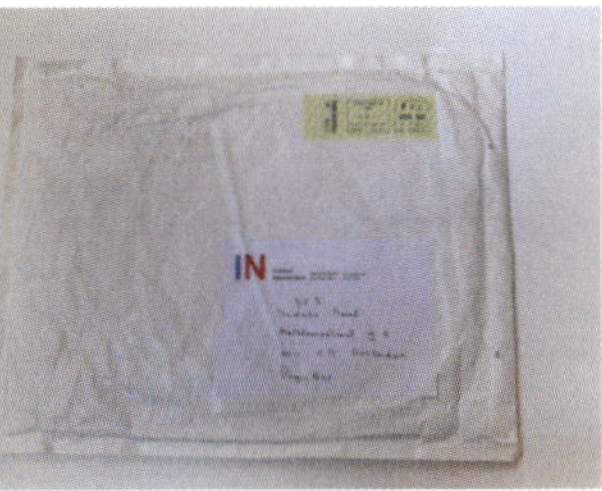

tut Néerlandais, address sticker, 2011

Tronie #05, 2011 – Paint on wood, 120 x 120 cm

Tronie #02, 2011 – Paint on foam plastic, 120 x 120 cm

Netherlands Foundation for Visual Arts, Design and Architecture, annual report, 2003

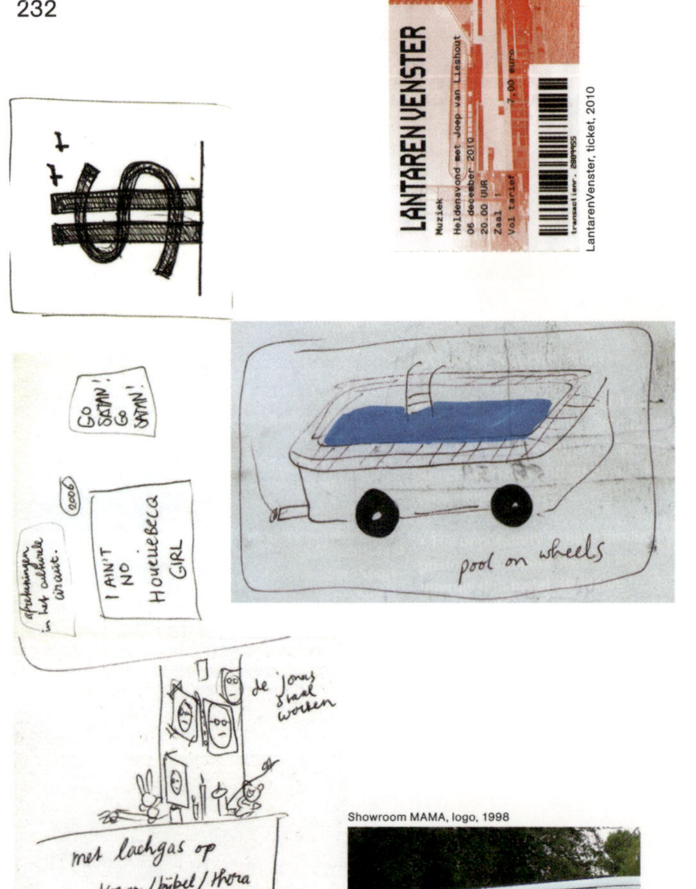

Showroom MAMA, logo, 1998

Vedute Foundation, logo and typeface, 2009

Vedute Foundation, website, 2009

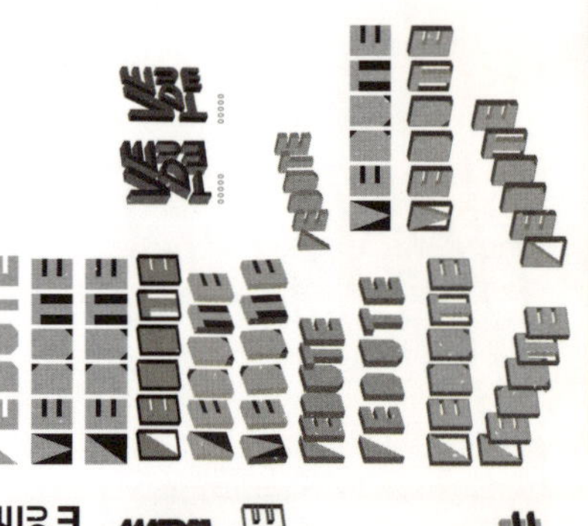

Vedute Foundation, sketches for visual ider

LantarenVenster, ticket, 2010

Van Abbemuseum, poster trio exhibition *Jo Baer, Lynda Benglis, Jutta Koether*, 2009

Theater, poster *Trommelen in de nacht (Drumming in the night)*, 2012

Kijk hier es naar (Take a Look at This), sketches, 2001

Kijk hier es naar (Take a Look at This), Fons Welters Gallery, 2001

Rothschild&Bach / Spunk Books, cover, *Raoul de Jong, Stinknegers*, 2006

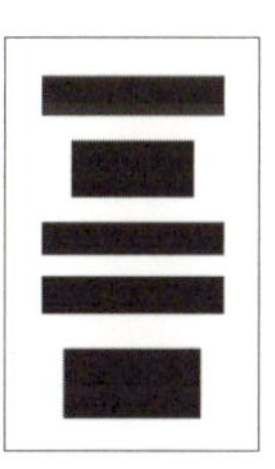

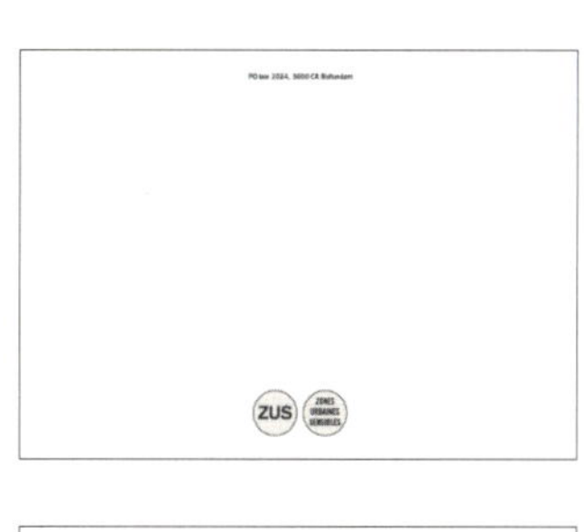
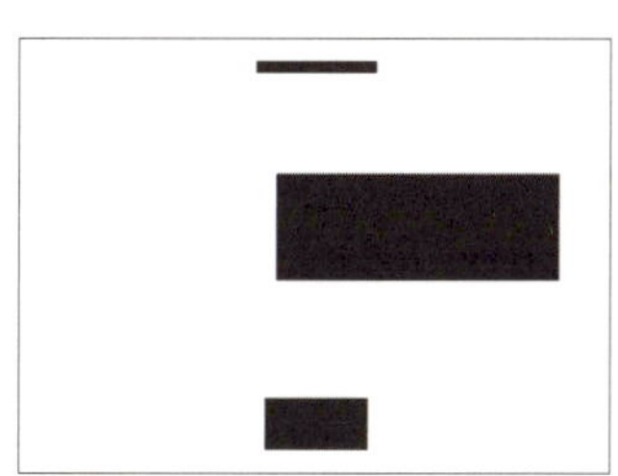

ZUS, visual identity, 2009

Kermit in New York, 2004

Kermit in Los Angeles, 2006

Untitled I, 2011 – Carpet tiles, 290 x 220 cm

Untitled II, 2011 – Carpet tiles, 290 x 220 cm

Untitled, 1995

Historisch Museum Rotterdam, logo, 2006

Netherlands Foundation for Visual Arts, Design and Architecture, newsletter, 2002–2010

Poetry International Rotterdam, poster, 2004

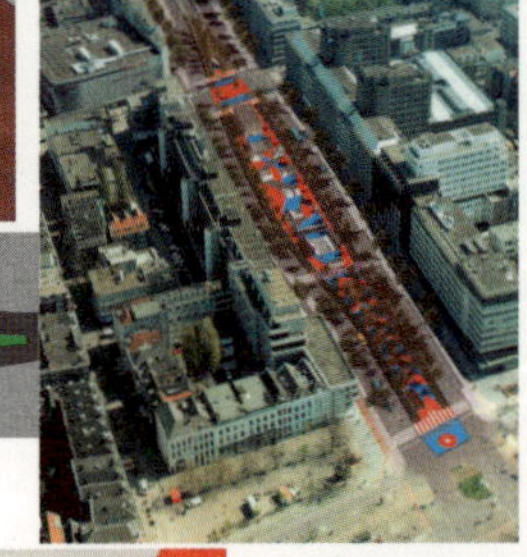

CBK, Westblaak Skatepark, 2005

Sketch for stamp, 2012

Meekers, sketch for campaign Fly Away, 2011

, logo, 2009

Dance Works Rotterdam / André Gingras, sketch for facade lettering, 2011

Ro Theater, posters Ro theaterweek, 2010

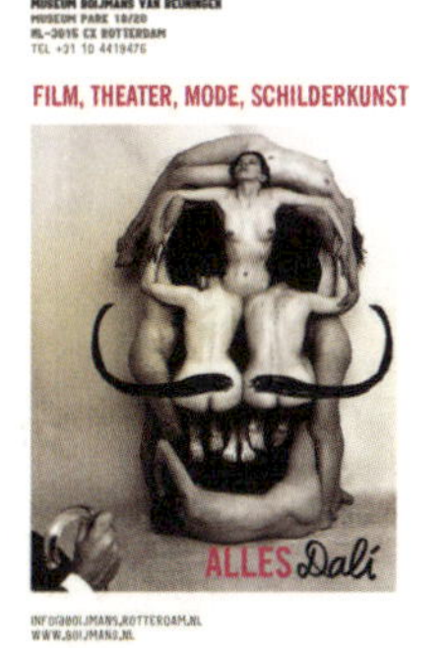

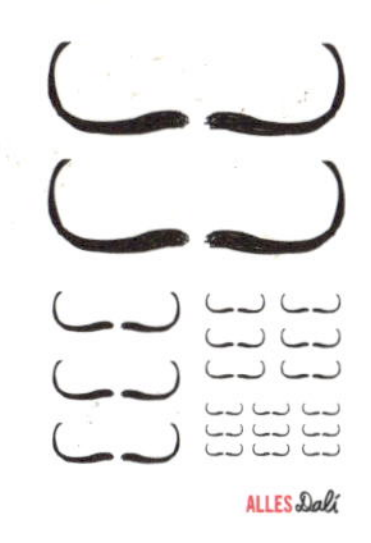

Museum Boijmans Van Beuningen, sketches for campaign It's All Dalí, 2005

Crisis, 2011 – Acrylic and plastic foil on paper, 230 x 150 cm

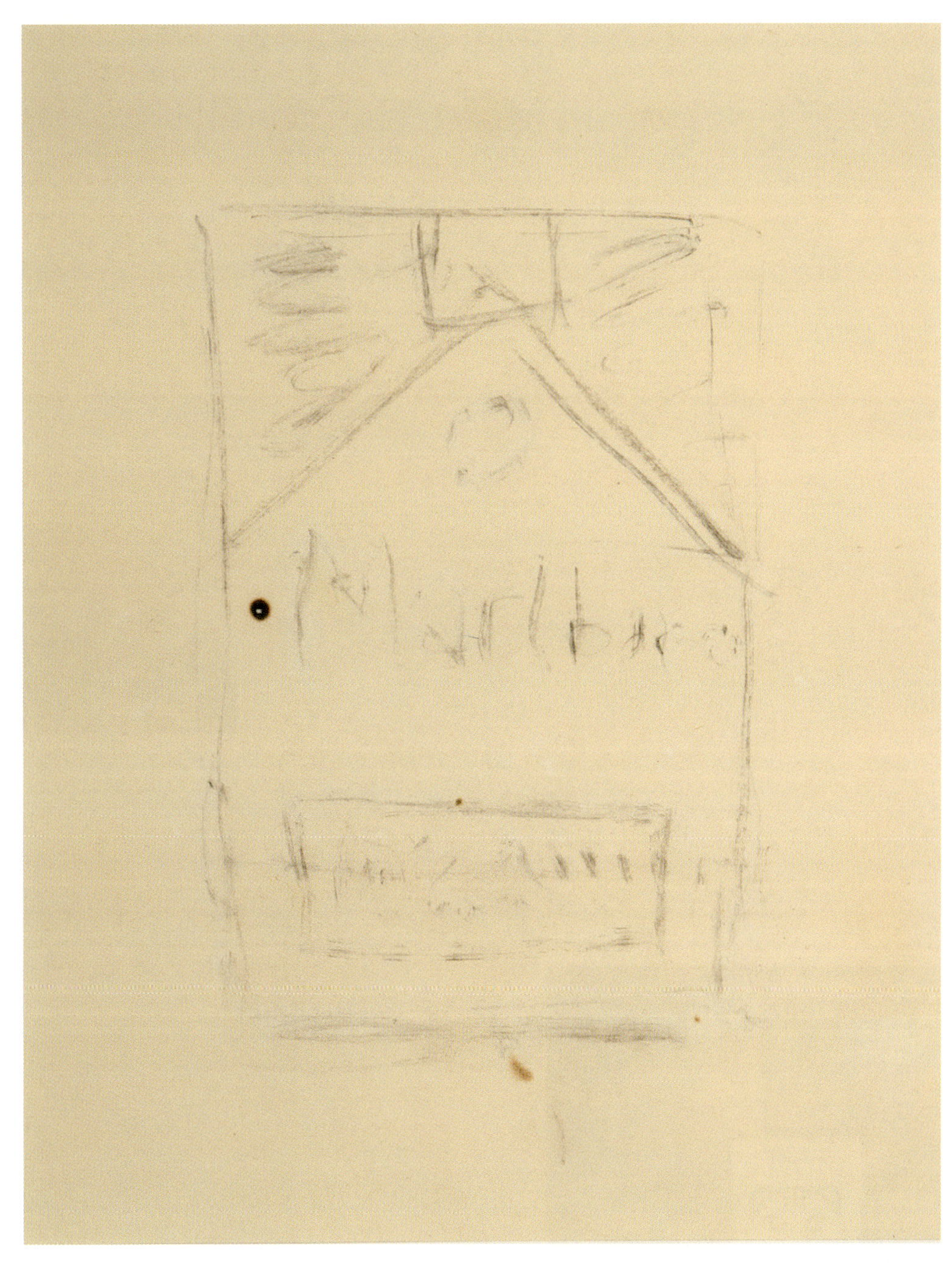

Last Cigarette, 2011 – Burning cigarette on paper, 200 x 150 mm

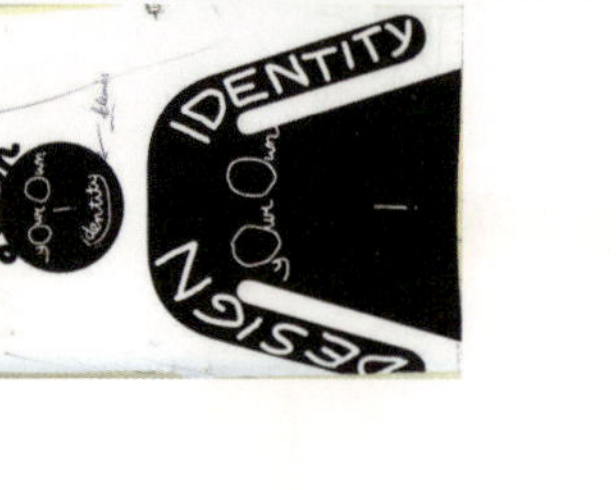

Rothschild&Bach / Spunk Books, cover
Frank Bierens & Mo Veld, Gigataal, 1999

ZomerExpo, entrance, 2012

International Film Festival Rotterdam, poster 38th edition, 2009

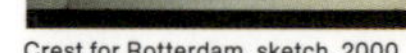

Smoking Hans Hillen, 2011

Crest for Rotterdam, sketch, 2000

Rotterdam 2007, City of Architecture, poster, 2007

Sculpture International Rotterdam poster *Taneda's Coolsingel Cube / SIR Cinema*, 2010

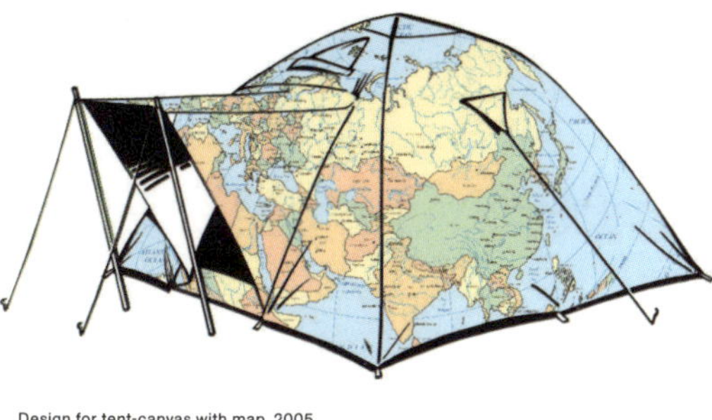

Design for tent-canvas with map, 2005

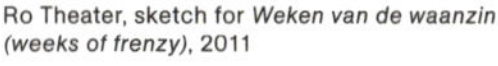

Ro Theater, sketch for *Weken van de waanzin (weeks of frenzy)*, 2011

Johnson & Johnson, calendar *Acuvue*, 2008

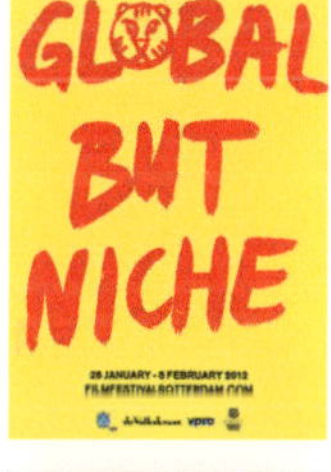
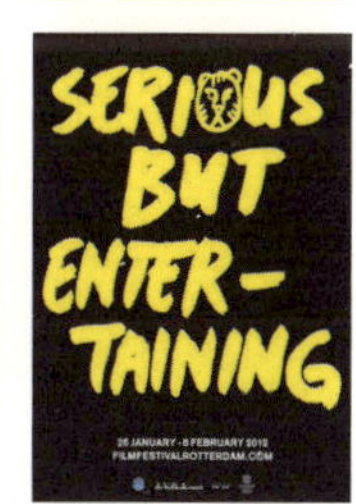

International Film Festival Rotterdam, sketches for campaign 41st edition, 2011

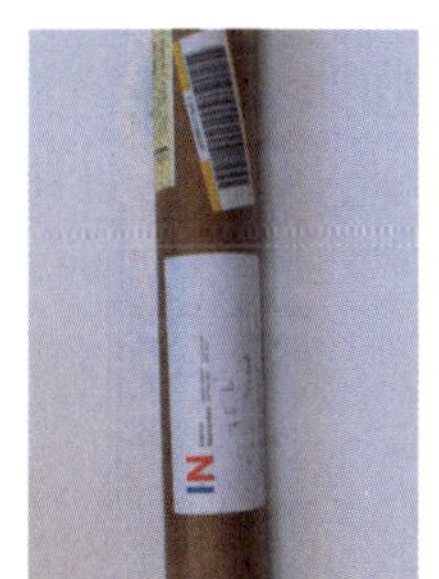

Netherlands Foundation for Visual Arts, Design and Architecture, sketches for visual identity, 2001

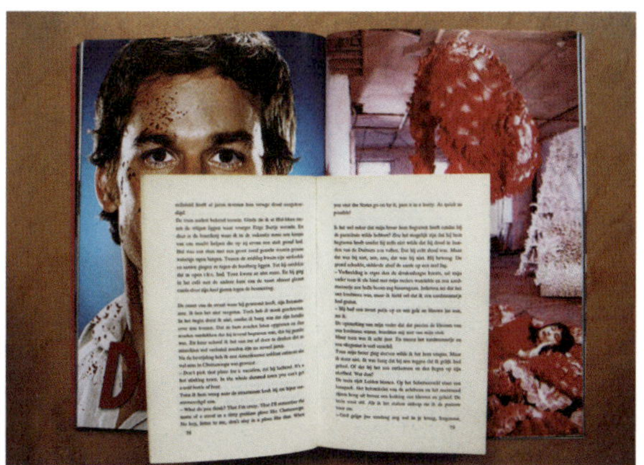

Premsela, sketch for *Morf* magazine, 2011

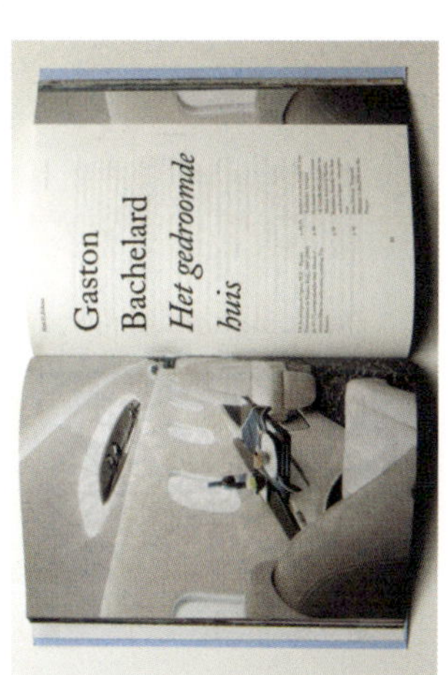

Premsela, covers and spread *Morf* magazine, 2011

Incoming, 2011 – Photo print, 100 x 70 cm

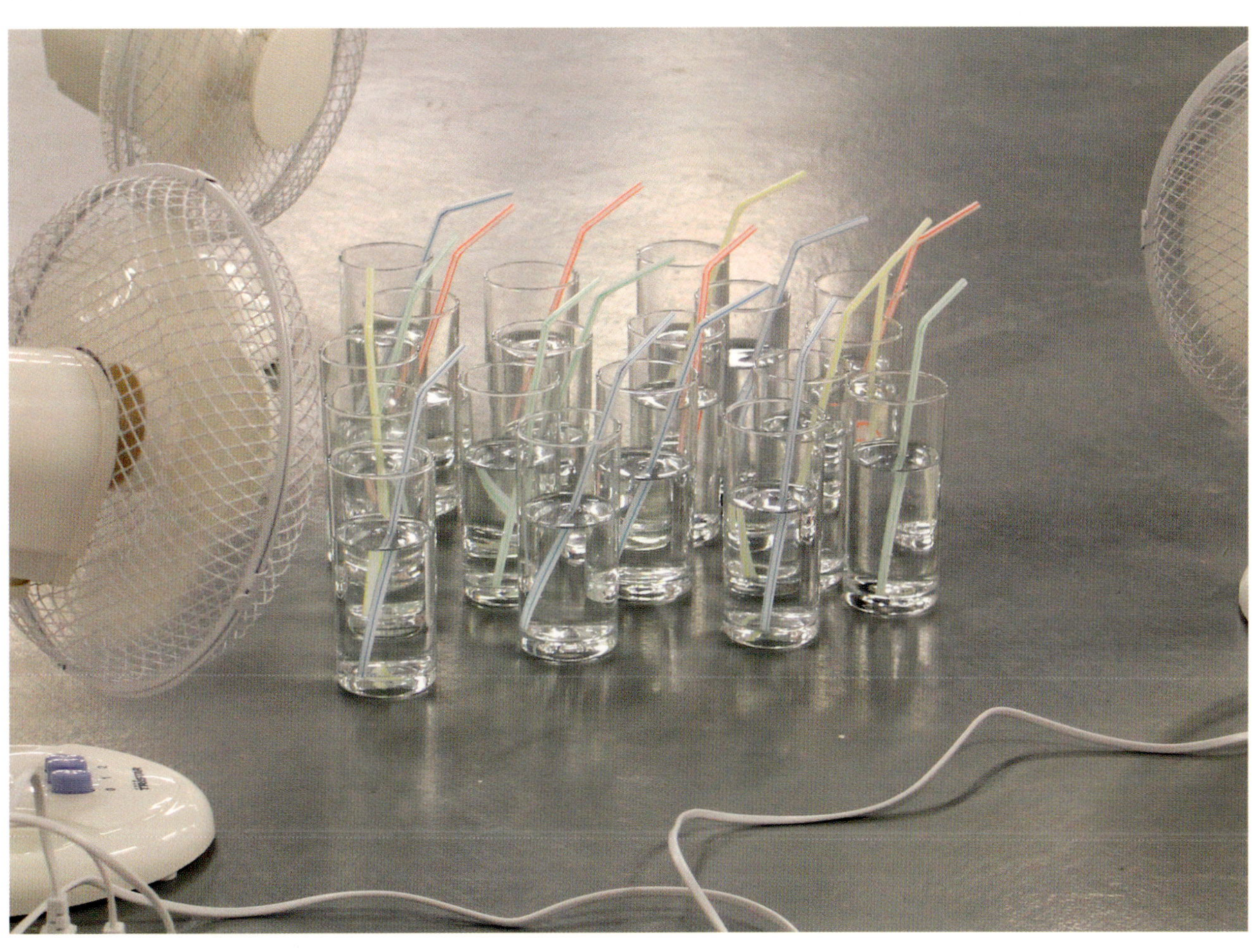

Migratory Birds, 2011 – Installation, fans, glasses, straws and water

Loves all colours, 2005

Logos in the Wild, 2010

The Final Solution, 2013

Metropolis M, cover magazine, 2012

SCULPTURE INTERNATIONAL ROTTERDAM

Sculpture International Rotterdam, logo, 2009

Photo, 2006

Institut Néerlandais, facade design, 2011

Shit Alphabet, 2005

Ro Theater & 75B, invitation Reuzen (Giants), 2011

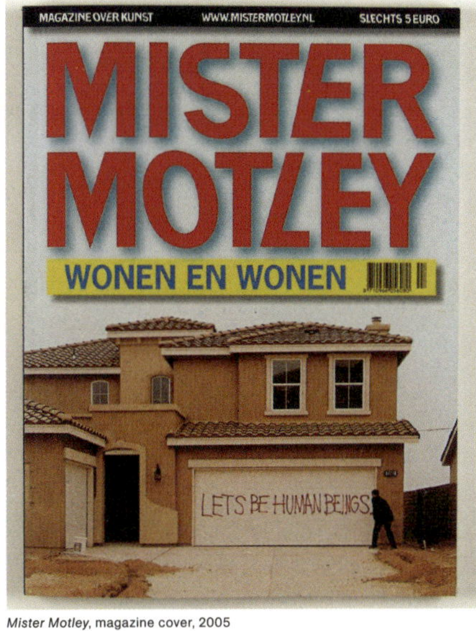

Mister Motley, magazine cover, 2005

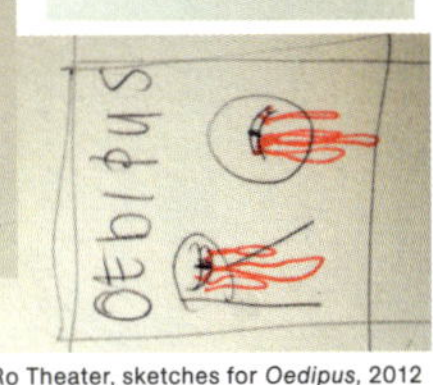

Ro Theater, sketches for *Oedipus*, 2012

Untitled, 2011

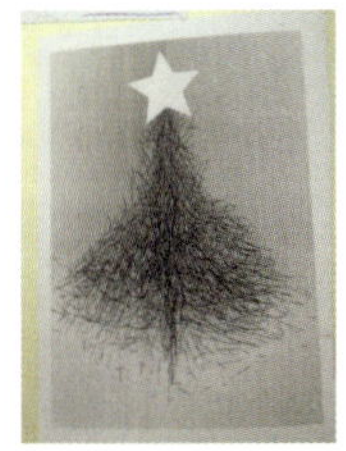

Christmas, 2008

Van Abbemuseum, poster *Sheela Gowda.
Open Eye Policy*, 2013

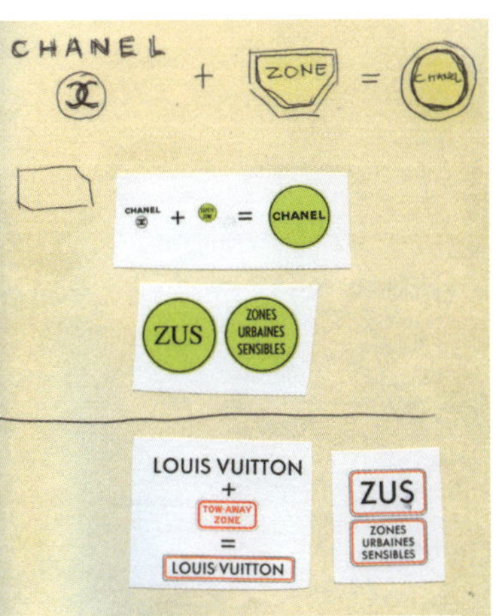

Ro Theater, poster *Oedipus*, 2013

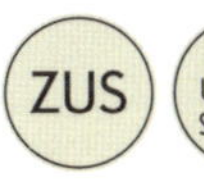

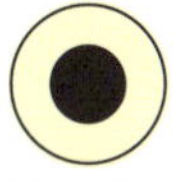
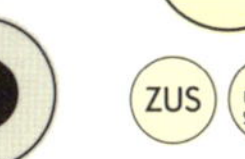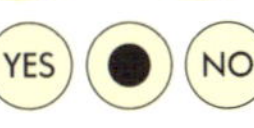
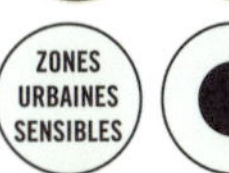
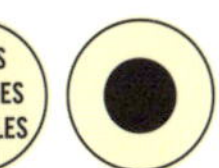
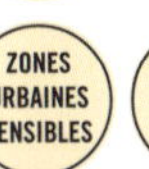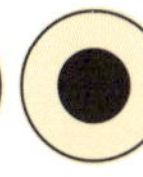

ZUS, sketches for visual identity, 2009

Exhibition Nuevos Disenadores Holandeses, Laus, Barcelona, 2001

Rotterdam Design Prize 2007, sketches for visual identity,
edition 2007

Church, 2012 – iPhone drawing on inkjet print, 220 x 150 cm

Canal House, 2012 – iPhone drawing on inkjet print, 220 x 150 cm

Sistine Channel Changing, 2006

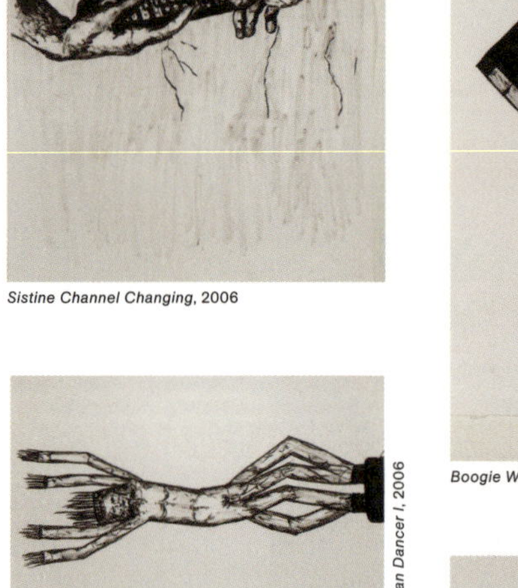
Vitruvian Dancer I, 2006

Boogie Woogie Blitz, 2009

Dyson Gnome, 2010

hoestende mensen
Objet trouvé (coughing people), 2002

De Unie, font, 2010

De Unie, rear of business card, 2010

Van Abbemuseum, campaign, 2008

Waterfront, logo, 1998

RijksakademieOPEN 2008
Sarphatistraat 470, Amsterdam
www.rijksakademie.nl

zaterdag 29 en zondag 30 november
11:00 – 19:00 uur

toegang inclusief publicatie €4
met kortingspas €3
weekendkaart €5
kinderen tot 12 jaar gratis

meer dan 50 kunstenaars uit de
hele wereld tonen hun werk

Aanmelden voor de residency 2010
tot 1 februari 2009

Sponsor: APG

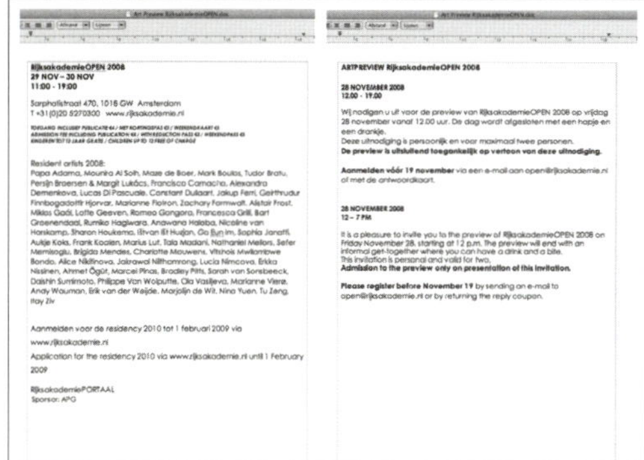

RijksakademieOPEN, items, 2008

VEDUTE

PRESENTATIES NIEUWE
MANUSCRIPTEN VAN:

VEDUTE SALON 2012

JURGEN BEY &
RIANNE MAKKINK
MARIEKE VAN DIEMEN
MAARTEN KLOOS
JAN JOOST PESKENS
PATRICK TANGHE
ANDRé THIJSSEN

UITNODIGING
Het bestuur van Stichting Vedute nodigt u met veel plezier uit voor de onthulling van zes nieuwe manuscripten, wederom bij ARCAM in Amsterdam. Door de verschillende disciplines en talenten van de makers belooft zondagmiddag 25 november een unieke middag te worden. Wij kijken uit naar de presentaties van een rijk palet aan werkstukken waarmee onze collectie zal worden verrijkt.

Bestuur Stichting Vedute
Dirk Sijmons (voorzitter)
Daan Bakker
Maaike Behm
Jonieke van Es
Peter van der Heijden
Behrang Mousavi
Roosmarijn Ubink

Over Stichting Vedute
44 x 32 x 7 cm
Stichting Vedute is opgericht in 1991. In ruim twintig jaar is haar collectie ruimtelijke manuscripten uitgegroeid tot 190 objecten. Het zijn driedimensionale werken die in gesloten vorm 44 x 32 x 7 cm meten en zijn ontworpen door gerenommeerde ontwerpers die daarmee hun gedachten over ruimte visualiseerden.

WEBSITE
Meer informatie over de collectie, foto's, teksten en films van de gerealiseerde manuscripten zijn te vinden op www. vedute.nl

DATUM
Zondagmiddag
25 november 2012
Start:
13.15 uur, einde 17.30 uur
Aanmelden is niet nodig.

LOCATIE
ARCAM
Prins Hendrikkade 600
Amsterdam
Zie voor routebeschrijving en parkeren: www.arcam.nl

Met dank aan:

Vedute, invitation, 2012

International Film Festival Rotterdam, Tiger Award, 2009

CoDarts

codarts
university for the arts

rotterdams conservatorium
rotterdam conservatoire

rotterdamse dansacademie
rotterdam dance academy

rotterdam circus arts
rotterdam circus arts

rotterdam classical music academy
rotterdam jazz academy
rotterdam pop academy
rotterdam world music academy
muziektheateracademie

Codarts, visual identity, 2005

rotterdam jazz academy

rotterdam pop academy

muziektheater academie

rotterdam academy for classical music

rotterdam academy for worldmusic

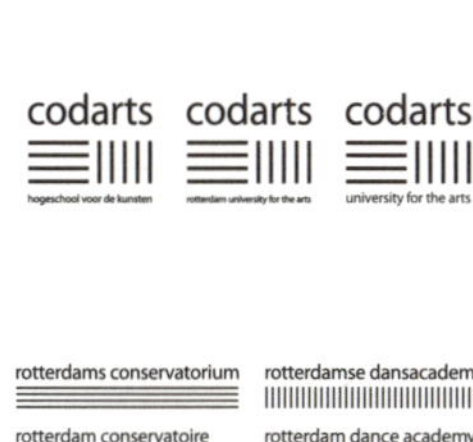

codarts
hogeschool voor de kunsten

codarts
rotterdam university for the arts

codarts
university for the arts

rotterdams conservatorium
rotterdam conservatoire

rotterdamse dansacademie
rotterdam dance academy

circus arts
circus arts rotterdam
circus arts academy

Tronies (TENT, Rotterdam), 2011 – Overview (part 2)

Photo, 2011

LantarenVenster, posters, 2012

Museum Boijmans Van Beuningen,
proposal flyer, 2002

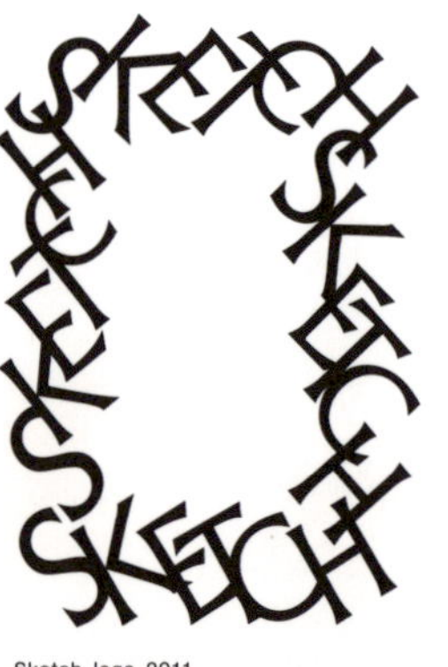

Sketch, logo, 2011

Rotterdam 2007, City of Architecture, poster, 2

Photo, 2002

On the Road, 2012

International Film Festival Rotterdam, poster 37th edition, 2008

Untitled, 2011 – Ink on paper, 260 x 150 cm

Achim Treu & Richard Cameron, 12" *Fluffy Target*, 2005

Codarts, Codarts Personal, 2007

ZomerExpo, sketches for campaign *Aarde (earth)*, 2012

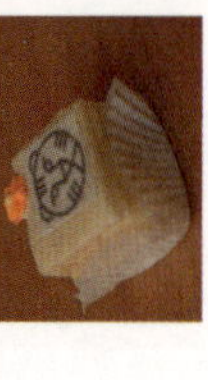

Rotterdam 2007, City of Architecture, poster, 2007

256

For Afke, 2013

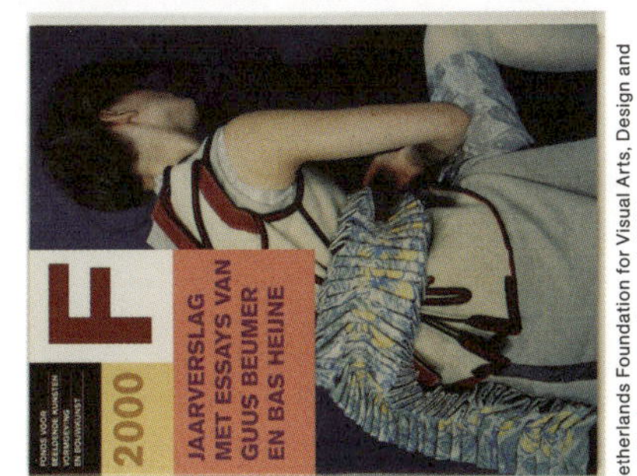
Netherlands Foundation for Visual Arts, Design and Architecture, annual report, 2000

Institut Néerlandais, poster *Rembrandt et son cercle*, 2010

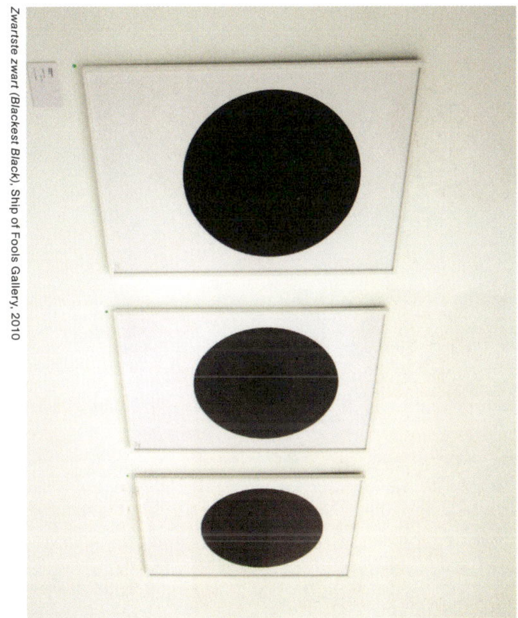
Zwartste zwart (*Blackest Black*), Ship of Fools Gallery, 2010

Museum Boijmans Van Beuningen, poster *It's All Dalí*, 2005

Netherlands Foundation for Visual Arts, Design and Architecture, envelopes, 2002

International Film Festival Rotterdam, sketches for campaign 41st edition, 2011

6TH St
1400 E
STOP
DON'T BU

Don't Buy This (Los Angeles), 2006 – Intervention, acrylic on paper

Meekers, sketches *Helaas pindakaas*, 2012

She Is So Cute, 2006

Van Abbemuseum, poster *René Daniëls*, 2012

ZomerExpo, catalogue, 2012

Van Abbemuseum, poster *Heartland*, 2009

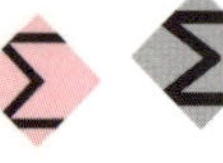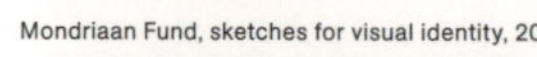

Mondriaan Fund, sketches for visual identity, 2011

(Handy for in the home. Whatever / Doesn't matter)

Van Abbemuseum, sketch for *Becoming Dutch*, 2008

260

(the sceptic think-tank
no use
never will be
don't believe in it)

Ro Theater, logo *Snorro*, 2010

Now & Wow, poster, 2005

SKOR, flyer *Polder Cup*, 2010

If there are any questions, we'll be happy to answer them, 2010

Photo, 2006

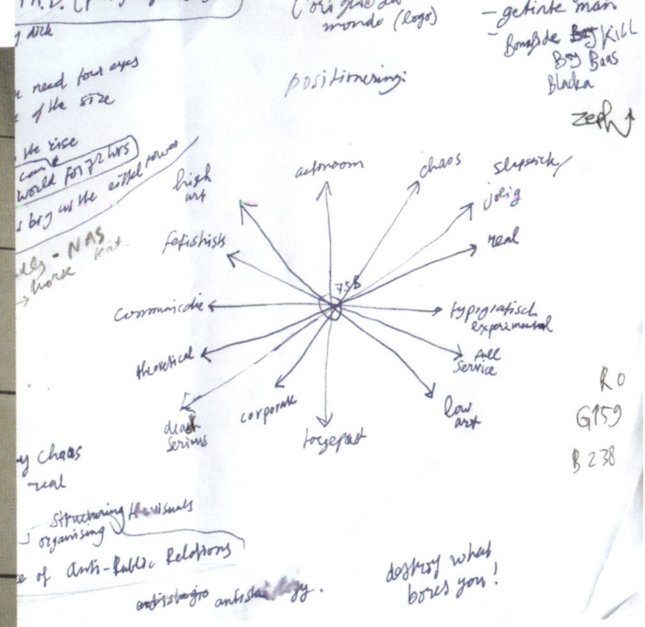

IN MEMORIAM
ANDRÉ GINGRAS

André Gingras (1968–2013)

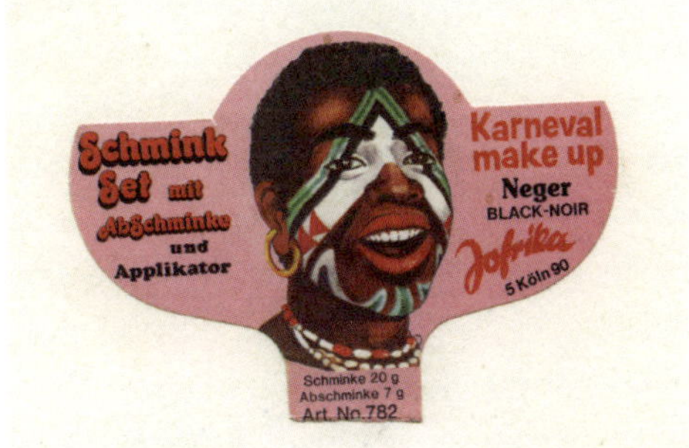

Objet trouvé, 2001

One with the Freaks (triptych), 2011 – Paint and marker on hardboard, 180 x 180 cm

Moonsick, 2011 – Spray can paint, tar and dirt on plastic, 120 x 120 cm

Biographies

Rens Rogier Muis (Rotterdam, 7 August 1974) lives and works in Rotterdam. Muis switched in 1993 from a training as a teacher to the Rotterdam Academy of Visual Arts. In 1995 he began his career with designs made with a fellow student for De Vlerk alternative pop/rock venue. Muis co-founded 75B in 1996, graduated in 1997 and then resumed work with 75B. In 2004 he graduated in Arts and Cultural Management at Rotterdam's Erasmus University. Muis has been a consultant on various committees for, amongst others, the Rotterdam Department of Art & Culture, Rotterdam Art Council (RKS), Netherlands Foundation for Visual Arts, Design and Architecture (Fonds BKVB; specifically the Foreign Residencies, Design and BKVB Live) and Domain for Art Criticism. In 2006 he was *artist in residence* at the Art Center College of Design in Pasadena. In 2007 he published with NAi Publishers *Graffiti in Rotterdam*, a book about the history of graffiti in Rotterdam since the mid 1960s. At present Muis is on the editorial board of Rotterdam Art Publications Foundation. He has published numerous articles, has held professorships and has given lectures, workshops and guest lessons at academies in the Netherlands and abroad.

Pieter Cornelis Vos (Utrecht, 2 July 1971) lives and works in Rotterdam. Vos was co-founder of 75B in 1996 and graduated from the Willem de Kooning Academy, Rotterdam, in 1997. He then resumed work with 75B. In 2001 Vos sat on the editorial board of *Hard Pop*, a book published by Showroom MAMA. In 2006 he was *artist in residence* at the Art Center College of Design in Pasadena. Articles published by Vos include 'HHHH Humobisten', in *Een Dure Grap* (2006); 'Concrete Jungle', in *Nieuwsbrief* #11, a newsletter issued by Fonds BKVB (2007); 'Alles wat goed is, komt in 2040 van Rotterdam', in *Rotterdam 2040* (2010); and 'The Happy Ending of Queenie and the Graphic Designer, A Fairy Tale', in *Sensation, Theme Promo & Campaign Graphics* (2012). He has lectured on graphic design and idea development at the Willem de Kooning Academy, Rotterdam. Vos has sat on numerous committees and has given workshops and lectures in the Netherlands and abroad.

The 75B Team
Annieka Bruyn van Rozenburg
Geneviève Kooijman
Merel Snel
Lea Sormani
Loes Verstappen

Robert Beckand (The Hague, 15 August 1972) was co-founder and left 75B on 30 June 2009

Former team members
Thijs van Beijsterveldt, Salome Kazeze Mhango, Iris Holtkamp, Joseph Hughes, Barteld Riemeijer, Meinhard Spoor, Marije Stijkel and Julia Visser

Exhibitions / Events (a selection)
Arts, a farce in two acts (i.c.w. Jetse Batelaan), TENT, Rotterdam 2012
A Perfect Day, Art in Drawings, Westergasfabriek, Amsterdam 2012
Easy, Maassilo, Rotterdam 2012
RE: Rotterdam, Rotterdam 2012
Face Value, TENT, Rotterdam 2011
Artefacts I & III, Vivid Gallery, Rotterdam 2010
Love Design Delirium, Kunstraum Niederoesterreich, Vienna 2008
75B 10x10, Blaak 10 Gallery, Rotterdam 2007
Dutch Graphic Design 1990-2001, American Graphic Institute Arts, New York 2002
COLOUR! The Exhibition, Artoteek, Schiedam 2001
Nuevos Disenadores Holandeses, Laus, Barcelona 2001
Kijk hier es naar (Take a look at this), Fons Welters Gallery, Amsterdam 2001
Exorcism/Aesthetic Terrorism, Museum Boijmans Van Beuningen, Rotterdam 2000
Mooi maar goed, Stedelijk Museum, Amsterdam 1999
Do Normal, San Francisco Museum of Modern Art, 1998
Holland International, LACE Gallery, Los Angeles 1998
Patch 'n Paste, Showroom MAMA, Rotterdam 1997

Publications
75B Posters, with contribution by Hanneke Briër, self-published, Rotterdam 2010
75B LAX, with contributions by Joshua Trees, Lisa Nugent, Nik Hafermaas & Simon Johnston, Veenman Publishers, Rotterdam 2008
75B 10x10, with contribution by Boyd Coyner, Veenman Publishers, Rotterdam 2007
Look (Symbol Soup; 8) in ass. with Peter Jeroense, Thames & Hudson, London 1999
Dutch Design Dead, Holland International, self-published, 1998
Pictobook, self-published, Rotterdam 1997

Bibliography (a selection)
Robert Klanten, Floyd Schultze and Anna Sinofzik (eds), *Introducing: Culture Identities: Design for Museums, Theaters and Cultural Institutions*, Gestalten, Berlin 2013
Oscar van Gelderen, Erik Brus et al., *Rotterdam (De Nieuwe Stijl)*, Lebowski, Amsterdam 2012
'A B&W Elephant', 360° *Concept and Design Magazine* #11, 2011
Henk van Gelder, 'Test: Affiches op straat', NRC Handelsblad, 5 November 2010
'75B', *ID Pure magazine* #23, 2010
Marleen Luijt, 'Deze tijger heb je zo nagemaakt', *NRC Next*, 16 January 2009
Harmen Liemburg, 'Boys to Men', *Items*, December 2008
Bart de Haas, 'Weltschmerz', *Vormberichten* #05, 2008
Area 2. 100 Graphic Designers, 10 Curators, 10 Design Classics, Phaidon, London 2008
'Affiche met Wilders gaat het museum in', *Trouw*, 3 June 2008
Cristian Campos, *Graphic Design in Holland*, MaoMao, Barcelona 2008
'75B. Ratable to Themselves', *[kAk] magazine* #03, 2007
Aaron Betsky and Adam Eeuwens, *False Flat. Why Dutch Design is So Good*, Phaidon, London 2004
'Dutch Delights', *idN Magazine* #02, 2003
Gert Staal, Sybrand Zijlstra and Ineke Schwartz, *Apples & Oranges. Best Dutch Graphic Design*, BIS Publishers, Amsterdam 2001
Exorcism/Aesthetic Terrorism. Fiery temperaments in contemporary art, Museum Boijmans Van Beuningen/ NAi Publishers, Rotterdam 2000

Awards (a selection)
Golden Award, China International Poster Biennial, 2011
Dutch Design Award, Eindhoven, 2010
Nomination, Festival international de l'affiche et du graphisme, Chaumont, 2010
International Museum Communication Silver Award, Brussels 2007
The Best Dutch Book Designs 2003, 2007 and 2009
Nomination, NPS Culture Prize, 2000
Double Nomination, Rotterdam Design Prize, 1999 and 2001

Commissions (a selection)
CBK Rotterdam & LP2, *Cor Kraat, made in Rotterdam*, exhibition design and campaign, 2012
Anne van der Zwaag and Nederlands Fotomuseum, *Zwart-Wit*, campaign, 2011
Mondriaan Fund, visual identity, from 2011
Institut Néerlandais, visual identity and communication, from 2011
MORF, magazine design, from 2011
Metropolis M, magazine design, from 2011
LantarenVenster, visual identity and communication, from 2010
Dance Works Rotterdam/André Gingras, visual identity and campaigns 2010–2012
De Unie, visual identity and communication, 2010–2012
Ro Theater, visual identity and campaigns, from 2009
Sculpture International Rotterdam, visual identity and communication, from 2009
ZUS (Zones Urbaines Sensibles), visual identity, from 2009
Van Abbemuseum, Eindhoven, visual identity and campaigns, from 2008
International Film Festival Rotterdam, visual identity and campaigns, from 2007

Codarts, visual identity and communication, from 2005
The Netherlands Foundation for Visual Arts, Design and Architecture, visual identity and communication, 2000–2011
NAi Publishers / 010 Publishers / nai010 publishers, design of various publications, from 2000
Now&Wow, visual identity and communication, from 1999

Collections
SFMOMA, San Francisco
Stadsarchief Rotterdam
MOTI, Breda
Museum Rotterdam
Stedelijk Museum Amsterdam
Private collections

Credits

This publication has been made possible by the generous support of the Mondriaan Fund.

With thanks to Erik Brus, Boyd Coyner, Martijn van Ham, Anne Hoogewoning, Hans Oldewarris, Lot Piscaer, Martijn Poel, Onno Poiesz, Eva Roolker and Edwin Veekens

Compilation, editing and graphic design by 75B
Authors Rens Muis and Pieter Vos
Text editing and project coordination Hans Oldewarris
Text correction Els Brinkman
Translation from the Dutch John Kirkpatrick and Vic Joseph (text Rens Muis)
Illustration credits All images 75B
Photography 75B, Jan Adriaans, Bram Belloni, Peter Cox, Max Dereta, Linda Druijff, Emiel Efdée, Bob Goedewaagen, Aad Hoogendoorn, Jarr Geerligs, Job Janssen, Richard Niessen, Bram Saeys, Ari Versluis
Printing Veenman+, Rotterdam
Binding Jansenbinders BV, Leiden
Paper Astralux, 115gr and Muncken Pure Rough, 100gr

nai010 publishers is an internationally orientated publisher specialized in developing, producing and distributing books in the fields of architecture, urbanism, art and design.

Available in North, South and Central America through Artbook | D.A.P., 155 Sixth Avenue 2nd Floor, New York, NY 10013-1507, tel +1 212 627 1999, fax +1 212 627 9484, dap@dapinc.com
Available in the United Kingdom and Ireland through Art Data, 12 Bell Industrial Estate, 50 Cunnington Street, London W4 5HB, tel +44 208 747 1061, fax +44 208 742 2319, orders@artdata.co.uk

Printed and bound in the Netherlands

www.75B.nl / www.nai010.nl

ISBN 978-94-6208-040-9